THE
ESSENTIAL
PUNK
ACCESSORY

SNIFFIN'GLUE
AND OTHER ROCK'N'ROLL HABITS

MARK PERRY

London • Tokyo

ACKNOWLEDGEMENTS

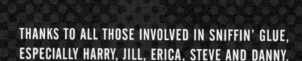

THANKS TO ALL THOSE INVOLVED IN SNIFFIN' GLUE,
ESPECIALLY HARRY, JILL, ERICA, STEVE AND DANNY.

EXCLUSIVE DISTRIBUTORS
Music Sales Limited,
14/15 Berners Street, London, W1T 3LJ.

Music Sales Corporation,
257 Park Avenue South, New York, NY 10010, USA.

Macmillan Distribution Services,
56 Parkwest Drive Derrimut, Vic 3030, Australia.

Every effort has been made to trace the copyright holders of the
photographs in this book but one or two were unreachable.
We would be grateful if the photographers concerned would contact us.

SNIFFIN' GLUE
AN INTRODUCTION

When I started the *Sniffin' Glue* fanzine back in July 1976, little did I know how important and influential it was to become. It was an essential ingredient in the UK punk scene, less by design and more through being in the right place at the right time.

Before punk happened I was basically living the same sort of life as any other teenage music fan. Having being born in 1957, the early Seventies rock stars provided the soundtrack to my teenage years. The first gig I went to was The Beach Boys at the Royal Festival Hall in 1971 and from then on I went to as many gigs as possible. I was obsessed with rock music and spent most of my money on either records or concert tickets, much to the displeasure of my parents. My dad's cry of "turn that racket down!" is ringing in my ears even now. I used to read all the music papers at the time - *Melody Maker, Sounds, Disc* and, especially, *New Musical Express*. I hung on to every word of writers like Mick Farren and Nick Kent.

I loved Glam Rock - David Bowie, T. Rex, Roxy Music, Mott The Hoople etc - and by 1973 I could be spotted stumbling about in silver stack heeled boots, purple loon pants, stripey tank top, brown satin jacket and shoulder length hair. This is only time in my life that I've dressed remotely outrageous. Even during the punk years, I never looked quite so silly. At the time I lived with my parents in a council flat in Deptford, in south east London, and I remember feeling quite nervous walking about. Most of the kids in our area were skinhead types or soul boys, and I once got beaten up outside Lewisham Odeon for looking like a 'poof'! The good thing about living in London was that you could easily jump on a bus up to the West End, so a lot of my time was spent in the records shops of Soho. Most Saturdays I would be up there, even after school sometimes. I left school in 1974 and started working for William & Glyns Bank, first in the City and then in South Kensington. There seemed to be plenty of jobs going back

then but it was a pretty limited choice, either the building trade, factory work or banking. I choose the latter because it seemed like the easiest and cleanest option! My mum was quite happy because she thought I'd end up being a bank manager. I hated it, it was boring. I was perfect punk material!

Early in 1976 I started reading in *NME* about a new 'punk' scene which was developing in New York. Like London's pub rock scene, it revolved around small venues such as CBGBs and Max's Kansas City. The *NME* writers made it all sound new and exciting and I could sense that this was not an R&B scene, which is basically what the UK pub rock scene was all about. The band that really caught my imagination was The Ramones - Joey, Dee Dee, Johnny and Tommy. Nick Kent wrote about their first album and as soon as I read his review, I couldn't wait to hear it.

I bought the first Ramones album on import and it completely blew me away. I'd never heard anything so exciting. The tracks were only about two minutes long and they were singing about sniffing glue, baseball bats and chainsaws, with song titles like 'Blitzkrieg Bop' and 'Beat On The Brat'. They played at breakneck speed with a basic line up of vocals, guitar, bass and drums. It was as if progressive rock had never happened. I was completely sold on it.

In early July 1976, The Ramones came over to Britain for the first time, supporting The Flamin' Groovies. I saw them at the Roundhouse and Dingwalls and they were even more exciting live. The energy was amazing.

At the gigs I met other like minded kids, such as Shane McGowan and Brian James. Brian told me about his new group, The Damned. I began to realise that these people were starting to call themselves punks and I felt that this was the start of something important.

A few days after the Ramones gigs, I asked the guys at Rock On record stall in Soho Market, one of my regular haunts, whether there were any British publications covering the new music because, apart from the New York magazine *Punk*, I had seen nothing. He jokingly said I should start one up myself. I obviously took his suggestion seriously because I went straight home and started typing the first words of my magazine - *Sniffin' Glue and Other Rock'n'Roll Habits*. I pinched the title from the Ramones' song 'Now I Wanna Sniff Some Glue'. I thought that if anything summed up the basic approach of the new music, it was this lowest form of drug taking.

I put the magazine together with the same 'back to basics' approach as the music that it was to feature. The main text, if you could call it that, was typed out on an old children's type-writer that my parents had bought me as a Christmas present when I was about 10. The 'headlines' and limited 'graphics' I scrawled out in black felt tip pen. It was raw but it put across the punk message perfectly. It celebrated the DIY ethic but was also the very best I could do at the time. Even in the first issue I identified punk as a scene separate from the established rock scene but, because of my openness, it included reviews of old favourites Blue Oyster Cult alongside the obvious ravings about The Ramones.

Once I'd finished putting the mag together I got some copies printed up on a Xerox machine (in my girlfriend's office) and took them to the Rock On stall. They could hardly believe that I had gone away and actually put a magazine together. They bought the copies I had printed and gave me some more money in advance to get some more printed in a proper copy shop. Rock On also helped me distribute it to other shops like Compendium in Camden and Bizarre in Paddington. Once people saw it, the shops had no trouble selling it. It seemed that there were plenty of kids, like me, who were eager to read about the emerging punk scene. It was still small but it was growing all the time.

By this time, August 1976, I started hearing more about the new British bands, groups like The Sex Pistols, The Vibrators, The Damned and The Stranglers. I started making a lot of new contacts through the fanzine. I also got invited to gigs on the guest list and also went 'on the road' with Eddie & The Hot Rods, which was a big deal for me at the time. This was the first time I really saw myself as a journalist because I ended up in the back of the van to Hastings with Caroline Coon from *Melody Maker* and Jonh Ingham from *Sounds*. My life was changing very rapidly.

The second issue of *Sniffin' Glue* came out in late August 1976. I felt much more confident with the magazine now and I realised that I could keep it going as long as I wanted. I was getting so much positive feedback. I started knocking around with Caroline Coon and my relationship to what I saw as my previous life was getting more and more strained. By September, I'd left my job at the bank and shocked my parents by hacking off my long hair with a Woolworths DIY hair cutter and started sticking safety pins through my clothes.

Caroline took me to see The Sex Pistols at the 100 Club and my life was changed forever the moment the band took the stage. They looked and sounded like nothing I'd ever seen before. Stunning but disturbing at the same time. Less a celebration of the rock ethic, more like a nail in its coffin. The club was only half full but the atmosphere was electric. I flung myself in and jumped up and down at the front of the stage. My satin jacket was ripped to shreds. Goodbye to glam rock!

At the gig I met up with Brian James again and arranged to interview The Damned for the next issue. Brian became *Sniffin' Glue*'s first cover star. Yes, issue three had photos, which we had no problem getting hold of. By this time the magazine was so hip that loads of people wanted to contribute and, most importantly, didn't want paying. Also, by this time, an old school friend, Steve Mick, was helping out with some of the writing. Later, I got another school friend, Danny Baker, involved.

EDDIE
AND
THE
HOT
RODS

Gorillas

i'M a
LaZy
Sod

BuZZCOCKS

NEVER MIND
THE BOLLOCKS
HERE'S THE
Sex Pistols

THE
JAM

CHELSEA

The Boys

The 100 Club Punk Festival took place in late September and we responded a few days later with a special issue - issue three and a half. We only printed a few copies which were quickly snapped up. Because of our basic DIY approach we could get things on the street very quickly.

Issue four followed in October 1976 and featured the first ever interview with The Clash, a band which was quickly establishing itself as the most important punk band in the UK. After talking to them, I realised that this wasn't just about music anymore but an attitude that went beyond clothes and fashion. *Sniffin' Glue* was at the heart of it all and from now on it was as though we had a mission to spread the punk word. You certainly couldn't read about Blue Oyster Cult anymore!

In November, Harry T Murlowski joined the team, as 'staff' photographer and general business manager. Up 'til now, I had worked from my tiny bedroom in my parent's council flat. With Harry joining, we moved the whole 'operation' to a backroom in the Rough Trade record shop in North Kensington. It was our first real office. We felt like a proper magazine! Later, in February 1977, we moved again, to an office at Dryden Chambers, Oxford Street which Miles Copeland let us have. Because of my position and influence as *Sniffin' Glue* editor, Miles offered me the chance to have my own record label and Step Forward was born. Within six months I'd gone from bored bank clerk to magazine editor and record label boss! Only in punk rock! Also in a short time, the *Glue* itself had gone from being a homemade fan letter to a firmly established part of the growing punk scene.

As the scene evolved and faced the contradictions of success, *Sniffin' Glue* reflected those concerns and, as can be seen in the following pages, was unable to remain unaffected by the need to make money. In a way, once we started taking ads we'd already signalled the beginning of the end. I didn't want the *Glue* to become just another magazine, so I ended it on issue 12 in September 1977, just over a year since the magazine first hit the streets. That last issue featured a cover mounted flexi-disc featuring the first single of my band, Alternative TV. We printed 20,000 copies, a far cry from the 100 or so print run of the first issue.

The punk scene hadn't gone away but there was no need for a magazine like *Sniffin' Glue* anymore. When it started it filled a gap in the market but by the second half of 1977 everyone was writing about punk rock. It was no longer an underground scene. Punk bands were signing up to established labels, had singles in the charts and were playing places like the Rainbow and the Roundhouse. The punks, in a way, had become the new establishment. For me the early magic had gone and I felt that most punk groups were playing it safe and had lost that initial sense of adventure. For my part, although no longer editor of the UK's premier punk fanzine, I continued to have a say through my label Step Forward Records and my band, Alternative TV.

This book collects together every *Sniffin' Glue* magazine that I published and is a blow by blow account of the most exciting music scene that Britain has ever produced. Thanks again to all those involved in *Sniffin' Glue*, especially Harry, Jill, Erica, Steve and Danny.

MARK PERRY, MARCH 2009.

SNIFFIN'GLUE
OPEN UP YOUR EARS AND BLEED

This is not meant to be a definitive guide, just my own favourites
of the records that either influenced, defined or captured the spirit of punk.
It's broken into three parts:

THE ROOTS

PUNK

AND POST-PUNK

I've resisted the temptation of putting Alternative TV in the list although
some people insist that our first album 'The Image Has Cracked' is essential listening!
A lot of the best punk was released on 7"singles and for a brilliant collection
of the best of these check out the 5CD boxed set '1-2-3-4 PUNK & NEW WAVE 1976-1979'
on the Universal Music label.

In the listing I've mentioned the original labels that the albums
were released on. With subsequent licensing and CD reissues,
some of these may have changed.

THE ROOTS OF PUNK
(PRE 1975)

The Doors: The Doors (Elektra)

The Velvet Underground: White Light/White Heat (Verve)

The Deviants: Disposable (Stable)

T.Rex: Electric Warrior (Fly)

The Flamin' Groovies: Teenage Head (Kama Sutra)

Alice Cooper: School's Out (Warner Brothers)

The Who: Quadrophenia (Track)

New York Dolls: New York Dolls (Mercury)

Mott The Hoople: Mott (CBS)

Iggy Pop: Raw Power (CBS)

PUNK
(1975-1977)

Patti Smith Group: Horses (Arista)

Ramones: Ramones (Sire)

The Damned: Damned Damned Damned (Stiff)

The Stranglers: Rattus Norvegicus (UA)

The Clash: The Clash (CBS)

Television: Marquee Moon (Elektra)

Sex Pistols: Never Mind The Bollocks (Virgin)

Suicide: Suicide (Red Star)

Talking Heads: Talking Heads '77 (Sire)

Wire: Pink Flag (Harvest)

POST-PUNK
(1978-1980)

Elvis Costello - This Year's Model (Radar)

Magazine - Real Life (Virgin)

Public Image Limited - First Issue (Virgin)

The Pop Group - Y (Radar)

Doll By Doll - Remember (Automatic)

The Jam - Setting Sons (Polydor)

The Slits - Cut (Island)

Joy Division - Unknown Pleasures (Factory)

The Clash - London Calling (CBS)

Dexy's Midnight Runners - Searching For The Young

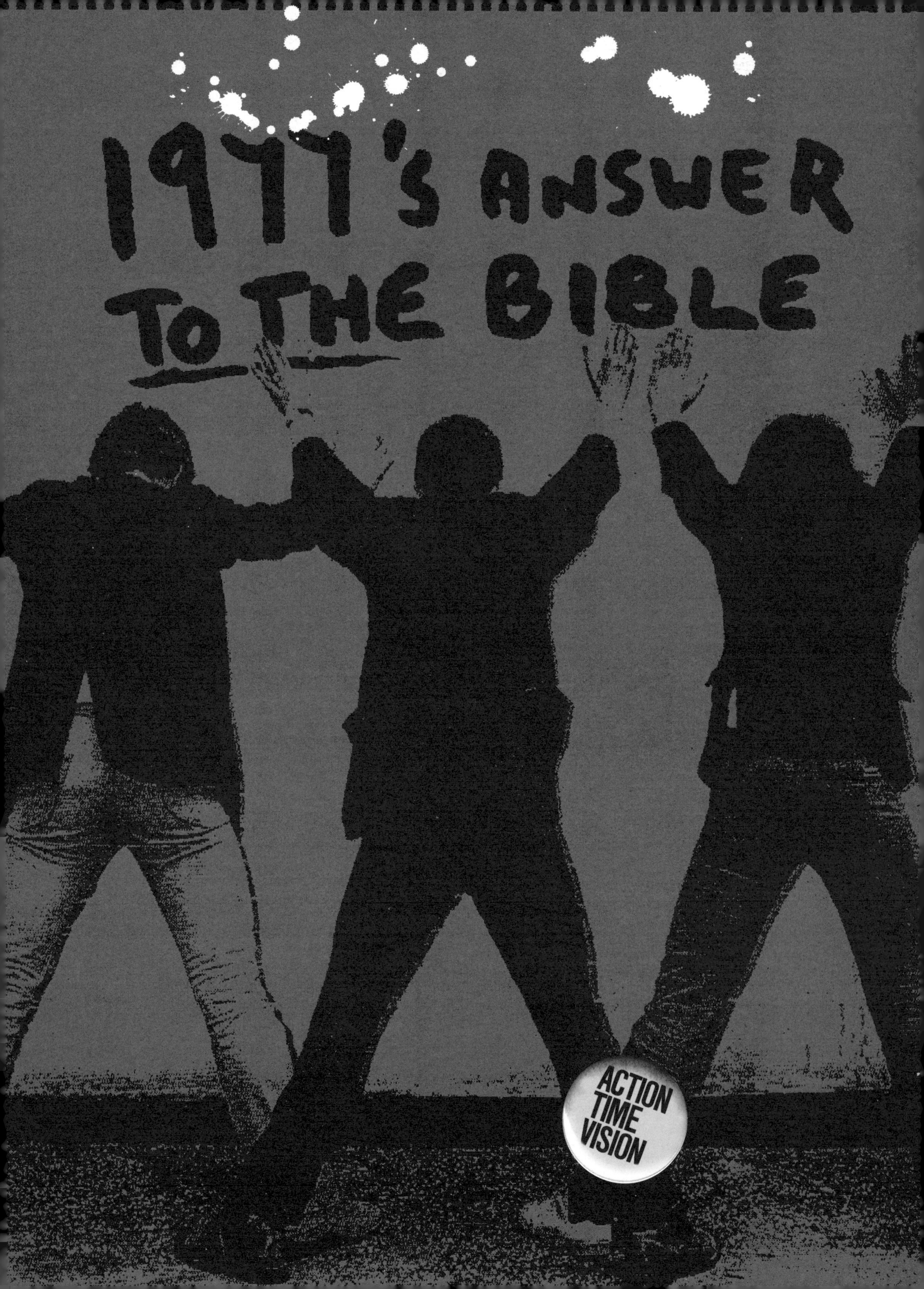
1977's ANSWER TO THE BIBLE
ACTION TIME VISION

SNIFFIN'GLUE
THE ORIGINAL ISSUES

SNIFFIN'GLUE..
+ OTHER ROCK 'N' ROLL HABITS FOR PUNKS! ①

15ᵖ

NO.1 OF MANY, WE HOPE!

THIS THING IS NOT MEANT TO BE READ...IT'S FOR SOAKING IN GLUE AND SNIFFIN'.

IN THE FIRST ISSUE:

THE RAMONES

ALBUM & CONCERT REVIEWS!

PLUS

BLUE OYSTER CULT

RE-REVIEW OF ALL THEIR ALBUMS!

+ PUNK REVIEWS

ALBUMS, SINGLES & CONCERTS!

MP's SNIFF CONTENTS:

The Ramones were in London this month and to realy get into the fact we've put this little mag/newsletter together.It's a bit amatuer at the moment but it is the first go isn't it,I mean we can't be Nick Kents over night can we.In this issue we lean heavily towards being a Ramones fan letter but later on we hope to bring you pieces on the following: Flamin'Groovies,MC5,Nazz/Runt, Runaways,Iggy Pop and the Stooges,Lenny Bruce,Roogalator,Dr.Feelgood,Eddie and the Hot Rods,Earthquake,New York Dolls, Jonathan Richman/Modern Lovers,Mothers Of Invention'66/68,Count Bishops,Sex Pistols,101'ers,Stranglers,Raspberries, Television plus any other punks who make and do things we like.

With the Ramones in this issue are Blue Oyster Cult,who have just released a great new album which we review along with all their other pieces of black plastic.The review sections try to tell you about things rather than give boring biased opinions,which we all have but there's no room for it in fanzines.We believe rock'n'roll,and especially'punk rock',is about enjoyment and <u>nothing</u> else-leave the concepts to the likes of Yes,Mike Oldfield etc.I hope you enjoy sniffin'(sorry-reading!)our little contribution to the punk culture,it would make us sniff glue if you did!

See yer,

Mark P.

'NOW I WANNA SNIFF SOME GLUE,
NOW I WANNA HAVE SOMETHIN' TO DO,
ALL THE KIDS WANNA SNIFF SOME GLUE,
ALL THE KIDS WANT SOMETHIN' TO DO'.

-Ramones'76.

SNIFFIN' GLUE....is chucked together by Mark P(Me)with help from Rick Brown from Tunbridge Wells(Kents answer to Detroit), Louise(My lovely lady),Rock On-Soho Market(Who supply most of the records and happen to be the best record shop in London),Airfix(Who supply the sticky stuff) and the music itself!

All feedback(i.e-angry letters)to:

Mark P,
24 Rochfort Hse.,
Grove St.,
Deptford,
London,SE8 3LX.

In issue 2 we wanna do something on the Flamin'Groovies and early Mothers('Wowie Zowie','Hungry Freaks,Daddy'etc).I just hope we can get it together.

UNTIL THEN-KEEP ON SNIFFIN' YOU PUNKS!

PUNK ROCK LIVES

SPLIT OPEN THE TUBES, IT'S THEM.

FLAMIN'GROOVIES/RAMONES/STRANGLERS-Roundhouse.
The ol'Roundhouse just reeked of glue last Sunday night.The Ramones,armed with miniture base-ball bats beat the hell out of all contenders for the'most exciting band of the year stakes'.The Groovies failed,in my opinion,because they stuck to rigidly to the'Beatles/Thank Your Lucky Stars'format but the Ramones blasted out none stop.It was all modern and hard.The guitar of Johnny was pounding out riffs at fantastic rate and Tommy,on drums,was incredible-he was so tight it was unbelivable. DeeDee,bass guitar,was weird-every song he counted in one,two,three,four wether it was in that beat or not.Joey was in compleat control of the audience,taking a laid-back stance,has he lean into he's vocals.Everything was right-the clothes, giving away base-ball bats and the music itself.They kick off with'Loudmouth'in a set which included all their album(I think)and some other songs which I'd just love to hear on plastic.It was all predictable but who cares,it was f'ing fantastic.
A word about the Stranglers-great!I can't wait to see 'em again, their sound is 1976.The Stranglers are a pleasure to boogie too-sometimes they sound like the Doors,other times like Television but they've got a i.d. of their own.

RAMONES(Sire-album).
The Ramones are what 1976 punk rock is all about.They are kids,I'm a kid and you are kids-you must be if are reading this shit.The Ramones give me power and freedom and that's what I want. I've had their album for weeks now and yet every time I spin it,it does me in,I can't sit down-I have to MOVEEEEEEE!
The Ramones are:

Joey Ramone-lead vocals.
Johnny Ramone-guitar.
DeeDee Ramone-bass.
Tommy Ramone-drums.
They look great-leather, jean and rubber.Each Ramone carries a tube (giant size,of course)and a bat(for beatin' brats).They are REAL PUNKS!
Their music is fast,simple and instantly likable.They hav'nt got much melody but they've got enough drive to make up for it.'Blitzkrieg Bop'bursts out of the speakers.Everything's full on,wait till your mum and dad are out(or wife if your unlucky)and turn it all UP!'Beat On the Brat' takes the pace a bit slower with crazed lyrics,next follows'Judy Is a Punk',then'I Wanna Be Your Boyfriend'and'Chain Saw'with lunatic power-saw intro.

Our anthem,'Now I Wanna Sniff Some Glue' crashes in and we're of into the stickist song around.Side one closes with'I Don't Wanna Go Down the Basement'which has a fantastic Bowie-'Hang On To Yourself'type riff.
Side's rockin'in a flash with'Loudmouth',everytime ol'Louise goes on a bit I play her this-IT SHUTS HER UP. 'Havana Affair'is great-still moving,still suprising every second.This track features a great'train going through a tunnel'riff that knocks me head off!'Listen To My Heart'is good but'53rd & 3rd'is great,smashing senses with it's plodding riffin' chorus.The album ends with three jivers- 'Let's Dance','I Don't Wanna Walk Around With You'and'Today Your Love,Tomorrow the World',which ends with a tiny bit of feedback.By this time you're coughing up blood and spitting all over your Led Zeppelin albums.
'Your a loudmouth baby,so I'm gonna shut you up!'They shut everyone up!

FLAMIN'GROOVIES/RAMONES/STRANGLERS
-Dingwalls.
This gig was lousy......
basically'cause I'd been thrown out by the time the Ramones were into their third song. It was a good night outthough thanks to a few realy good guys who were all PUNKS!It's realy nice to be able to talk to people who are enthusiastic about the punk-rock scene.It's people like these who can make something of the scene instead of posing in flashy clothes and being'hip'.I'd like to mention Steve Walsh who's one of the most dedicated punks I've ever met and a great band,the Damned,who could realy do things this year.Go and see'em and find out for yourselves(I'm sorry I didn't turn up at the 100 Club,I'm sure you were great)
The music I did hear was as good as the Roundhouse.I hope the Groovies were more raw though,I'd hate to go off of them.

RE-REVIEW:

BLUE OYSTER CULT

The clever thing about the Cult is the way in which they choose the subject matter for their pieces.They are interesting to listen to lyrically as well has musically-this sets them apart from loads of other heavy-metal bands who seem content with just blowing your head off. Even though they're'deeper'than other HM bands the riffs come first.They reach for the ultimate in heaviness and they're are always grasping it.In my opinion they're THE heavy band-from the opening riff of 'Transmaniacon MC'to the closing chords of'Debbie Denise'they're the best band to ever touch a stun-guitar.

THE BLUE OYSTER CULT:

Donald(Buck Dharma)Roeser-lead guitar,vocals.
Eric Bloom-vocals,stun-guitar,synthesizer.
Allen Lanier-keyboards,guitar,vocals.
Joe Bouchard-bass,vocals.
Al Bouchard-drums,guitar,vocals.

Their Albums:

Blue Oyster Cult(CBS'72).
An absolute classic They've not matched it for it's freshness. A spacy feel swamps all of the tracks, the harmonys are perfect and the playing is superb.The songs range from the beautiful, 'Last Days Of May',to the shit-kicking, 'Cities On Flame With Rock and Roll'.Simply great Cult.

Tracks:Transmaniacon MC/I'm On the Lamb but I Ain't No Sheep/Then Came the Last Days Of May/Stairway To the Stars/Before the Kiss, a Redcap/Screams/She's As Beautiful As a Foot/Cities On Flame With Rock and Roll/ Workshop Of the Telescopes/Redeemed.

Tyranny and Mutation(CBS'73).
This is much heavier,over all,than the first album but just as suttle and melodic when it has to be.Side one is pure rock,it must be the heaviest studio side of an album in rock history.Deep Purple are kicked in the head as'The Red and the Black' storms out of the speakers...'O.D'd On Life Itself takes the pace a bit slower(a fantastic song)and then the guitars of'Hot Rails To Hell'slice out of nowhere,then pull back to a sort of a Hawkwind type riff with Stun-guitar well on top of the mix.By this time your pulling your hair out with ecstasy. Finally the sidesbrought to a stunning end with'7 Screaming Dizbusters',and chirst side two's on in a flash man!More riffs,solos, great songs and your dead by the end of it all.A Killer!

Tracks:The Red and the Black/O.D'd On Life Itself/Hot Rails To Hell/7 Screaming Diz-busters/Baby Ice Dog/Wings Wetted Down/ Teen Archer/Mistress Of the Salmon Salt.

Secret Treaties(CBS'74).
After the sexual experienced gained in listening to the last album this comes over as more laid-back.This album is the Cult being a bit more serious than before,everything is more thought out.It's big and broad,a monster and probably their best effort so far.There are not so many 'killer riffs'as on the first two,altough it does peak,on'Dominance and Submission' (Which happens to be my favourite ever Cult track)and'Harvester Of Eyes',it is all up there.The songs are all interesting,they have a sense of mystery about them so you just want to play the album again,to try and understand it.A brilliant album.

Tracks:Career Of Evil/Subhuman/Dominance and Submission/ME 262/Cagey Cretins/Harvester of Eyes/Flaming Telepaths/Astronomy.

On Your Feet Or On Your Knees(CBS'75-double)
Realy,I think that they needed this release,so they could sit back and think out their next move.The album has been taken by some to be their best album but it's obvious to anyone who's heard the Cult albums that it's just a great bit of fun.All the killer-riff tracks are here along with a couple of oldies,namely'I Ain't Got You'and the horrible'Born To Be Wild'.The recording is near to'Kick Out the Jams'noise wise that is.No tracks'cut the studio version to pieces except perhaps'Harvester Of Eyes'which features a great synthesizer riff,which ain't on'Treaties'.The drums are mixed far to low so to get the best sound you have to turn the album fall on.It doesn't do your head much good but who cares if they die young listening to the Cult!

Tracks:Subhuman/Harvester Of Eyes/Hot Rails To Hell/The Red and the Black/7 Screaming Dizbusters/Buck's Boogie/Last Days Of May/ Cities On Flame With Rock and Roll/ME 262/ Before the Kiss,a Redcap/Maserati GT(I Ain't Got You)/Born To Be Wild.

MORE BOC ON THE NEXT PAGE!

CULT CONTD.

Agents Of Fortune(CBS'76).

       'Secret Treaties'was aiming
to this.'Agents'is completly differant
from what Cult have done before.It is a
mixture of styles that works very well.
The tracks are shorter than before but
with much more melody(altough they've never not had that).This is the Cult searching
-they don't find on'Agents'but the next one
should be IT.Still'Agents'is with us now !
Side one kicks off with'This Ain't the Summer Of Love',a great rousing driving song.
The popish'True Confessions'follows with
a realy nice vocal from Lanier.Next comes
the great'(Don't Fear)the Reaper'WhiłŁ
features the best harmonys the Cult have
ever done.This tracks a Cult classic.Ł.
'E.T.I(Extra Terrestrial Intelligence)'
comes in nice with a lovely wavey guitar
intro,a nice'funky'track.Side one ends with
the atmospheric'The Revenge Of Vera Gemini'
with Patti Smith helping on vocals-another
realy good track.

       Side two starts with a couple
of out-and-out rockers,'Sinful Love'and
'Tattoo Vampire'with a shit-kicking drum/guitar
speedy intro.More atmosphere follows with
'Morning Final'a story of death and then
'Tenderlion'a great Cult tour-de-force.It
all ends with the,almost soft'Debbie Denise'
they almost sound middle-of-the-road in this.
An album of moods and experiment ,Cult
show that they ain't heavy-metal'dummys'but
the can realy perform.More please!

       Well,that's all their off-
icial albums.There's also;

The Soft White Underbelly(Bootleg'72).

       You may be able to pick this
up somewhere.It's much better than the
official live offering but it is very short
and dear.It was recorded in 1972 and realy
shows the band at it's best.They're realy
tough and biting,even stunning at times and
that's something for a bootleg.
       It was originally released by
CBS as a promotional E.P,that's probably why
sound's so good(All this was told to me my some
heavy Cult fans one hot night down the Marquee,or was it?)Anyway,it's a great bootleg
compared to most.

Tracks(With times):The Red and the Black
(4:35)/Buck's Boogie(5:18)/Workshop Of the
Telescopes(3:40)/Cities On Flame With Rock
and Roll(4:42).

NEXT WEEK(ALRIGHT,NEXT QUARTER)WE SHOULD
HAVE A RE-REVIEW OF THE EARLY MOTHERS!
I bet you can't wait.

I DIDN'T NO WHAT TO PUT HERE

SO I WROTE THIS!

THE S.G. REVIEW SECT.

We review things as they come,so
albums,singles and gigs are all
mixed together to form one very
large,very informative review section:

RUNAWAYS (Mercury-import album).

I've always hated girl
bands,singers etc.Rock'n'Roll's for
blokes and I hope it stays that way.
Girls are good for one thing and for
one thing only-going shopping for
glue.This album though is an ex-
ception.I realy think it's got
something.

For a start,it's prod-
uced and writen by the wonderful
Kim Fowley.He's got a great little
band here and it shows as soon as
the album kicks off into 'Cherry
Bomb'which sets the pace for the
whole album.It's tight driving punk
rock all the way,there's loads of
lovely groans and sighs from the
girls(All under 18,by the way)which
should move a few punks-all the way
to the toilet.They sound a lot like
the New York Dolls half the time
and it's all right by me'cause I
love'em.Other tracks are'You Drive
Me Wild','Is It Day Or Night','Thun-
der',Lou Reed's'Rock and Roll','Lovers'
'American Nights','Blackmail','Secrets'
and the Alice Cooper like'Dead End
Justice'.

This albums a lot of
fun and so's the cover.It must be
the cover of the year-five lovely
girls spread over it,as you say
girls'you drive me wild!

I can't wait to inter-
view'em.

TELEVISION-LITTLE JOHNNY JEWEL(Ork-import
single).

This single is fantastic.
We've heard about'em but now were hearing
it for ourselves.The song is dead slow
but what a killer it just bursts with
pent-up enegy.It opens with a strained
bass riff and then in cames this out
of key guitar,which is a cross between
Barry Melton and Frank Zappa,and it's
so punky it's brilliant.The voice is
pure Lou Reed but even more dead-beat·
as side one fades out you can't wait to
get it over to'Little Johnny Jewel'Part 2
and your not disapointed the guitar solo
will burst your glue tubes.I can't wait
for a f'ing album from these guys,it
should be wild to say the least.Go out
and listen to this single and tell if
I'm wrong!

EDDIE AND THE HOT RODS-WOOLY BULLY(Island
-single).

This IS the Hot Rods 2nd
offering and it is a great example of the
lads style.Side 1 is produced by Andy Mackay
and is a good rollin' rendition of the old
Pharaohs hit,I don't think they should have
let him blow though.Side 2 is the great
'Horseplay(Weary of the Schmaltz)'which kills
WB for excitment and power.It obviously comes
from the sessions that produced the excellent'Writing On the Wall'/'Crusin In the
Lincoln' single and features a brilliant
guitar solo from Dave Higgs along with a
tight harp riff from Lew Davies(who's no
longer a Rod).I can't help thinking when
I listening to this that the Rods were
much better with a harp player.It's still
great but it could be better.Read on:

EDDIE AND THE HOT RODS/VIOLENT LUCK.
Marquee Club 22/6/76.

This gig came about after
Automatic Man had to cancel,and what a gig
it was to!I don't know where the hell Violent Luck come from but I just hope I see
'em again as soon as possible.They look like
the Stooges,and they sound like a cross between Mott the Hoople,New York Dolls and the
Stooges.They hit us with a great set which
included a fantastic version of the Groovies
'Slow Death'and many excellent original
numbers.The lead singer smashed a mic-stand,
climbed the amps,kicked another mic-stand
into the audience-actually hitting some kid
and insulted three girls,telling them to
f'off!The band are realy tight and some the
guitar playing was stunning.If anyone's
reading this who knows where I can see'em
again get in touch.

After that onslaught the
Rods had to realy play and they did to.Barrie
Masters was full of enegy as he lead the band
through a great set which included all their
recorded songs,'69 Tears','The Kids Are Alright'and a POWERFUL version of the Stones
'Satisfaction'.Yet another sweaty night with
Eddie and the Hot Rods,when will they ever
let up?I hope they never do.

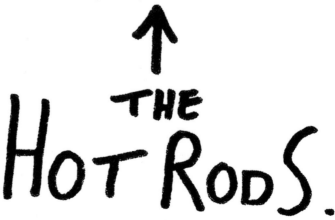

THE HOT RODS.

SNIFFIN' MORE NEW TUBES.

REVIEWS ②

THE 101'ERS-KEYS TO YOUR HEART(Chiswick
                                -single).
               This is a really good song
done realy well by a great band.Rock'n'
Roll/boogie-woogie at it's sweaty best.
They're not a heavy band,so they rely on
sharp andchrisp playing.The 101'ers are
nice and snappy.Side two is another good
song-'Five Star Rock'n'Roll Petrol'which
boogies just as good as'Keys'.
               The Count Bishops also
record for this small,but already classic,
label and I hope there's a lot more goodies
to come from it.

CAPTAIN BEEFHEART-DIDDY WAH DIDDY(A&M-E.P).
               This is not new and it's not
easy to get,but what a brilliant performance
by the Captain.He pouts,grunts and plays
some mouth-harp that will get you high.This
is early it's ancient-1964's the year but
it doesn't matter.Other tracks are'Frying
Pan','Moonchild'and'Who Do You Think You're
Fooling?'.It's raw R&B that kicks in the head
everything the Captain has done since.
               If you wanna buy it get in-
touch and I'll give you an address.THE WORLD
WILL FINALLY KNOW WHERE?

"BABY,BABY WHAT AM I GONNA DO,
 ME GLUE'S ON FIRE AND IT'S STICKING TO D.O!"
"D.D?"
"YES...DONNY OSMOND!"
"LET HIM BURN"
"YOU FIEND!"

I JUST GOT HIGH SNIFFIN' THE COVER OF THE NEW '101'ERS' SINGLE! IS THIS NORMAL?

TODD RUNDGREN-RUNT(Bearsville-import album).
               This was made when Todd was
the punk,he's not anymore but who cares when
there's stuff like this available.I reviewed
it'cause it's only just been made available
again and it's realy good.I thought that To-
dds last four albums were too cold.He seemed
to surrounded his self with banks of sound
and there wasn't enough of the punk shining
through for my liking.
               'Runt'was made in 1970 and
shows Todd in a exhilerating mood.He is some
-times soft but mostly enegetic.It starts of
-f with the shuffling and funky,'Broke Down
and Busted'and carries on through'Believe In
Me'and'We Gatta Get You A Woman',two very
melodic'popish'songs.'Who's That Man?'takes
the pace much faster and features a great
Beck-type solo from Todd.Piano rippling and
a great driving riff,a classic!'Once Burned'
is soulful and nice but'Devil's Bite'is real
rockin and takes side one too a stirring fin
-ish.Side two starts as one finished,with a
powerful rocker-'I'm In the Clique'with a
real rollin'drum-solo.'There Are No Words'
follows and is rotten,sounds like a cross
between Dave Crosby and a monastry.Next ple-
ase.A great medley follows,three great soul
tunes with a splash of punk-spirit-'Baby,
Let's Swing','The Last Thing You Said'and
'Don't Tie My Hands'.The last cut,'Birthday
Carol'is the last thing in concepts not too
long,not tooshort,a brilliant mixture of
rock styles.
               This is a classic album,and
it's great to be able to replace my worn
copy!

THE LAST PAGE.

'Heh ho,let's go!Heh ho let's go!'

That's what it's all about,right! This thing called'punk-rock!The weekly music papers gave the Ramones a hard time,didn't they,'cause they don't f'ing understand that's why.They put down their songs,stances and even their enjoyment.The reviews of the Ramones gig just sums up the whole dumb atitude of the'best-sellers'towards punk-rock.They treat it like some kind of freak-show to be laughed at,I don't know why their bother.One paper's gonna have an'A-Z Of Punk-Rock'next week just to be hip-why don't they stick th Queen and all that trash that drive around in expensive cars.The weeklys are so far away from the kids that they can't possibly say anything of any importance to punk-rock fans.I can't spell,I wouldn't win any awards for literature but at least I don't write down to yer!

Enough of this talk about shit.Somebody said to me the other day that there's no such thing as punk-rock,"Todd Rundgrenss the only punk!",he exclaimed.No body can define punk-rock,it's all about rock in it's lowest form-on the level of the streets.Kids jamming together in the dad's garage,poor equipment,tight clothes, empty heads(nothing to do now you've left school)and model-shops.Punk-rock's all those things.Shit,there's something happening in London now.We've had some incredible gigs and great scenes.London's got a <u>scene</u> goin', we don't need New York we've got it Here. The Sex Pistols,Eddie and the Hot Rods,the Damned,Violent Luck(Now called Sister Ray), the Stranglers,the Vibrators,and the tasty Roogalator to name but a few.

We've got to make somethin' real happen here.Most British rock is past it now but the punk scene isn't.Let's build our own bands up instead of drooling over the NY scene.I'm not putting that scene down but if we've got somethin'goin'on here we wanna make it better.We're gonna try to do a bit for the scene but it's all up to you-the kids(and of course,the guys who feel young). London punk is great so let's go!

THE DAMNED ARE GREAT.

THE LONDON SCENE-PUNK WISE!

←

Let's go,let's go,yer man lets f'ing go!

ANOTHER BIT ABOUT THE RAMONES.By ?

The Ramones are here,the Ramones are there,the Ramones are f'ing everywhere....well,that's the way it seems at the moment.With the Ramones you've got the style the power and the primitive rhythms.They're what makes us write this piece of bog-paper they're worth it.The Ramones have that cult feel,they'll never be fully excepted and I hope it stays that way.We wouldn't have punk-rock if it wasn't for the cult aspect of it all.

The Ramones are classic,and they are best off being a cult band.Sniffin' glue dosn't make it at Hammersmith Odean.The Ramones are ours(I'm talkin'to yer,punks!) and by the shits I hope they stay ours.'Beat On the Ingham,beat on the Ingham,beat on the Ingham with a base-ball bat!'

Goodbye all you punks stay young and stay high!

WOW!
I'M A
STAR!

SNIFFIN' GLUE...
+ OTHER ROCK'N'ROLL HABITS FOR PUNKS! No.2

AUGUST '76.

ARE YOU DOWN FROM THE LAST ISSUE YET? IF SO READ ON, YOU PUNKS!

THE SMUCKS IN THIS ISSUE:

THE FLAMIN' GROOVIES

EDDIE AND THE HOT RODS
IN HASTINGS!

BBOS

JONATHAN RICHMAN AND THE MODERN LOVERS.

♥ REVIEWS

HEARTBREAKERS

NEW YORK REVIEWS!

& THE BRATS.

PUNK REVIEWS
INCLUDING THE DAMNED.

MP's SNIFF. LET'S GO.

Funny,my piece in SG No.1 was realy easy to write.I went on about SG's place in today's sociaty and how we're better for you than the weeklies are.Now,in this second issue I've got nothing at all to talk about. The month ain't been made that great by the departure of two SG helpers,Louise and the denim clad Rick Brown(who didn't do sod all anyway).In comes the great Steve Mick,who's ready to write some brilliant pieces,plus another girl(I'm still trying to choose one) to take Louise's place.

There's been some good gigs most of which you can read about in here.On the record side there's the Jonathan Richman albums which are reviewed and not much else. Also in this issue there's a Flamin'Groovies re-review(after the Roundhouse I thought that we needed one)and a New York page,featuring the Brats and Heartbreakers.I would have chucked a Hammersmith Gorillas bit in but I couldn't get it together.By the way,their new single's great.'She's My Gal''s the A-side and on the flip there's'Why Wait Till Tomorrow'.They're both realy good tracks.It's out soon.

See I've completed my column it's f'ing easy,once you get going.I hope you like the first issue and I hope you like this one more,if you don't you can go and read the MM or some other shit and die just like'em!Why don't you do that,Dan-druff or better still,why don't you enjoy yourself!

Mark P.

BACK ISSUE DEPT.

IF YOU WANT THE FIRST ISSUE WE HAVE A FEW LEFT.IT FEATURES THE RAMONES, BLUE OYSTER CULT AND LOADS OF OTHER PUNKS!PRICE ONLY 25p INCLUD.POST.

'SNIFFIN'GLUE...'is stuck together by Mark P with help from......now let's think.Special thanks to Roger of Rock On,the tall one with the moustache in Rock On(I always forget his bloody name), Larry of Bizarre,Gloy Glue(Airfix let me down)and the noises themselves.

The next issue gonna be the greatest mag you ever saw,the shit is let loose when you open it!No realy,it's gonna look new,spankin'new if I can help it. It should have-the Damned(if I can get them to do an interview),the Hammer-smith Gollys...sorry,the Hammersmith Gorillas and anything else that I can lay me'ands on!

ENJOY YER SNIFFIN' SELVES TILL THEN!

Note: Punk drawings donated by the very wonderful(So he says)Jonh I.

Sniffin'Glue is aimed out,now and again by: Mark P,
            24 Rochfort Hse.,
            Grove St.,
            Deptford,
            London,SE8 3LX.

All words-Sticky Situations Productions.

ALL DONATIONS TO ——————>

SG No.2 - AUGUST 1976

CRUSIN' DOWN TO HASTINGS WITH EDDIE AND THE HOT RODS

EDDIE AND THE HOT RODS-Hastings,17/7/76.

Hastings'a typical old seaside town:deck chairs,flabby white flesh baskin'in the sun and a pavillion at the end of the pier.When rock'n'roll cruised into town it headed straight for the aforementioned Pavillion.We left London at 3.00 and were down there by half 6.00,not bad,considering we couldn't find the A.1.I had a right ol'suprise when I found out that one of the guys in the van was Jonh Ingham,who I'd put down a month earlier for his Ramones review in Sounds.He said he doesn't mind the album now,I'd still like to beat him over the head with a base-ball though.

Lovers tiffs apart,it was a great ride down with Barrie Masters,the Rods singer,at the wheel and everybody else shoutin'directions.When we got there the place was empty except for a few liggers and the support band hangin'around the hall.A sound check was tried but not only did the hall have a shity sound but Dave Higgs,lead guitar,wasn't around so everybody went for a walk.

Paul Gray's only young but he's a real drivin'bass player.His main influence,he told me,was Lemmy.Paul first got his playing together jammin'along to his ol' Hawkwind records.He now listens to the MC5 and the Stooges.All the Rods have differant tastes in music,but it all forms together to make the Rods sound.It's a sound that is total enegy.If you've ever seen the Rods you'll know the buzz you get from'em,well,it's the same off stage.They are constantly joking and fooling around.Their roadies are great guys to,especially Dean,who was openin'bottles with his teeth!Half a crate in 50 seconds his teeth were fallin'out afterwards but he don't care,rock'n'roll's all that counts. There's also Ed Hollis,their manager,who's a character and a walkin''book of rock'.

Waiting through the support band was murder,they came on like a third-rate Taste.At half-ten the Rods were on,burstin'straight into!Get Across To You'which had the small but happy crowd up and boppin'. It was great at the front,these kids in Hastings were even fighting for badges,wild! Every move Barrie made was cheered,when he and Dave did the leap-frog bit in'Crusin'In the Lincoln'the mob went crazy!This is where rock'n'roll realy counts,at the end of a pier

in front of rock-starved kids.No review could describe the great vibe in the hall. I just wish you could have been there,it was amazin'.The Rods done two encores and than,back in the dressing-room for a well earned rest.Paul looked half dead,he reckoned he had a temperature of a 100 ever since the Marquee gig a week earlier.The others wern't so bad,Barrie and Steve Nichol the drummer rung out their stage clothes while Dave looked as cool and unconcerned as usual.In time we were on our way back to London.It was a quiet journey back,only disturbed by some weird noises coming from the radio.'Metal Machine Music'had nothin' on this racket!

Those kids down in Hastings will realy remember the Rods.They work bloody hard to make everybody happy, they've built up a great live act and a great sound.Ed Hollis is a lot to do with it,sohas Dave Higgs-guitar,Barrie Masters-vocals,Paul Gray-bass and Steve Nichol-drums plus their great road-crew.They're one hell of a unit,I hope they go on for f'ing ever!

Mark P.

INGHAM IS HIP!

THE FLAMIN'GROOVIES

GROOVIES AT THE ROUNDHOUSE.

I've never realy gone much on revival bands.Sha Na Na,Fumble and all that lot always leave me a bit cold.It's the act they put on,sure,you can boogie to'em but they seem too rehersed,so it's like watching old men making out they're enjoying themselves are the Groovies falling into that trap?

They came on in all the gear, haircuts,even a violin-bass,not so bad but the music,that's where they went wrong.They had trouble keeping in tune'cause the heat and their new sixties type songs are so perfectly arranged that an out of tune guitar noticed.If they'd have got down and boogied it wouldn't have mattered but they stuck to their sixties formula.They failed'cause of it.What's available on plastic is great though so here it is:

SG'S GUIDE TO THE GROOVIES ON PLASTIC!

Sneakers(Skydog 10"EP).

Orginally released in San Francisco in a limited edition of 2,000 by the group themselves.This is a re-release.It shows the Groovies at they most primitive and what a distinctive sound the Groovies had,even in 1968.All the songs are interesting especially the bustlin'and exciting 'The Slide',which powers along like only the groovies could.

Tracks: Golden Clouds/The Slide/Prelude In a Flat To Afternoon Of a Pud/I'm Drowning/Babes In the Sky/Love Time/My Yada.

Supersnazz(Fan).

Another re-release,it was first released by Epic in 1969 in very small quantities.Again it shows the distinctive sound of the Groovies.Their writing was also bubbling coming out in the form of such classics as'Laurie Did It'and'Brushfire'.The highpoint of the album for me though is their renditions of'Somethin'Else'and'Pistol Packin' Mama'which are both amazing.It's stupid picking out tracks'cause it's all brilliant!

Tracks: Love Have Mercy/The Girl Can't Help It/Laurie Did It/A Part From That/Rockin' Pneumonia and the Boogie Woogie Flu/The First One's Free/Pagen Rachel/Medley:Somethin' Else & Pistol Packin'Mama/Brushfire/Bam Balam/Around the Corner.

Flamingo(Karma Sutra).

A change of label and style.It all adds up to a'no holds barred'heavy album which is bustin'with enegy.They hardly let up on an album which must be oneof the all time best.'Headin'For the Texas Border'and 'Roadhouse'(their own song)are perfect exam-

-ples of heavy-rock,where they use the main riff just enough for they'm to stick in your mind.You have to hear the excitment on this album to believe it,another brilliant album.

Tracks: Gonna Rock Tonite/Comin'After Me/ Headin'For the Texas Border/Sweet Roll Me On Down/Keep a Knockin'/Second Cousin/Childhood's End/Jailbait/She's Falling Apart/ Roadhouse.

Teenage Head(Karma Sutra).

The follow up to'Flamingo'that should have made'em.Instead it was forgoten just like all their other records.Again,it's a classic with a mixtures of styles,all done perfectly.The feel on this album is amazing.'Teenage Head'is great,with a stunning riff and so is'High Flying Baby'with a realy nice slide guitar.A lot of it sounds like the Stones but still you've got that distinctive Groovies feel on all the tracks. 'Teenage Head'is a monster!

Tracks: High Flyin'Baby/City Lights/Have You Seen My Baby?/Yesterdays Numbers/Teenage Head/32-02/Evil Hearted Ada/Doctor Boogie/ Whiskey Woman.

The Groovies on the above records were:

Roy Loney-lead vocals,guitar.
Cyril Jordan-lead guitar,vocals.
Tim Lynch-2nd lead guitar,vocals.
George Alexander-bass guitar,vocals.
Danny Mihm-percussion.

After'Teenage Head'failing to do anything the Groovies came to Britain to join United Artists where they recorded two singles with Dave Edmunds:

Slow Death/Tallahassie Lassie(UA)

This single is a classic and should always be remembered as such.It's a anti-drugs song that is the Groovies at their very best.'Tallahassie Lassie'is another solid track.A great single!

Married Woman/Get a Shot Of Rhythm and Blues (UA).

Not as good as'Slow Death'but still a good solid single,performed like only the Groovies could.

UA didn't give them anough push and they both failed.The Groovies then had nothin'so they began to break up.

(All the records listed here are readiliy available if you keep your eyes pinned.I've out singles that are on albums.'cause they're impossible to get anyway).

CONTD.

GROOVIES PART TWO

There's two records from around this period:

Grease(Skydog ep).
Recorded in 1971,this is what the Groovies should have sounded like at the Roundhouse.It's all hard heavy metal rock that blows even the hard-nuts'brains out.

Tracks: Let Me Rock/Dog Meat/Sweet Little Rock'n'Roller/Slow Death(live version).

Alive Forever!(More Grease)(Skydog single).
Both tracks over 5 minutes and they're both amazing.Deatails as above.

Tracks: Jumpin'Jack Flash/Blues From Phillys.

In the 1974 the Groovies were goin'again,the line up was and still is to-day:

Cyril Jordon-lead guitar,vocals.
Chris Wilson-lead vocals,guitar.
James Farrell-guitar,vocals.
Dave Alexander-bass guitar,vocals.*
David Wright-drums.
*should be George Alexander of course!

You Tore Me Down/Him Or Me(What's It Gonna Be)
(Bomp single).
Released with the help of Greg Shaw and'Who Put the Bomp'this is from the Dave Edmunds sessions.It's a great song with full Edmunds production takeing it to the great accolade of being my fav single of last year.Side two is the old Raiders,done with lovely style and respect for the orginal.

Shake Some Action(Sire album).
This is the Groovies sixties album.'You Tore Me Down'was only the start of it.I realy like this album,it's all good wholesome stuff.Best tracks are the title track and the great'I Can't Hide but it's all on the same level-it's a good album.

Tracks: Shake Some Action/Yes It's True/St. Louis Blues/I'll Cry Alone/Misery/Please Please Girl/Let the Boy Rock'n'Roll(Which is available as a single backed by'Yes It's True')/Don't You Lie To Me/She Said Yeah/Sometimes/I Saw Her/You Tore Me Down/Teenage Confidential/I Can't Hide.

'Shake Some Action's what I need,to let me bust out at full speed'So why didn't they at the Roundhouse.This kid that I met there summed it all up-"Four years I've waited to see this f'ing band and they come on like the Beatles on'Thank Your Lucky Stars'!"

Mark P.

For the best history of the Groovies read Greg Shaw's great article in'Who Put the Bomp'No.13-Spring'75.

ROCK ON

The ROCK ON Commercial Pitch
No use telling ya 'bout the Groovies records, the Ramones records etc. etc.ya know we got them,so with thesubtlety of Alan Freeman's nylons I ll just zap you with little gems like......

The JAGGED EDGE- You Can't Keep
A Good Man Down (£1)
On Gallant Records, these guys come on like a psyched out Standells with an Augie Meyer sound alike on squeaky Vox, and a star maracas player who periodically wipes out the entire band with great walls of shuffling beans.Defiant vocalist refuses to miss out on his nookie just because his chick has left him in the lurch- you just can't keep a good man down.

The STACCATOS- Gypsy Girl/Girl-£1.
Two great stances in one- They got a great line in frustration these boys; on one side their Gypsy Girl with crystal ball has just phased out, backed by more Standells rhythm guitar and cymbals changing key into a "hey,hey,hey" chorus. More muted, imploring flip

Southwest F.O.B.- Smell Of
Incense (.75)
A real H.I.P. record this one Consciousness expanding lyrics about everpresent fullnesses and such like- Farfisa organ with choral hook- you can almost smell the joss sticks- pop psychedelia made by people who regularly score sand and incense in ounces.
-Acid Kitsch.

Shadows Of Knight- Lightbulb
Blues (.75)
Flip of "Oh Yeah"with Killa riff and crazed vocals from Jim Sohns.

Spades -- You're Gonna Miss Me
£2. Repress.
Roky pre ELEVATORS-version of their big single. Such an authentic garage sound you can smell the carbon monoxide. Minus the ELEVATORS wobbly noise trademark , but Roky's vocals are as nasal and sensational as ever; great harmonica, almost in the right key

That's some of the 45's you can get from us most any time.There's usually lots of one offs by garage owners with funny names. Ask to hear them. See ya.

WE DIDN'T COME HEAR TO MESS AROUND, WE'RE ROCK'N'ROLLIN'YER

THE BRATS-82 Club,5/12/75 1st set(I think).

The drums bounce into action and the band steam into a powerful version of the Yardbirds''Stroll On'with that great riff well on top of the mix.The guitar's realy flowing and singer is realy crass.

"We didn't come here to mess around,we're rock'n'rollin'yer baby!"the singer pouts and they power into'Keep Doin' What You're Doin'',the guitarist,Forest Hills, realy works on this one.Next comes'If You Can't Rock,You CanRoll'which is heavier than the single.Once again the guitar is on top and all over the place,workin'hard.I Might Not Be the Only Rock Star On Earth,But I'm Sure Gonna Try and Be the First Rock Star On the Moon'is a great song,with the singer makin'the most of the good lyrics-"Ma,I'm leavin'soon,to be the first rock star on the moon".Great stuff!

'Empty Love Affair'follows and is good,they sound like the Dolls on this one.The guitarist does a real good solo at the end that takes the band into a great blues song.They deliver the blues well,especially the guitarist,who's got a great sense of dynamics.Back to rock'n'roll with'Hot Lips'which struts along well,then'You're My Girl'which has a great chorus with rumblin' bass drivin'it along.'Be A Man'is much the same,tough drivin'rock."I'd be a man if I could,but I'm not yet a boy and that's good" they sing.The set ends with the strutin' 'Qudalude Queen'opening with a real solid riff,"She's a real gold digger,a one night gigggr,I8ve never met a girl that was any slicker.An all night groover,a drug abuser don't you try to win her or you'll be a loser".It's all good stuff ain't it.There'll be no beatin'on these Brats!

BRATS-Demos.

Their studio sound is a lot cleaner than the live Brats.Both'Qudalude Queen'and'Be A Man'are both good rock songs and would be great singles.'Qudalude Queen' is particuly good,with Forest Hills-guitar using a fuzz affect on the riff.The others on the demo tape were'Seventeen',a horrible song,done with big production,and the fantastic'Criminal Guitar'."It's a teenage nightmare,rock'n'roll's against the law!"and"Ever since the trains stopped runnin'with been liming in a Subway car".It's about kids in hiding'cause they play rock'n'roll and it must be their best ever song.I hope these tunes find a way out on plastic,they deserve to.

Don't write for a tape'cause I aint even got one.I could only get a quick listen'

HEARTBREAKERS-C.B.G.B,9/7/76 1st set.

One of the best bands around ▬▬▬ these are and they sure know how to rock.The drums are like a machine-gun and the Heartbreakers slip into the great rockin','Goin'Steady'.The drumming's realy sharp and the band boogie along on top of it."One,two,three,four"and we're into another great rocker'Chinese Rock'.The vocals are sneering all over the place,"I'm living in a Chinese rock,all my best things are in hock.I'm living in a Chinese rock,everything is in the pawn shop!".Then,straight into'Pirate Love'and again the drummings' realy sound.There's a great guitar solo as well,which drives the song along at a fantastic pace.'Can't Keep My Eyes On You' is next,with a realy weak vocal.It's just right for this song though.You could tell that they were realy enjoying themselves. It all ends with the powerful'Flight'which has a nice little guitar riff comin'in now and again.They sing together on this and it sounds great.It all ended then,what a pity,they were f'ing fantastic!

New York rock ain't to bad. The punk-scene is happen,these are just two of the bands.It's like,there's a lot of new enthusiasm coming from either young kids or older rockers who've had enough of f'ing about.Let's hope the same sort of thing happens in good'ol'London.

Rykr Amrpe,signin' off from New York.

HEARTBREAKERS

AND

THE BRATS

THE ROADRUNNER! ♡

JONATHAN RICHMAN + MODERN LOVERS

THE MODERN LOVERS(Home Of the Hits-import).

    Most of this album was rec-
orded a few years ago with John Cale produ-
cing.The story is that,Cale recorded these
tracks with the band and then advised them
to re-record them and get'em out.They've
been lying around ever since.Noting the cult
appeal of Richman,following his amazing'Roadrunner'single,Berserkley probably saw fit to
release'em.They're still in the orginal form
that the Lovers recorded'em.The sound of the
early Modern Lovers is hard to describe,but
it's certainly a great record.Richman himself is brilliant throughout,and the Lovers
ain't bad either.

    An earlier version of the
'Roadrunner'track opens the album.It's much
faster than the single and the sound is very
much like the early Doors.Richman sings like
a madman over the pounding riff and the organ,
from Jerry Harrison,is all over the place.
'Astral Plane'is even more like the Doors
with the organ well on top and Richman's voice
phrasXing the eerie lyrics perfectly.'Old
World'keeps up the pace.The Richman lyrics on
this one are great,conjuring up images of
the past.There's a fantastic guitar/organ
bit that knocks me out,"Right!We'll say good
bye to the old world and we'll have the new
world".

    'Pablo Picasso'is weird,all
about the artist's sex appeal.It's sung over
a dreary beat that just keeps on repeating
itself and it's another killer,killer,killer,
killer!

    Side two starts with'She Crac-
ked'and it's just that...cracked!It's taken
at a maniac pace with guitar and organ fighting for position.'Hospital'is about love
and is slow,so slow it nearly stops.Richman's
excelleant as usual.'Someone I Care About'
brings us back to speed,the movement they
get is amazing,using a realy simple riff to
great advantage.'Girl Friend'takes us down
again to another love song and shows Richman
being gentle.Not for long,after'Old World'
Richman changes his sights to the new—"I'm
in love with the U.S.A,I'm in love with the
modern world!".'Modern World'is another fantastic rocker,a work of art!

    Why this album was bumming
around for so long I don't know,but I'm
just glad it's available now.F'ing fantastic!

Modern Lovers: Jonathan Richman-guitar,lead
vocals.Jerry Harrison-piano,organ,vocals.
Ernie Brooks-bass,vocals.David Robinson-drums.

JONATHAN RICHMAN & THE MODERN LOVERS
    (Berserkley-import).

    This album is Jonathan's new solo
outing.Altough he still uses the Modern
Lovers as the title of his group it's a
whole new sound,mainly'cause Harrison,the
organist on'ML'is not on this.The line up
is Richman and Robinson with Leroy Radcliffe-guitar,vocals.Greg'Curly'Keranen-
bass,vocals.The sound is a lot lighter
than the early Lovers as are the songs.The
first track is'Rockin'Shopping Centre'.It's
a great boogie with a realy nice,twangy
guitar sound.

    "Back In the U.S.A'by Chuck Berry
as done by the modern Lovers!"Richman
shouts and it's a realy good version.Next
the silly love song'Important In Your
Life'with lovely Mothers'type harmonies.
Richman goes crackers...as he sings about
his favourite place'New England'.More silly
harmonies and it's fab,I love it!The plod-
din''Lonely Financial Zone'follows and is
Richman's look at...I don't know,work it
out yourself!"In the lonely financial zone
by the sea,I have walked under moon and
stars".

    'Hi Dear'bowls side two in,it's
swingin'but sad.She'll never love'im.Back
to fun with'Abominable Snowman In the
Market','Hey There,Little Insect'and'Here
Come the Martian Martians'.Three snappy
rockers and they'll kill yer!Richman is
brilliant,the lyrics are great!

    'Springtime'is just Richman on
accoustic and is realy good.He is happy—
"I'm glad I'm teasesd by the breeze,I'm
glad I'mteased by the trees..I'm even
glad I'm teased by this need to share!"
An accoustic'Amazing Grace'ends the album
with great style.It just somes up Richman's approch to his music,he lives it and
he loves it!

    'Roadrunner''s juat part of it,
both these albums are classics!

For the rest of Richman:

BERSERKLEY CHARTBUSTERS,VOLUME ONE
    (United Artists).

    A compilation album with four
Richman tracks,which first came out in the
form of two singles-'It Will Stand','The
New Teller','Government Centre'and the
famous'Roadrunner'.They're all classics!

    Also on the album-Earthquake,
Greg Kihn and the Rubinoos.All good stuff.

"I'M IN LOVE WITH THE U.S.A"

THE S.G. REVIEW SECT.

THE DAMNED-Nashville,15/7/76.

The Damned are among us!It was all so obvious at the Nasville.They were only the support band but they realy turned on the style.It's bands like this that could blow the lid off the London punk-scene and make everybody listen.The Damned just scream out with enegy,they are brash,flash and loud!

The lead singer is just right moving across the stage like a panther searching out it's pray.The band come up behind him with a rough tough sound that just pounds out.Sometimes the Stooges flash to mind, and the Dolls but through it all is the Damned.The image is black,the music is black-damned by the volume.Half-hour into their set and the drummer went crazy.He's been solid all along but now he just goes mad, kicking his kit into the suprised front tables.In a mass of confusion the band trundle off stage only to return again for two more numbers,by this time they were brilliant.I reckon they could've gone on all night but they were pulled off'cause they were only supporting.

The Damned are fantastic,they are controlled madness and one of the best new bands I've seen for years.They realy liv-up to my expectations.Look out for an interview!

RAMONES-BLITZKRIEG BOP(Sire-single).

This is a fab single.Don't listen to what the OLD men are saying,the Ramones are the best.'Blitzkrieg Bop'and on the flip,the storming'Havana Affair',a great introduction to the album of the year.A killer(literally)for discos as well, just think of the new dance-the'BB'.You stuff a tube of glue up yer nostril,beat the DJ with a base-ball bat and run around shoutin''Hey ho,lets go.Hey ho,let's go!' Think it'll catch on?

THE STRANGLERS-Nashville,20/7/76.

The Stranglers are a good band but not yet there.Know what I mean,the're yet to blow my head but the're getting there. The brand of rock is hard to describe,it's like the Doors,but it's got more life.It's almost bouncy sometimes,they just seem to cruise along,partically on'Sewar'which is a stunning piece of rock.

The group consists of a very straight looking drummer,who keeps a very soud beat throughout,a organist,who looks like he's just come home from Woodstock(real hippy looking),a bass player who looks like a Ramone(leather,jean,rubber)and a singer/ guitarist who just looks scruffy.Togother they add up to one of the most orginal groups I've seen on the pub circuit. "Sorry,I got excited!257@539=740

THE DAMNED

THE BRATS-KEEP DOIN'(WHAT YOU'RE DOIN')
                    (Whiplash-single).

A real good rollin'band with a realy good single.Great for parties...no realy,it's got a ringin'guitar riff that you 'll always remember.Great work all over from the guitarist,Forest Hills.Side two's the tough'If You Can't Rock(You Can Roll)',that sounds like the Groovies in places.Probably 'cause of the ripplin'piano and nicely sung chorus.If you can't rock,you can roll...to this realy good single(They're somewhere else in this issue so go and look for'em).

BEAT ON THE DJ.

SNIFFIN' GLUE...

AND OTHER ROCK'N'ROLL HABITS, FOR ~~PUNKS~~ GIRLS! ③ SEPTEMBER '76.

THE MAG THAT <u>DOESN'T</u> LIKE GIVING YOU 'UP TO DATE' NEWS ON THE MUSIC SCENE. PRICE-25pence.

THE DAMNED ☆ SEX PISTOLS WITH ☆ IGGY POP +

BLAH, BLAH !

'Allo,this is the third issue and this is where we either get stale or really bowl you over.I don't like the mag ....it should be fucking fantastic,but it's just cruisin'at the moment.There's somethin' new in this issue,we've got photos..at least I hope we have.The BIG thing in this one is the Damned interview,which is pretty good. There's also a little bit on the Sex Pistols and quite a lot of Iggy Pop...it's not bad at all really!

The thing that's been bugging me at the moment,is...what seems to be,a gig shortaged.It's like New York's got a few clubs with'punk'bands playing every night.Perhaps there's a couple of bands playing a few sets between'em.I mean,guys don't go there to see one special band,they'll dig the atmosphere and that.There's bands in London that need that type of scene...I must admit that it's picking up at the moment.The place to be was the 100 Club,they've had some really good'punk'tuesdays and there was the'Punk Festival'down there.The success of those gigs proves that there's loads of kids who are interested.Places like the Nashville are alright but they care more about blues/rock bands than modern punk bands,like the Damned,who were pulled off stage while supporting S.A.L.T.'cause they were"playing over their time".A band like the Damned ought to be able to play two sets a night or all night even!

We should put the boot in to this type of unsureness(is that a word?) and somethin'about it.Eddie and the Hot Rods, the Sex Pistols,the Damned,the Clash,the Count Bishops,the Gorillas,Roogalator,Sister Ray, Stranglers,the Jam,Buzzcocks,Slaughter and the Dogs....they all need'good'gigs and there is probably a lot more bands.Get along and see all the'punk'rock you can'cause that's the only way somebody's going to be interested in opening some sort of club,for these bands and others like'em.I may be sounding dramatic but I wanna go out and hear the sounds that I like every night,I wanna have to choose what gig to go to.We need somethin'happening daily,if it don't get that way we can forget the whole thing right now!

I hope you enjoy the third issue.......

Mark P.

S.G. 3

'SNIFFIN'GLUE...'is put together using a stapler with Ofrex 50/60 staples and a helping hand.Also'on the team'are Mark P(the Editor),Steve Mick(the serious writer)and that's all.

Contributions from: Micheal Beal(photos and help with the layout),Roger Armstrong ('Rock On'plug column)and C.C/Jonh(some pics).

Other mentions to:Phil,Larry,Tim,Nick,Chi, the New Beatles and Steve Walsh(the FACE).

The next issue is going to have nothing to do with the Sex Pistols,the Clash and the Stranglers.It's only a rumour....

Address of the mob(to send letters,gifts, press-kits,records to review etc.):

S.G,
24 Rochfort Hse.,
Grove St.,
Deptford,
LONDON,SE8 3LX.

All gaff-Sticky Situations Productions.

BACK ISSUE DEPT.

No.1 had the Ramones and Blue Oyster Cult.

No.2 had Eddie and the Hot Rods,the Flamin' Groovies,the Brats,the Heartbreakers, and biggy review of Jonathan Richman/Modern Lovers albums.

ANOTHER THING I BETTER MENTION IS THAT THEY'VE ALL SOLD OUT!Collectors items already?

Apologies to Bryan James for spelling his name wrong throughout the Damned interview.Is a pretty good bloke,that Brian is.......he won't mind!

Gossip........the Vibrators are quite a new band to the scene,but,as original Damned lead-singer Steve said,"they won't get anywhere'cause the drummer's got long hair!".Very true... ...the Vibrators seemed lost against all those stares from the Pistols audience,all they could muster was,"we all know you're so cool",poor band.......so Nick Lowe is not a punk, poor bastard........seems like ex-NME editor,Allan Smith,is only too pleased to give his address to strangers on underground trains,who'pose as fanzine writers....and he's got big ears.......some women came up to Mark P.at the Nashville,a few weeks back,she didn't like his views on women-rockers and she was gonna suprise him real soon,we can't wait.Another female has been on to us,her name is Chi,she'll be writing some stuff for the mag... don't worry,I'll check it before it gets seen by humans.....the Jam arn't a bad R&b band, but their following at the'Upstairs At Ronnies'Disco last week,were childish heavies who would be better off in the army,saving our great coutry from the threat of Facism......END

DAMNED. INTERVIEW.

The DAMNED are Brian James-lead guitar, David Vanian-lead vocals.Ray Burns-bass and Rat Scabies-drums.Their manager is Andrew Czezowski.They've been the Damned for only a few months but Brian,Ray and Rat were in Nick Kent's band,the Subterraneans,who you'll be hearing more of next issue.David's doing his first singing job in the Damned so it's a great mixture of just enough experience and new,young ideas.What follows is untogether so it's great.One,two,three,four-

SG-You've not played many gigs,what's happening?
RAT-We'll play anywhere that'll have us except pubs.
SG-Except pubs?
RAT-You realy get a shitty reputation for one thing and it's very difficult to break out of the pub circuit.Most of the pub audiences like to sit,have a drink and chat about the weather ...we're too loud for pubs anyway.
SG-There isn't anywhere else really.
RAT-Places like the Nashville are alright.It would be nice to get a tour or somethin'.
SG-The songs you play.....
RAT-They're all our own songs except...the only ones that ain't ours are'Help',the Dolls one,'It's Too Late'and the Stooges'number, '1970'.
SG-What sort of stuff do you listen to?
BRIAN-I listen to the Stooges and the Dolls.
ANDREW-All their influences are the same,that is why they came together.
RAT-No they're not...
BRIAN-You like Dave Clark!
RAT-It's not that....it's like,yea Dave Clark started me playing but I mean....I was very young when Dave Clark came in.
SG-What about the stuff you see playing in pubs?
RAT-There ain't nothin'!
BRIAN-There's nothing going on so far in this country,you tell us what have you seen?
SG-To us there's no good or bad...
RAT-To get the scene going...
SG-It's no good putting bands down,it's great that there's bands trying.
RAT-The biggest thing around at the moment is the Rods.The Pistols are trying to make a dent but whether they will or not I don't know.About the only two bands...I don't know about Sister Ray'cause I ain't seen'em yet.
SG-What you think of the Rods?
BRIAN-They're alright,they need to progress a bit though.They're going back on old stuff but they're good though.
DAVID-They do generate excitment don't they?
RAT-I really like Eddie and the Hot Rods and you,Barrie Masters....we've all got differant influences,getting back to that.Ray used to listen to Marc Bolan until he discovered Iggy Pop.

DAVID-Until he got Iggy's t-shirt he means!
SG-He tried to swop me that...Iggy's shirt for a Marc Bolan t-shirt!
RAT-You...
RAY-I was talking about somethin'else.
RAT-That's what we got has a bass player...
SG-He wears a nice line in shades.
RAY-I bought these for 5p would you believe?
RAT-No,basically... our music fires off so well'cause we hate each other....
SG-Every band says that!
RAT-It's true...we don't see each other at all socially.
SG-What have you done before the Damned?
RAT-I was on holiday like...that's the last thing I was doing.We all had varied backgrounds.
RAT-Yea,I was a toilet cleaner...yer,print that!
DAVID-I'm still working as a grave digger, a guy who digs graves,he don't dig'em he digs graves....
RAT-Yea,we don't see each other at all socially,we hate the sight of each other and (pointing at David)I'd kick his head in if I got half the chance!

PUNK ROCK?

RAT-You can call it punk-rock but I don't think I like that definition..Punk!
BRIAN-It's the word people use...
RAT-Yea,but it's like a tag,the thing is I hope it don't go to far....I dunno,what's a punk?
SG-It's a ruffian,isn't it?
DAVID-The actual definition means worthless.
BRIAN-No one playing in a band's worthless!
RAT-You've got to have talent to some degree to get up on stage to do it!

3

BRIAN-If someone says you're a punk,it don't mean they think you're stupid....
RAT-It's just a slag down,I can see how the tag came about but I don't see how it applys to me.
DAVID-Or anyone else in this group!
SG-How would you describe your music?
DAVID-There isn't a name at the moment.
RAT-It's not rock'n'roll but it's like....
DAVID-It's music for NOW!
BRIAN-Power music...
RAT-Get up of yer arse music!We'll drive you out to the other bar in the Nashville!
SG-They were sitting there stunned at the Nashville,when you were supporting S.A.L.T.
RAT-We've had that at a few gigs...well two of 'em.Our second gig we just played and there was nuthin',except we were throwing bottles at some guys things like that.Afterwards they were calling for an encore.There was nothing after every song but by the end they went mad!
SG-What about the stunt at the Nashville,you know,kicking the drums?
RAT-It wern't a stunt,we was playing so badly well I was anyway,and that number just wern't goin'right.I couldn't take anymore,it had to stop and I knew that ounce I got rid of that initial outburst it could go a bit better, which it did.Except S.A.L.T.closing the curtains on us,we was into our last number when they done it as well.Then again,it looked good I suppose.It was a laugh afterwards,you expect hippys to be friendly people but...
SG-S.A.L.T.really wanted to get you off...
RAT-...'cause we was too much of a threat to them.
DAVID-We didn't even do our fifty minutes.
RAT-We was contracted to do an hour,but it was still great,the guy from Chiswick,Roger Armstrong came up and asked us to do somethin'.
SG-You gonna do it?
RAT-It'll be a one off deal.
SG-It's all rock'n'roll on Chiswick at the moment.
RAT-I think rock'n'roll...you mean the 101'ers single?
SG-...and the Count Bishops,great rockin'stuff!

THE LONDON SCENE.

RAT-Who wants to see and hear 45year old rock stars?
BRIAN-45 year old people!
RAT-What about the sixteen year old kids on the streets who ain't had no life,they're the ones we're going for.
ANDREW-We wanna satisfy the young audience.
SG-We need a club in London where you've got it every night,like New York at the moment!
RAT-In New York there's loads of clubs...
BRIAN-There's only about three or four...
RAT...more than there is over here though ain't there?
BRIAN-There's a scene,there's not that sort of community feel here.

RAT-Joey Ramone was saying that they all know each other.There's competion but they are all good mates as well.
SG-That's the feeling we should get here.
BRIAN-That's what'Sniffin'Glue...'is all about.
DAVID-That's what we wanna do,make people do somethin'rather than just sit and talk about it.
BRIAN-There's no fun around at the moment.
RAT-London's a real dead town anyway,like that Pistols thing we done,it was'uncool' to clap another band,you know?
BRIAN-But Johnny's alright.
RAT-Yea,I like Johnny Rotten...
SG-Ask the Rods what they think of'em!
RAT-I don't think they're very fond of them somehow.
BRIAN-It's sad,the Stranglers as well.
DAVID-It's a shame'cause really all these young bands should be friendly,it should be a whole scene.
RAT-I think we're the only bands that talks to the others on a friendly level..except S.A.L.T.!It works both ways,if you're good to a band they'll work with you.One good turn deserves another,it don't seem that way with a lot of'em.
ANDREW-That's where the punk tag relates to the scene.
SG-Are you associated with Sister Ray?
BRIAN-I know the singer and the guitarist.
SG-They're really good...
ANDREW-They're a bit dated though.
SG-They sound a lot like Mott the Hoople...
ANDREW-...and sixties R&B!
RAT-He's a good guitarist.
BRIAN-Yea,Kelvin,the singer's good too.
SG-Getting back to you,what song are you hoping to do for the single?
RAT-We're thinking of doing a slow twelve-bar actually,called'My Baby Left Me and I Ain't Got a Shirt On My Back'and it goes de, do,de,dum,da,de,do.It goes from E up to A up to B-flat and back to E again!

YEA?

RAT-It's like a vicious circle..still hassling gigs...you get on to an agent and ask"come down and see us'cause we're looking for an agent".They say"OK maybe I will".Of curse they don't come so they ask for a tape and we take'em one and they say"We can't really tell from that".They won't give you a fucking gig to start off,at one of their places....it's such a vicious circle!

4

THE DAMNED

"YOUR PRETTY FACE IS GOING TO HELL".

RAT—Dave Vanian,what makes you tick?
DAVID—Tick,tick,tock!I havn't got an image
on stage,whatever I do is just like.....
RAY—Chuck Berry smells!(He had to get that in).
DAVID—....images,I don't like anything con-
trived.I think images should come naturally,
just do what happens at the time-work off the
audience.A panther?Thats mostly'cause I hate
the audience.No I don't really,we love all
the punks!
RAT—Keep on booking us kids....
RAY—Buy our records!
RAT—There's to much plasticness around....
ANDREW—Yea,in the record business!
RAT—Funny man,no,there's too much posing.
DAVID—They're being far to serious about the
image a not about the music.Like,we're here
to have a bit of fun.
RAT—Just do what you wanna do,that's why my
kit went over,It just happened!

RAY

MP

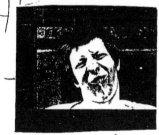

↑ RAT

STRAIGHT PIECE OF PUNK WRITING?

      People looked around and
stared.There were seven of us sitting in a
Whimpy bar on a Sunday afternoon.The Damned
really stood out from everyone else,they looked differant-an odd crew of tearaways who
might suddenly burst into bovver.
      Ray,the bassist of the band
couldn't even afford a cheeseburger and as
Rat stressed,having sussed the layout of the
joint,"It might be difficult to run out the
door with seven of us!".
      The band havn't played many
gigs yet but we know they're good.I started
asking Ray why he liked Marc Bolan'cause he
was wearing a T.Rex t-shirt(Which he got off
of me-MP)."I like'Get It On',that's good",he
replied.Ray's the only member of the band
who's into Bolan and claims that Bolan was
his only influence.Ray has been playing bass
for a couple of years,so he says,and claims
he started after seeing Bolan on'Top Of the

5

Pops'.

      "He doesn't play bass though?"
      "No",replied Ray slowly,"but
I don't play bass like anyone else,you know"
      "No,that's true",laughs Rat.
      When the band are together
they just play loud and fast,whether it's a
concert or a rehearsal.There was no rehearsal today,somebody was'borrowing'their gear.
However,Ray seemed to be more irritated
about not being able to buy a cheeseburger.
He just sits there quietly,not in the mood
for talk but boasts-
      "I don't need no practice".
      "What do you think audiences
most like about the band?"
      "The enegy!",Rat replied
firmly.I asked the band where they hope to
be playing next year.
      "Stockwell",answered Rat"We
wanna do a tour of Andrew's house!"
      "Yea,We wanna play my dad's
garage",joined in Dave,"We don't want to
play to audienced".
      "Don't you care about audi-
ences?",I asked.
      "No!",insisted Dave.
      "Audiences bore you?".
      At this point Rat came in
and clearly explained what was meant,"Do
they bore us,only when there's no response".
      "What do you do then?"
      "We don't responed back,if
they throw things it's fair enough,you know'
You get a reaction,if they like it.Good or
bad...it's a reaction!"
      "We don't usally get a non-
reaction",cut in Dave.
      "Well,we did at St.Albans
didn't we?",somebody chirped in the back-
ground.
      "No,no",argued a couple of
the band,"Throwing beer and bottles,it was
very good!"
      They settled down and I aske
Rat what made him take up playing.
      "Failed me 11+so I thought
I'd get me own back.No,I dunno...I just
like hitting things-inner frustration".
      "Shall we go?",someone sug-
gested.
      "Yea,good idea".
            Steve Mick.

      Well I must say that was
the biggest lump of crapy serious writing
I've ever read.I promise it'll never happen
again,here's what really happened in the
Whimpy bar-MP.

RAT—I'm the only one with a dynamic personality in the group.
SG—Shut up!Where do you hope to be playing
next year?
RAT—Stockwell,we wanna do a tour of Andy's
house!

LAST BIT OF THE 'ORRIBLE DAMNED!

DAVID-We wanna do by dad's garage.
SG-You gonna cram an audience in?
DAVID-We don't play to audiences,only cock-
roaches.
SG-Audiences bore you?
RAT-Only when there's no response.
SG-What do you do then?
RAT-We don't responed back.If they throw bot-
tles it's fair enough,you know?
BRIAN-Good or bad,it's a reaction....but when
you get absolutely nothin'....
SG-It's like playing to a brick wall!
BRIAN-Yea,right!
DAVID-When we get nothing we usually try har-
der.
BRIAN-We don't usually get a non-reaction...
RAT-Well,we did at St.Albans though,didn't we?
BRIAN-No,throwing beer and bottles....very
good that.
SG-What do you think audiences most like ab-
out the band?
BRIAN-The enegy.
RAT-I think that's our main selling point.
SG-It's not just your dynamic stage person-
ality then?
RAY-They like me as well...
RAT-It8s my dynamic stage act!
RAY-They like me.
RAT-Why do they like you Ray?
RAY-They come to see what sunglasses I've got
on.
SG-Do you wear a differant pair each night?
RAY-I keep on losing'em.
(What goes in here is a chat about shades,we
join the converse when it gets back to music)
SG-Do you feel frustrated,not being able to
reherse today?(Somebody had'Borrowed'their
gear)
RAY-No.
SG-You don't care?
RAY-I care but it doesn't get me down.
SG-How long have you been playing for?
RAY-A couple of years or so...
SG-Would you say that you had any influences?
RAY-No,not really....
SG-You just thought that you'd like to play.
RAY-I don't play like anyone else,you know?
SG-Does it irritate you...not being able to
buy a cheeseburger?
RAY-Yer,that irritates me!
SG-Do you practice much?
RAY-I never practice!
SG-What,do you just play when you're together?
RAY-Yea,I don't need practice.
SG-You reckon it was just born in you to play?
RAY-Not really...I saw Bolan on'Top Of the
Pops'.
SG-He doesn't play bass though,does he?
RAY-No.
SG-What made you lot play?
RAT-Failed me 11+ and I thought I'd get me
own back.No,I dunno...I just like hitting
things.To relieve that inner frustration!
                    <u>THE END</u>

6

L.B.R.
BRYAN JAMES
. RAT SCABIES
. RAY BURNS
DAVE VANIUM

**********<u>THE DAMNED-STOP PRESS</u>***********
          Andrew Czezowski is now
<u>not</u> the band's manager.The new manager is
Ron Watts,the guy who got'punk-rock'down the
100 Club.I don't know the reason for the
change.Also,the band are recording a single
for the Stiff label,not Chiswick!More details next issue....that's all.

PISTOLS 2

SEX PISTOLS-Any club,any date.

I can't remember what really happened at the-club to be honest.By the time
the Pistols made it on stage the place just
wasn't the same anymore.I mean,it wasn't the
-club,it was'The Sex Pistols'Club'!

The Sex Pistols are a force,you
get that feeling from their audience and it'
sticks in your mind.The clothes,the hair and
even the atitude,of the audience has a direct link to the band.On a club level it's a
weird thing,even I've got cropped hair now,
you just can't help getting into it!As the
Pistols pounded out their'music'the image
was in every corner of the club.Their sound
is pure enegy,you can't describe it in stupid words-you've got to experience to under-
stand.I just liggered in the tense atmosphere,posing,like the other punks(or were the-
y?).You get that feeling at the Pistols gigs
that everyone's posing so they can't really
be punks can they?Punks are carefree,and I
mean completly....you know,like a football
who kicks in someone's head and don't care
a shit.Yer,the Pistols crowd are not punks,
they're too vain.But what's wrong with that
so am I.

After their set they mingled with
the audience(mostly friends)and I confronted
Rotten,who tends to be a bit bored with ever-
ything:
SG-Do you like shocking your audience?
Rotten-Yes.
SG-Would you be dissapointed if the Pistols
audience became unshockable?
Rotten-Well,I think that was a stupid ques-
tion and you were stupid to ask it!
SG-Alright....what makes you write the songs
then?
Rotten-The audience.
SG-You gonna continue writing in the same
vein?
Rotten-It's what the audience wants.
SG-Suppose the audience gets bored with the
way write?
Rotten-Oh,man....
SG-Suppose you get bored with us asking you
questions?
He didn't seem very bothered af-
ter that one!
Everyone's against the Pistols.
I'll stick up for their music but the image,
I dunno.There is a need for'em in the clubs,
they've already proved that.It's great to
see'em.....they've been banned and all that,
but that makes their gigs even better.I reckon they're an important band'cause they'll
sound great on record(the Pistols'tapes are
very good),all they've gotta do now is get a
contract........Polydor?
Oh,yer Rotten's this decades
FACE!

Mark P/Steve.

ROCK ON

NUCKERS - Open Up Your Mind
On the gloriously psyche-
delic pink,powder blue and multicoloured
"Rembrandt"label.Opens,deceptively,with
some pretty guitar chords,then lapses into an ominous marching rhythm,with threatening farfisa organ underpining the
guitar.Suddenly!!!-"When you've run away
and there's no place to hide"-sings a
man sounding remarkably like Billy J.
Kramer;-he stops singing for a moment and
in storms this great fuzzed out distorted
psychobloose guitar-back comes the Billy
J.Kramer sound-a-like encouraging you to
"open up your mind now,see the rivers
overflowing",as the fuzz guitar makes
strangulated noises all over the place.
And so after a false ending they disap-
pear hand in hand off into the psychedelic sunset of cosmic effluence.

MOUSE & THE TRAPS - Sometimes You Just
Can't Win/Cryin'In Side.
- L.O.V.E.Love/Beg,
Borrow and Steal.
Both issued 1968 in this
country on President(PT 210&174 respect-
ively)it is the same Mouse as(Ronnie Weiss)
"Public Execution"on'Nuggets'."Sometimes"
is a lovely,wistful ballad,with Mouse's
Dylanesque voice backed by some great
chording on a clangy Fender electric-
piano.Despite the strings it maintains
it's credibility remarkably.Flip intros
with the inevitable Farfisa squek,but
lifts almost innediately with a fantastic Fabs rhythm guitar and backing vocals
arrangements- very classy."L.O.V.E.Love"
sounds like it's title-a bit lightweight
maybe,with a certain nostalgic ring for
all you flower children out there."Beg,
Borrow and Steal"hoever really goes over
the top,MOCK-SITARS!!!,no less,lead in-
toan aggressive rocker with one of those
insistant repetitive ascending guitar
riffs,that really burns into the brain
cells.These actually do turn up in junk
shops and markets,well worth 10p.

LOU REED - Nowhere At All.
"Not available on L.P",it
says on the single,the flip of"Charley's
Girl"-a sludgey'eavy guitar riff and a
very clacky bass drum gradually bring in
reinforcements and bury Louie in a mass
of off-the-shoulder riffs.Still avail-
able-rush out and help support your favourite drug abuser!
Roger'psychedout'Armstrong.

(Was Roger alright?-Ed).

7

OPEN UP AND BLEED 'IGGY POP!

IGGY AND THE STOOGES-METALLIC K.O(Skydog album).

'Open up and bleed',is the subtitle of this album.It's just what Iggy does,over forty-minutes of power and menace. All those days of looking at pictures of the 'Ig'are gone,"I wonder what he's saying?".Now you've got a chance to hear it,boy!This album shows that Iggy was <u>the</u> posuer,<u>the</u> image and <u>the</u>'heavy metal kid'!Forget Rotten for a while,you've <u>never</u> heard crowd/performer abuse like this,and what's so perfect is that the music is boosted by it.The first side's patchy but side two is perfect Stooges,just enough of everything!RAW POWER....

On this record the Stooges are James Williamson-lead guitar,Scott Thurston-piano,Ron Asheton-bass guitar and Scott Asheton-drums.The cover reckons-'the last ever Iggy and the Stooges show,Michigan Palace Detroit'73-74'.Who cares?What matters is the legend that's on it,I know that every guy,including me,would have loved to do what Iggy done.He's just one of those guys that are unbelieveable,his actions and words were just right.He knew when to give up and what's left are memorys like this album.Iggy came from a small town near Detroit,Ann Arbor,he was into the blues for quite a time.He played drums in various local bands before realising that he wanted to play <u>his</u> music.The first Stooges gigs were as support to theMC5 and the gigs picked up from there.Iggy story from around this period-

"We used to have this jam called'I'm Sick'and we did a song at the same time called'Asthma Attack'.What that was,right about the time we recorded I got this big disease and practically died.Lost about twenty pounds.I was just up in this room for about three weeks,just one my back.I literally couldn't move.Couldn't do nuthin'.But I did not want to go to a doctor because I don't like to do those things at all,because they're very....they sap one's strength.

"So we had to do a show right in the biggest part of my sickness... I was completely...just in total..I can't describe what kind of sickness it was,except that it was everything at once.

"The funniest thing was that when I was really sick,I had to literally by the will come up on stage and when I got on stage,I was white as a sheet.It was this way,we did about three jobs.While I was sick,'cause we could never afford to turn down even one job.'Cause our backs were against the wall.This was right when we got signed by Elektra,September and October of '68.

"We did'I'm Sick','Asthma 8

Attack'and one other song about being sick and nobody believed us,everybody thought it was this way of saying'I'm Sick Of All This' I was singing songs about what I was really into-during'Asthma Attack'I would weeze you know,for real.On those jobs I couldn't even dance on stage.I just barely had to get up and sing and I would fall down there and lay by the mike in pain,you know,I was in real pain.People were booing'cause they thought it was a put on and they're going"What's This" you know?That was one of the oddest little things!"

Iggy knew of one thing and one thing only-performing,that's what he does on this album,fucking fantastic!

<u>Tracks</u>:Side one-Raw Power/Head On/Gimme
Danger.
Side two-Rich Bitch/Cock In My Pocket Louie Louie.

Iggy Pop story from Zigzag by Dave Marsh. (Zigzag No.17 if you want the article,there' a couple of great photos as well).

HOT FROM THE PUNK FEST. / PUNK SINGLES \ GIRLS?

EDDIE & THE HOT RODS-LIVE AT THE MARQUEE
                    (Island EP)
        All you lot out there should
have this by now....if you ain't,GET IT!
Tracks:96 Tears','Get Out Of Denver'and a
medley of'Gloria'and'Satisfaction'.

COUNT BISHOPS-TRAIN,TRAIN/TAKING IT EASY
                    (Chiswick-single)
        A double A-side from the four
piece Bishops.Best side for me is'Taking It
Easy',written by bassist Steve Lewins,it's a
powerful rocker with some really neat guitar work.'Train,Train'is more laid-back but
it's got some great powerful drumming and
more good guitar work.Altough they play well
on both cuts,I reckon the materials letting
'em down.The songs are OK but they're not
memorable...they ought to really think about
their next release otherwise they're gonna
put out another single that's only'good'and
not great.Check out their first release on
Chiswick-'Speedball(EP SW1)',on which they
do some oldies.

GORILLAS-SHE'S MY GAL(Chiswick-single).
        As I said in the last issue
this single's really good.It seems that they
have dropped the Hammersmith from their name
it doesn't change the sound though.It's a
great swinging rocker with the band really
moving.The B-side is a slower sixties type
tune,'Why Wait'til Tomorrow',which is another good tune.The Gorillas capture the feel
of the sixties without being a revival band.
I hear they played a great set at the French
punk festival,it'd be good to see'em live in
London.I hope all you punks have got their
first single,their amazing version of the
Kinks''You Really Got Me'on the Penny Farthing label...they're a great band!

NICK LOWE-SO IT GOES(Stiff-single).
        He's no punk but this is still
a nice first release for the new Stiff label.
Lowe is a pub-rocker,from the early days with
Brinsley Schwarz to the punk fest the other
day with the Girls.This is a great record,B-
side is'Heart Of the City',both songs are re
ally catchy.Simply,a single to get.
        I hear there's a Roogalator
single due on Stiff soon,should be bloody
good!

TYLA GANG-STYROFOAM/TEXAS CHAINSAW MASSACRE
                    BOOGIE(Stiff-single).
        Stamped on the paper cover of
this single is-"ARTISTIC BREAKTHROUGH!DOUBLE
'B'SIDE".What a goodie......again,no'punk'-
rock but this is a shit-kicker.It's got mov-
ment that'll fucking rock yer speakers.Every
thing is great,the voice,the slide-guitar...
it's a bleedin'killer!I mean I really hated
it at first,it sounded too Canned Heat-ish
but it's a grower.Next please,Mr.Stiff....

9

POLI STYRENE JASS BAND-DRANO IN YOUR VEINS
                    (Mustard).
        This is a weird item from a
band I know nothing about.The B-side's,
'Circus Highlights'and it's pretty good.
Get it at'Rock On'if you dig sixties type
punk-rock,oh yer it sounds like the Floyd
in'67 here and there......

HOT KNIVES-LOVIN'YOU(K.O.-single).
        This is hardly'knockout'as
the label suggests.The guitar solo's not
bad but the whole thing's so pedestrian.
The flip's just as stunning,'Around the
World'and it's got a jump on it,fucking
thing.
        I forgot to mention,there's
two ex-Groovies in the line-up,Danny Mihm
and Tim Lynch,and Cyril"I'm a punk"Jordan
produced the bleeder.....it still doesn't
save it.

POPPEES-IF SHE CRIES(Bomp-single).

WACKERS-CAPTAIN NEMO(Bomp-single).
        These two have been out for
some time,I think,but I only got'em the
other week.They're both available'cause of
Greg Shaw,as was Bomps first release,the
Groovies''You Tore Me Down'.These two are
alright but that's all.
        The Poppees are a Mersey-sound
revival band and they really sound like
the Beatles,you sure they ain't the Fab
Four,Greg?The B-side is Lennon/McCartney's
'The Love Of the Loved',which was written
for Cilla Black.Both sides are done well,
and you'll like'em....if you're into a
'Come Back Beatles'trip that is!
        The Wackers are a differant
kettle of glue altogether,they're a drag
in a totallly differant way.'Nemo'is a
sprawling song that is just boring.The B-
side is a bit better,it's'Tonite'.I mean
I really like this bands albums but this
single.....why don't Bomp get the long-
lost'Wack and Roll'album released,now
that would be something.How about it,Greg
baby?

VELVET UNDERGROUND-WHITE HEAT(ep).
        This is a bootleg and if
you try you'll be able to get it.The
tracks are studio outakes from about'69.
It's real groovy...if you like the VG.If
you don't like'em,pretend that you never
read this.Tracks:Foggy Notion/Inside Your
Heart/I'm Sticking With You/Ferryboat Bill.

Hold on,dig these lyrics sung by Maureen
Tucker on'I'm Sticking With You':

"I'm sticking with you,
 'Cause I'm made out of glue,
 Anything that you might do,
 I'm gonna do too".

Get it for those lyrics....sniffers!

S.G. PIN-UP . IGGY POP.
+ FRIEND!

VO.1 IN A SERIES ☆ KIGGY+FRIEND
10

SNIFFIN' GLUE...
AND OTHER ROCK'N'ROLL HABITS
FOR... ~~YOU~~ WHO CARES!

28th Sept '76.

THIS ISSUE IS RARE.....RIP IT UP AND IT'LL BE RARER! Price: EMPTY YER WALLET, YOU BASTARD!

PUNK special

100 CLUB
100 OXFORD ST. W.1
7.30 till late
Membership not required

3½

"IT'S BACK TO JAZZ FROM NOW ON, WE CAN'T PLAY HERE AGAIN .... NOT AFTER TONIGHT"

+ BUZZCOCKS.

SEX PISTOLS
CLASH
SUB WAY SECT
SUZIE AND THE BANSHEES
AND FROM FRANCE
STINKY TOYS

AND THE WONDERFUL!!
VIBRATORS
OPEN 7.30 pm. 60p in

the Damned

PLUS STARS

WE'RE THE ONLY MAG, WHO KNOWS WHAT'S HAPPENING

100 CLUB PUNK FEST!

EVERYBODY THOUGHT THIS WAS A MUCKRAKING ISSUE BUT WE FOOLED YA ALL'CAUSE IT'S A VERY STRAIGHT AND DULL-A VERY UNSPECIAL'SPECIAL'!

This entire thing was written by Steve Mick....so now you understand why it's all very straight and dull. *SAVED BY MARK P. AT THE LAST MINUTE!*

OH NO HE DIDN'T THE LITTLE BASTARD! S.M.

<u>Yes,it's the'1976 100 Club Punk Festival!</u>

Monday:What a fucking great night,anybody who was anybody was there,it was an occasion not to be missed.A bunch of Discos and a few ageing hippies and popped down to see what was happening as well as the regular punk fans posing and liggering in the fun.There was a bit of a rumble but it wasn't too violent, it was a great night.

SUBWAY SECT.

The Subway Sect hit the stage first and had all the intellectual wimpeys cringing in horror and yapping about how the band couldn't play etc.The line-up of the Sect is:Vic Godard-vocals,Paul Smith-drums, Paul Myers-bass and Robert Miller-guitar, it was their first gig and I loved'em.They chew gum on stage and look vacant.The 4 songs they did were great.Oh yer,during the Sect's set I heard of a promising new band-the Fuckers(or Wankers-Mark P),the photos were great they've never played,that's why they're already a legend

SUZIE + THE BANSHIES.

After the Sect's set the buzz was going round about the Pistols follower, Sid,who was gonna play drums with the next band up-Suzie and the Banshies.Everybody was excited and thought that Sid was gonna pull out his chain and madly lash out at the poor drums.When they finally made it on stage,Sid was terrific,he kept a real clear drum tempo going which really lifted the band a cut above a few other punks currantly on the scene. the amazing thing was,that Sid had only been plaing the drums for one day.I spoke to Sid afterwards and he was really pleased and told me he enjoyed himself.

A few people spotted in the bar after Suzie's set were,Paul Weller,the Jam's guitarist and Mike Spencer,the New Yorker who used to front the Count Bishops.He reckons that the London punk scene is far superior to the scene in New York.Very true.

CLASH.

The Clash were really good. They seem to be getting better every time I see'em.Their set was more loose and expressive than before.They've dropped a member and they are probably the most powerful band on the scene at the moment.The response from the audience was pretty good but they're still yet to find their own audience.They're gonna start heading in clubs so they should soon build up a loyal following,theyfucking deserve it.

After the Clash,in the dressing room I got me Count Bishops badge ripped off,someone(a'clash')poundedit into the floor with the heel of his boot,"We'll get you a real badge",he said.Thank you, Mr.Clash!

SEX PISTOLS.

During the interval the Sex Pistols showed up.I approached Johnny Rotten,who was slouched over some chairs with Glen Matlock:

SG-Would you do'Top Of the Pops'?
Rotten-Great,why not?Should be good.
SG-There's a rumour going around that your song,'Anarchy In the UK'was made just to promote Malcolm McClaren's'Anarchy'shirts, is that right?
Rotten-No,that's just other bands jealous of us...anyway,the song came out first!
SG-Yea,but it's said that it was all planned.
Rotten-Well,all I can say to that is,"Yawn"!
SG-Just,"Yawn"?
Rotten-Yea!

The Pistols were fucking brilliant!They were really on form,there was kids on chairs,tables...the following they've got is amazing.No one in their right mind could say they"can't play",they're getting better every gig.No,there was <u>no</u> violence,they just played!

YER, IT WAS GREAT "."OH, YER?."

Tuesday:"It's back to jazz from now on,we can't play here again....not after tonight".

It had to happen,let's hope it don't happen again!It was a quieter night than Monday,except for the violence of course.

STINKY TOYS.

Stinky Toys opened the bill.They would have been great if they had done a few songs and then left but they played on and on and on and they sounded the same all the way through the set.The girl singer was a big girl-a real screamer,who looked like one of those SS birds in her drab shirt and black tie.She squealed and croaked and jerked and jostled and had a lot of power in her voice. No one could tell the words she was singing but all those wincing screams she sounded as if she was saying something.The songs I did know were,'Under My Thumb','Substitute'and a pretty good version of Bowie's'Hang On To Yourself'.Back to Francethough please,Toys.

DAMNED.

The Damned emerged next.They were really pissed off with things as they powered through their raw set.For a start,Dave Vanium mic kept cutting out plus there was loads of jeering from the"wonderful"Vibrators in the audience.The atmosphere was growing tense,it cracked when one of Bryan's guitar strings broke.15 minutes it took to re-string the thing,more jeers etc.Vanium was all overthe place when they restarted,throwing beer into the crowd and he ripped Chaotic Bass'Sex Pistols t-shirt.Suddenly there was a bit of violence at the front of the stage-a glass had been thrown.Dave jumped down into the crowd to see what happened,he was soon back on stage-"Which one of you bastards hurt someone near and dear to us...Come up here and we'll kick the shit out of you,you bastard!"

No one admitted throwing and the music raced on,the Damned were fucking great, it's a pity the atmosphere in the place didn8t match it.Suddenly,a heavy is on stage,the music stops-"There's three people waiting outside for an ambulance,if there's anymore glasses thrown we'll stop the show and have you all out!"

One more number and the Damned left the stage.Someone said the Damned are awful.Don't you believe it,there's no fucking pussyfooting with the Damned.They put everything into what they do.

"The Damned are better than most bands but they've got no good lyrics,I mean, you can't hear'em.The kids can't go,ru de dum de dum and remember the tune,and it'd stick in there heads so they can pass it on.With the Sex Pistols the kids really bop-that shows you they've made it,I mean,did you see any-

one bop to the Damned?They played Iggy Stooge,that was 1969,I mean,we're seven years on,this is 1976!",Malcolm McClaren said.He's got a good point but we think the Damned are saying something through their energy,the way they behave on stage, etc.They're certainly the most controversial band in London at the moment!

VIBRATORS.

The worst band of the whole two days,the Vibrators played a rather predictable set.Old rockers mixed with a couple of self-penned newies.You know, the Vibrators are just out of place,they give themselves a'tee,hee'name and make out they're punks.I don't reckon the should have been on the bill.Next...

CHRIS SPEDDING.

Spedding joined the Vibrators on stage for some real goodies,including 'Motarbikin''and'Hungry Man'from his great album.Two deserved encores and a suprise on-stage appeerence by Damned bassist,Captain Sensible.He sung a great lead vocal now and again,he said afterwards:
Captain-Yer,it was fucking great.Chris was waving at me,he really loved it!
SG-Spedding looked a bituncertain to me.
Captain-Some guy tried to get me off stage!

I wonder what Spedding really thought?No we didn't ask him.....

BUZZCOCKS.

Everyone seemed to be gone home for the Buzzcocks.It left us the chance to really listen to'em.Their sound is rough,very like the Pistols but that guitar sound!Fuckin'ell,it was a spitting, rasping monster.The Buzzcocks were Ok they fucking done well.They are:Howard Devoto-vocals,Pete Shelley-guitar,Steve Diggle-bass and John Maher-drums.They've got a loyal following up in Manchester and they're hoping to get some more gigs in London.

Steve Mick/Mark P.

The mob's policy:

THE WHOLE IDEA OF WRITING A LONDON PUNK FANZINE,CALLED'SNIFFIN'GLUE.',SHOVE PUNK-ROCK UP YA NOSES,GET ON BAND'S GUEST LISTS,PONCE DRINKS OFF OF WALLPAPERS & BECAME THE LAD TO INTERVIEW!

(...but we just love music-Ed)

Johnny Rotten photo on cover is by Ray Stevenson,Cheers!

OPE I DIE BEFORE I GET OLD. SG-3½

Here's a few words on the blank generation.

No Anarchy.

We don't want no anarchy,
We just wanna play outta key,
We don't want no rebel stance,
We just wanna play some high-school dance,
Why the fuck should we spray your clothes,
I just don't wanna be"one of those",
It's such a drag when they say to you,
"We wanna change things and so do you",
I got nuthin'more to say...'cept,just play!

Then.

Oh,yer,it was all about joss-sticks,
And beads,Mahler,Oz,It,
Now it's about you and me,
Give me some of that'ol reality.

Fuckin'Is Boring.

Fuckin'Is Boring,
So you must be too,
I just wanna kiss,
And look at you,
Go and get some inside-leg pleasure off some-
one else,
'Cause fuckin's destroys my mental health!

Ga,Ga,Ga,Ga,Ga,I'm a dummy,
Ga,ga,ga,ga,ga,I'm a punk,
Ga,ga,ga,ga,ga,I'm a hippy,
Ga,ga,ga,ga,ga,I'm a crap-face junior,who
can't write a word.

Butch.

It's a"I'm a woman,love me"scene,
Another one-way trip,
She's the one that's dragging me,
Into that whole'dummy'bit,
No,I won't upset her,
I'll just kick her in the teeth,
Yer,I'm a'so-called'chauvannist pig,
Makin'out I'm beef!

Poseur.

You're a fuckin'poseur,
Wether you're a'disco'or a punk,
You're a fuckin'poseur,
Wether you're a hippy or a'girl',
I'm a fuckin'poseur,
'Cause I'm writing this shit,
We're all fuckin'poseurs,
In our own poxy way.
Poseurs,poseurs,you lovely vain poseurs!

Who cares,who fuckin'cares!

I certainly don' t,baby!

I will not believe this is the
end of it all.The atmosphere is great,too
great to not believe that the scene will
go on,even with the 100 Club forgeting
'punk'rock for a while.The scene is in the
bands,in the fans who will go anywhere in
London to hear the music that they relate
to.Just look at the audiences that they've
been getting at the 100 Club,kids who have
to walk home or pay out for rotten taxis,
they're the ones that it's all about,the
music,the clothes,everything.The old guys
in the press are looking at it and thin-
king-"I wish I was young again".Yer,that's
what they're thinking.I've seen them guys
hold up the bay and get drunk'cause that's
all that's left for'em.Their music is dead,
the moment they realise it and starting
respecting the'new-wave',they'll have to
admit that it's the most exciting thing
to happen in British music for ten-years,
or more.

It's not just the press,it's
also the record companies.I don't wanna
see the Pistols,the Clash etc.turned into more AC/DCs and Doctors Of Madness.This
'new-wave'has got to take in everything,
including-posters,record-covers,stage pre-
sentation,the lot!You know,they'll be
coming soon,all those big companies out
to make more money on the'new,young bands'.
Well,they can piss off if they're hoping
to tidy up the acts for the'great British
public'.The Pistols will be the first to
be signed and I know that they'll stay
like they are-completly independent!
                    Mark'angry young man'P.

What's this:

I mean,imagine yourself in
this situation-being dragged down the 100
club to watch some'punk-festival',fuckin'
hell,I mean it's not on is it?Especially
when your press officer for(name band).The
bar's the best place to be,yer,sure,I'm
an old cunt,I care about music.Why should
I be nudged into liking a bunch of crap
like the Pistols who,"could be good buisness".I don't reckon I know it all but the
Pistols isn't music is it?It's a noise
that's all.I heard the same in'65 with the
Who but it all seemed to mean something
then,you know,when I was young.
(That was overheard at the 100 Club on Monday or was it.Still.....HOPE I DIE BEFORE
I GET OLD!-Mark P).

SG4 WILL HAVE CLASH, GORILLAS,
DR. FEELGOOD, + HOT RODS.

SG-THE 5-MINUTE RIP OFF

SNIFFIN' GLUE...
AND OTHER ROCK'N'ROLL HABITS, FOR THE NEW-WAVE! ④ OCT '76.

What,this isn't a joke.If you want something funny buy MAD.Anyway,this issue is priceless.

THE CLASH

BUZZCOCKS ✦ SAINTS ✦ PATTI SMITH
NEW LP.

THE STEVE MICK COLUMN... YEAH, SO WHAT! —MP

YAT-E YAT-E PRESS!

Don't it make yer sick?All these bleedin'reporters holding up the bar.getting drunk saying,they were there,they saw it all.They're washed up and old.I mean,take all this sensationalism crap about violence and punk-rock.If you wasn't at the 100 Club Punk Fest.and you read all that shit in the press about fights,blood and bottles you would be scared shitless!Fuckin'ell what was Giovanni Dadamo talkin'about?It sounded more like a feeble description of the Battle Of Hastings,everybody thinks of murder and massacre whenever punk-rock's mentioned now!

Three beer glasses were thrown by some idiot-alright,that was bad-but that can happen and <u>does</u> happen at many 'hippy'rock concerts.It's just stupid ,that's what it is,to blow up the violence on punk-rock and so badly distort the truth!

US AND THEM.

Something is happening, like,when the Jam recently played Upstairs At Ronnie's disco.It seems that a member of the Wild Boys(a group currently rehearsing) got mouth-wacked by a Disco-kid'cause he was wearing a Swastika armband and got branded as a"burner of Jews".It seems that the non-new-wave fans,you know,the'footballs'and the 'discos'are turning against us'cause we're out of line,we're differant and they can't understand it.

It's a bit silly,ain't it? I mean,we don't wanna'cause no trouble,we want to enjoy ourselves-possin'and liggering, shades and glue,sneers and bored expressions are all part of it.Punks are not girls,if it comes to the crunch we'll have no option but to fight back and fight hard!But it's silly 'cause who would really wanna badly hurt any one?

It's nothing new though,I mean,mods vs.rockers,skinheads against hippys,same old thing,you know? Anyway,hope you enjoy this issue,punks have been telling us we've got the best mag around.Well,of course we have 'cause we're broke,on the dole and live at home in boring council flats,so obviously we know what's goin'on!See you soon...

Steve Mick.

P.S:'ere,how comes that creep,Mark P.got his photo in SOUNDS and I didn't?Still...nicked his column this week,didn't I?Up yours,MP. Yati-Yati-Star!

YOUR FREE S.G. BADGE → 2

WHAT CRAP HAVE WE GOT THIS TIME?

Front-cover:Joe & Paul of the CLASH by Roco.

Page3-6:CLASH Interview by Steve Walsh.

6:PATTI SMITH/LOUREED-new albums reviewed by Mark P.

7:BUZZCOCKS by Steve Mick. JAM OUTDOORS by Mark P.

8:SAINTS by Mark P.

9:DR.FEELGOOD-newie reviewed by Rick SINGLES reviews by Mark P.   Brown.

10:Pin-up No.2: **FEELGOODS.**

"SNIFFIN'GLUE...'is the mag for you,
Mark P's the editor and don't care a shit,
Steve Mick's a writer,one of a glass,
And if you don't like the mag you can stick
it up you arse!"
Also sticking things in various places are;
Rick Brown(who's a fool for a banana)and
Steve Walsh(who's likewise for rolled-up
Jonathan Richman cover).

Special sneers to:Roco(CLASH photos)and all the other people I love dearly(you know who you are).

Address of the"most exciting mag ever"(my dad said that).

SG,
24 ROCHFORT HSE.,
GROVE ST.,
DEPTFORD,
LONDON,
SE8 3LX.

This mag is published by noone....well,what d'you except IPC or whatever it's called,I mean it's getting to the point when you(yes you readers,I'm talking to yer)actually like SG.Come on now,you alright?

Don't bother writing after back-issues'cause we ain't got none!I don't believe in old news,we gotta think ahead!

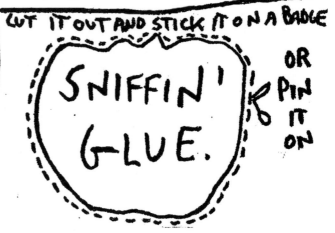

CUT IT OUT AND STICK IT ON A BADGE

SNIFFIN' GLUE.

OR PIN IT ON

THE VERY ANGRY
CLASH

"All the power is in the hands,
Of people rich enough to buy it,
While we walk the streets,
To chicken to even try it,
And everybody does what they're told to,
And everybody eats supermarket soul-food,
White riot!"

('White Riot'by the Clash).

MICK

The CLASH rehearsal studios
are situated somewhere between Dingwalls and
the Roundhouse.Inside it has been decorated-
pink and black colour scheme-by the band.The
downstairs studio,where the band rehearse,is
equipped with a juke-box,pink drapes hang
from the cieling-very tasteful.I talked to
three of the band(Micky Jones-guitar,Paul Si-
menon-bass and Joe Strummer-guitar)in the up
stairs office.

Mick tells me,he and Paul have
been together for about 6-months and with Joe
since the 101'ers broke up.They told me boredom inspires their songs-"It's just that I
can't stand not doing anything",Joe explained.

SW-What's the name about,why call yourselves
Clash?
Paul-Well,it's a clash against things that
are going on...the music scene,and all that
we're hoping to change quite a lot.
SW-Does this mean you're political?
Mick-Yes,we're definitely political!
Joe-We wanna be the apathy party of Great
Britain,so that all the people who don't vote
go out and don't vote for us!
Mick-We're really into encouraging creativity
...we ain't a bunch of raving facists!
SW-Are you a bunch of raving arnachists?
Joe-I don't believe in all that arnachy bol-
locks!
Mick-Yeah,arnachists believe in lawlessness..
look,the important thing is to encourage
people to do things for themselves,think for
themselves and stand up for what their rights
are.
SW-You hate apathy?
Mick-Oh,I fuckin hate apathy but I hate ignorance more than anything.
SW-Do you try to put this over in your songs?
Mick-All our songs are about being honest,
right?The situation as we see it,right?
SW-Right!So the songs relate directely to you
and your enviroment?
Mick-Right,otherwise we'd be writing bullshit!
SW-So,what do you want to happen today?
Joe-What I'm most aware of at the moment,is
that most people in London are going out
every night to see groups or something and
they're making do with rubbish and because
everything else around is rubbish,it's not

immediately apparant that it's rubbish.Peo-
are prepard to except rubbidh,anything
that's going.I mean,every single LP anybody plays me in any flat I go to and they
say,"this is good"...it's rubbish and they
have got nuthin'else to play...the thing is
they've got to think it's good,otherwise
they go insane...
Mick-...and it's all shit!
SW-What's shit?
Mick-All them records,right...you know,you
can't go out and buy a record'cause you
know it's just,like,fuckin'bollocks...just
a load of shit!
Joe-The only good one is that Ramones one.
Mick-Yer,the Ramones record is good.
(Doorbell rings-in strolls Mark P.to spoil
my fun).

HERITAGE.

Joe-It's our heritage...♪What are we livin'
for,two-room apartment on the second floor♪.
That's English,not what's goin'on now.
Mick-They're the most important English
band.Like Mott the Hoople's Ian Hunter always spoke to the kids straight and even
when they went to the States and they were
getting a bit flash and a bit dopey he still
used to sing about the dole and he had to
translate for the Americans and say,"look,
this is really the welfare".They don't
know what the fuckin'dole is,where as we're
all down the dole anyway,coppin'our money
off Rod Stewart's taxes!

3

In 1977,I hope I go to heaven,
Cos I been too long on the dole,
And I can't work at all.
Danger,stranger!you better paint your face,
No Elvis,Beatles or Rolling Stones,In 1977!"

('1977'by the Clash).

SW-What do you think is wrong with people
today?
Mick-They're apathetic...boring...boring
music bores me!Boring'cause it's not new,bo-
ring'cause it's not...
Joe-It's a lie...
Mick-...they ain't pushin'themselves nowhere
they ain't being creative.
Joe-Where's that picture of the George Hat-
cher Band?
Paul-Oh yeah,that's a real joke,that is...
Joe-We found this to be...
Mick-Hilarious,have you seen it?
(They hold up a advertisment for the George
Hatcher Band showing to members in typical
stage pose).
Joe-I mean,the whole thing is a lie,it means
nothing.
Mick-Except that they're on tour with Dr.Fe-
elgood.
Joe-All this crap like,oh yeah,they've got
long hair and his got his arm up here and
look at his cowboy shirt and the trousers.
SW-What have clothes got to do with it?
Mick-Well,this is what rock'n'roll's supp-
osed to look like...
Joe-It&s a state of mind.
Mick-What's the differance between this ad.
and the cover of last wecks NME,it's the same
pose ain't it?I think that's the same pair
of trousers,from'Jean Machine'.
(Mick was referring to the previous weeks'
cover-pic of the Rod's Dave Higgs).
MP-But they're a pair of trousers!
Joe-No,you can't say that's clothes and this
is music,it's a state of mind,a complete th-
ing.If anything was going on in that blokes
head he would do something about it.
Mick-To show he was a person,he would've done
something to himself.Now,he's just showing
that he's one of the many-a consumer,i.e:I
eat shit all the time!
SW-Everyone's a consumer,I mean,if you go
down to'Sex'and buy a pair of leather trousers your still a consumer.That's the odd
thing about the'70's,in order to change society you must first consume it.(You can tell
he's been to art-school-Ed).
Mick-Yeah,but if it comes out of creativity.
Some people change and some people stay as
they are,bozos,and they don't try to change
themselves in any way.
Joe-We deal in junk,you know,I just realised
that the other day.We deal in junk.We deal in
like,the rubbish bin.What we've got is what
other people have put in the rubbish bin.Like
Mick's shirt was gonna be put in the bin until he paid 10p for it.I mean,you ain't gonna
go down to'Sex'with yer ten quid stuffed in

4

yer pocket and buy some stupid...er...I
dunno,I've never even been down there.
Mick-I think it's a bit easy to go down
there and look great,I mean,there stuff's
pretty good.Looks good to me,but I think
the way we do it is much more accesible
to kids cos'anyone,at very little price
and it encourages'em to do something for
themselves.It's to do with personnal freedom...I don't think it's just the trousers
though,I mean,the trousers reflect the
mind.
Joe-Like trousers,like brain!

"WHITE RIOT,I WANNA RIOT!
WHITE RIOT,A RIOT OF ME OWN!"

SW-Would you say your image is violent or
suggestive of violence?
Mick-It reflects our'no nonsense'attitude,
an attitude of not takin'too much shit.I
don't like violence tough.
SW-What do you think of the aura of violence that surrounds the Pistols,I mean,
it can easily get out of hand.
Joe-I think it's a healthy sign that people arn't going to sleep in the back-row.
Mick-I think people have got to find out
where their direction lies and channel
their violence,into music or something
creative.
SW-Thing is,you talk about being creative
but say the thing got so popular that we
had all those fuckin'footballs and discos
and all that lot coming down to see Pistols
gigs,They'd take the violence at face value and go fuckin'crazy!
Mick-So you think it can get out of hand?
SW-You bet it can...
Mick-It got out of hand on Tuesday(100Club
fest-glass throwing incident).
SW-I reckon it could get worse.
Mick-I definitely think it could escalate
but the alternative is for people to vent
their frustrations through music,or be a
painter or a poet or whatever you wanna be.
Vent your frustrations,otherwise it's just
like clocking in and clocking out...clock
in at the 100 Club,every one comes in,
everyone clocks out,it ain't no differant.
SW-How much change do you want,d'you want
a revolution?
Joe-Well...yeah!
SW-A bloodless one or do you want just total
chaos?
Joe-No,I'm just not into chaos,and I don't
believe it when people say they are'cause
you've got to be a special type...
SW-Of maniac?
Joe-Well,a Frenchman,about 100 years ago
could be into chaos'cause it was possible
then,but nowdays,this is like sleepytown.
So,when someone tells me they're into chaos
I don't believe it.

CLASH!

Joe-What I would like to see happen is,very much...I realise a lot of people are quite happy,you know,at that market down the road from here.All them people,they're as'appy as sandboys and I'd just like to make loads of people realise what's goin'on.Like,all those secrets in the goverhmeht and all that money changing hands and every now and then it comes to light and someone gets sacked and someone else comes in the back-door,know what I mean?I'd like to get all that out in the open and just see what's goin'on.I just feel like no one's telling me anything,even if I read every paper,watch TV and listen to the radio!

RADIO.

SW-What was that with the radio at the 100 Club gig?
Joe-Well,all that was...I'd been lucky and bought a cheap transister in a junk-shop for ten-bob and it worked quite well.I'd been goin'around with it on my ear for a few days just to see what it was like.When someone broke a string I got it out and it just happened to be something about Northern Ireland.
Mick-A state of emergency...
SW-Yeah,bombs...I thought it was interesting I thought maybe it was part of the way you approach your audience.
Mick-That was part of it,but we've tried other things since then,like at the Roundhouse ...er...we'talked'to the audience...
Joe-But they were half asleep...
Mick-The ones who were awake were pretty clever.
Joe-I didn't think so,I mean,you could hear them,I couldn't.How can I answer smartass jibes when I can't hear'em?All I could hear was some girl sayin',"nyah,nyah,nyah!"and then every-one goes,"aha,ha,ha(Bursts out laughing)".If you can't hear what they're saying,then you can't really get out your great wit!
Mick-Well,I'm sure they were funny'cause everyone was laughing at'em but when Joe said something like,you know,"Fuck off,fatso!", there was just complete silence!
(More laughter).
SW-So,what do you wanna do to your audience?
Joe-Well,there's two ways,there's that confronting thing right!No...three ways.Make'em feel a bit...threaten'em,startle'em and second-I know it's hard when you see rock'n'roll bands,to hear the lyrics are but we're workin'on getting the words out and makin'em mean something and the third thing is rythmn. Rythmn is the thing'cause if it ain't got rythmn then you can just sling it in the dustbin!

"He's in love with rock'n'roll,wooaghhh!
 He's in love with getting stoned,woooagh!
 He's in love with Janie Jones,wooagggh!
 But he don't like his boring job,no-oo!"

(Janie Jones'by the Clash).

ANY INFLUENCES?

Joe-That's a tricky question...Paul's are the Ethiopians and what's that otherband?
Paul-The Rulers.
Joe-I've never heard of'em!
Mick-Up until now,I thought everything was the cat's knackers and every group was great.I used to go to all the concerts all the time and that's all I did.Until,some-how,I stopped believing in it all,I just couldn't face it.I s'pose the main influences are Mott thé Hoople,the Kinks,the Stones but I just stopped believing.Now, what's out there(points out the window) that's my influence!
SW-What changed your way of looking at things?
Mick-I just found out it wern't true,I stopped reading all the music papers'cause I used to believe every word.If they told me to go out and buy this record and that, then,I'd just go out and do it.You know, save up me paper round and go out and buy shit and now I'm in a position where I'm selling the records'cause I don't have much money and they're showing me how much my shits'worth!'Cause I paid 2 quid for them albums and they give me 10 pence down the record shop,that's how much they think you're worth!

MICK.

Mick-I've played with so many arse'oles and my whole career has been one long audition.Like,I was the last kid on my block to pick up a guitar'cause all the others were repressing me and saying- "no,you don't want to do that,you're too ugly,too spotty,you stink!"...and I be-lieved'em.I was probably very gullible and then I realised that they wern't doing too well and I said,ah fuck,I can do just as well!

PAUL

5

LONDON'S BURNING WITH BOREDOM,
LONDON'S BURNING,DIAL 999!"

SW-What do you think of the scene so far?
Mick-Well,it's coming from us,the Pistols,
Subway Sect and maybe the Buzzcocks,that's
it,there are no other bands!
MP-What do you think of bands that just go
out and enjoy themselves?
Mick-You know what I think,I think they're a
bunch of ostriches,they're sticking their
heads in the fuckin'sand!They're enjoying
themselves at the audience's expense.They're
takin'their audience for a ride,feeding the
audience shit!
MP-What if the audience say they're enjoying
themselves?
Joe-Look,the situation is far too serious
for enjoyment,man.Maybe whenwe're 55 we can
play tubas in the sun,that's alright then to
enjoy yourselves,but now!
Mick-I think if you wanna fuckin'enjoy yourselves you sit in an armchair and watch TV
but if you wanna get actively involved,'cause
rock'n'roll's about rebellion.Look,I had this
out with Bryan James of the Damned and we
we're screamin'at each other for about 3 hour
'cause he stands for enjoying himself and I
stand for change and creativity.
Joe-I'd rather play to an audience and them
not enjoy it,if we we're doin'what we thought
was honest.Rather than us go up and sing-
Get outta Denver,baby!Jand do what we didn't
think was honest.
Mick-If they enjoy us then they come withus.
If you ask me what I think of groups like the
Hot Rods,I think they're a load of bozos and
they're not telling the audience to do anything other than stay as they are.They're
playing old stuff and I don't think much of
their orginals.The situation is where the
Hot Rod's audience are bozos and it's easy
to identify with a bozo.I mean,obviousyly
they're goin'down...like,people queing outside the Marquee,they've got a great thing
goin'for themselves,but it's not to do with
change,it's just keeping people as they are!
SW-What do you think the scene needs now?
Mick-Ten more honest bands!
Joe-More venues...
Mick-More events!
Joe-...just more people who care,if we could
get out hands on the money and get something
together...immediately.None of the promoters
running any of the venues in London,care.Ron
Watts,the 100 Club bloke,has done something
but no one else really cares.They don't give
a shit about the music,not one shit!
                    END.

All CLASH photos by Roco.

Also,a mention to CLASH drummer,Terry Chimes,
who wasn't at the interview.
                              Steve Walsh.

PATTI SMITH

PATTI SMITH-RADIO ETHIOPIA(Artista-album).

Side one:Ask the Angels/Ain't It Strange/
Poppies/Pissing In a River.

Side two:Pumping(My Heart)/Distant Fingers/
Radio Ethiopia(a)Radio Ethiopia(b)Abyssinia.

        This album takes Patti a long
way from NYC,the sound is more like Blue
Oyster Cult.For me,the Patti Smith Band
have finally made it...as a band.Their
first album,'Horses'is good but this one
is great!
        'Ask the Angels'is a great
opener with a lovely rolling melody and
tasty Lenny Kaye lead-guitar work,the
finest I've heard from him.Patti,herself,
is just right,her voice is getting better
all the time.'Ain't It Strange'is almost
reggae,it's my fave track at the moment,
it's a pity Patti's lyrics are lost slightly in the production.'Poppies'is very
like the title track of the first album.
Patti describes a happening-"The gas in-
flicted her entire spine",the monologue
is haunting.
        'Pissing In a River'is not as
strong as the rest of the album.I can't
hear the words,not very catchy,boring big-
production ballard...
        'Pumping(My Heart)'wakes me
up,it's an out-and-out rocker,powerful
and great!My second fave follows-'Distant
Fingers',a song written by Patti with the
Cult's Allan Lanier(Maybe he's playing on
it?It's funky,there's a nice clickin'guitar
and off-beat drumming.It'd·be a good single,
there's a dramatic chorus.
        'Radio Ethiopia'-heavy intro,
lot's of moog jungle noises,pulsating riff,
vocals-totally bizarre,begins to sound
like space-rock,TOTAL CHAOS!This is great
Patti Smith,there's lots to listen to,lots
to understand,or is there?
        Whatever the meaning of any
song on this album it's still a goodie.
Touhhes of heavy-metal,pop,reggae,SciFi and
of course-punk!The real thing I get from
this is the feeling of the band,as a whole.
The thoughts of listening to a crazed NYC
poet are gone,they're now a killer punk-
band-probablyy the best in NYC.
                              Mark P.

LOU REED-ROCK'N'ROLL HEART(Artista-album).
        Sad to say that I wish
to denounce one of my heros.Sorry,but he's
said it all before.12 tracks that just go
onn and onn and onnnnnnn.....
                              Mark P.

BUZZCOCKS + THE JAM

It really shows the effect of the Pistols on an audience when bands start forming out of them.The Buzzcocks-Howard Devoto:vocals,Pete Shelley-guitar,John Maher-drums and Steve Diggle-bass are one such band they saw the Pistols at Manchester in June and from then on the Buzzcocks thought they could do better.Tired of all the"clever flashy groups"they knew ther could do better by just getting up on stage and singing about "supermarkets"and"boredom".

SM-Do you want anything changed in the band?
Steve-We like the way things are.Perhaps the sound could be improved.Like,I've got a Les Paul but Pete doesn't want to use it,he prefers to use his Audition guitar.It's broken at the neck but the sound he gets from it is what he wants.
SM-Do you like interviews or do they bore you?
John-Yeah,but I don't know what to say.
SM-What do you think of the music press,the way they treat the'new-wave"?
Pete-I like Giovanni Dadomo...
SM-Urhg,I hat'im.
Pete-...he did a good piece on us.
SM-Do you think they're too interlectual.As if they observe and don't know what it's all about.You,know,they just observe and look down on it all.
Pete-Yeah,I suppose so.
SM-Caroline Coon's about the best,she knows she's on the outside.
Pete-Oh,come on!Did you see what she was wearing at the'Screen'?That ripped t-shirt with safty-pins in it!
SM-Well,she's just enjoying herself,good point though.What do you think of London audiences?
Steve-They're alright,but it pisses me off a bit.When they just stand there,like,at the 'Screen On the Green',we were the first group on and the audience were very cold.
On stage,the Buzzcocks,undismayed by scant audiences,don't give a shit Their first number,'Breakdown'showed forcefully what they're about.Devoto,with cropped orange tinted hair,stands twisted infront of the mic,his head always turned away from the audience.Pete,with a razorblade earring dangling about his head,clasps his guitar and throttles out riff after riff that proves he don't need no solos.John's drumming in'Oh Shit'couldn't have been better,whacking away without a trace of feeling while Steve maintains the pace on bass.Rumbling away on such goodies as,'Big Dummy'.The audience don't know,the Buzzcocks don't know and even we don't know what they're about-but we all know they're good,very good!

Steve Mick.

THE JAM-Newport Court,Soho.16/10/76.

A really nice one by the Jam. It takes a lot of'go'to do something like this,yeah,play in the street.Honest,they played on the fuckin'pavement.The sound was a bit low,obviously,but everything was fine.
They're a resricted band'cos they play'60's R&B but within that structure they're great.Wearing suits and ties they played for a good half-hour and got two'encores'from the crowd who were a mixture of tourists,Chinese,and actual Jam admirers.They should be great at the 100 Club next week where they can get a better sound.Their equipment's good,the guitarists got a Rickenbaker(the type Pete Townshend used to play)and so has the bassist.It'd be great if they could start writing some stronger material,you,know,this sixties rivival thing's alright for a start but what we need now is more serious bands who have got something to sing about.The Jam are good but they've got a lot to think about(and change)before they break into the London-scene with any credibility.
Mark P.

GOSSIP/NEWS/CRAP

I hear that the Vibrators are to be Chris Spedding's backing band, should go well together.No,the Vibrators were actually good at the Nashville the other day.They dropped most of the oldies and played a loud and fast set...at the same the Stranglers were slightly boring,playing the same old set...EMI,good or bad for the Pistols?The Pistols,who are now ready to perform'anarchy'at major gigs throughout the country,obviously think it's a good thing...Steve'two-tone'Havoc has made it! Once your pin-up gets to the middle pages of the SUN your a star...Richard Hell EP due from Stiff,soon I hope...Mark P's band, the New Beatles,have split up.Some of the guys have gone back to playing the blues and one,a guitarist/bassist is looking for a"hot"punk band to play with...Sid Vicious has got a"weird"stage act lined up for his new band,which also stars Steve Walsh,SG writer...you see,they're all trying to be stars...two new bands have come along,the Boys,who are in the sixties mould and a more interesting bunch called,Chelsea... a big tube goes to Kris Needs of Zigzag. His Flamin'Groovies/Ramones articles and punk reviews over the past couple of months havn't been bad...us and them again.the Clash played London University the other day supporting Shakin'Stevens and some teds started trouble,still,no one was badly hurt these mixed music gigs are getting hairy though...till next time-bollocks!

7

STRANDED WITH THE SAINTS

THE SAINTS-(I'M)STRANDED(Fatal single).

My whole vision of Aust-
ralian rock'n'roll was darkened by the comedy
image of AC/DC.Who needs schoolboys when the
Saints prove that there's at least some life
'down under'(cliches,cliches!).This single is
a brilliant effort.The Saints recorded and
released it themselves.They're what rock'n'
roll's all about.They move-fast,loud,very
like the Ramones,but they're no take-off.B-
side is just as exciting,'No Time'-no solos
just power.Single of the year?It should be.
The Saints formed as Kid
Galahad and the Eternals in'73 and at once
found it hard goin',so they say-
"The original band started
with Chris Bailey-vocals,Ed Kuepper-guitar
and Ivor Hay-piano.We couldn't get a bassist
or a drummer because no one wanted to play
with us.We only managed to play at a few parties because audiences at the time didn't
want to hear our versions of R&B standards.
We eventually manged to get a drummer and
Ivor changed to bass to save time.We staged
our big debut at a local'Returned Soldiers
Hall',about 150 people turned up,half of who
walked out after the first number.Then after
the second our drummer walked out and we almost called it'quits'but we decided to keep
playing to the 30 people who were still with
us.Before the last number the manager of the
hall arrived with cops,turned off the power
and told us to"fuck off"!The cops told us
they would confiscate our equipment if we
didn't go,so we went.
"We retired from the music
scene for a while and then started off again
when we got a new drummer.We booked another
hall and the second dance was a bit more successful but we had to stop early again.The
hall manager was beaten up because he tried
to stop people pissing in his yard,which was
next-door.
"This brings us up to the
start of'75.We got another drummer,our first
date with him was at a'Communist Party Of
Australia'dance.We thought this might be our
first success but our fan-club got a bit over
enthusiastic and a fight broke out with the
Commies which we got dragged into.By this
time we were banned by all the local halls
so we broke up.
"After a couple of months
we decided to make another go of it,as the
Saints.This time,Ivor changed to drums and
we got another bass player and played our
first really successful dance.It was on New
Year's Eve around a swimming pool and the
audience was great.This booking got us another,put on by the newly started Queensland
FM Radio Station,about 500 people turned up,
half of who walked out but those who stayed
loved it.The guy who booked us was arrested
for selling drugs and the guy who took over

the station,hated us.So,after a few more
moderately successful dates we decided to
cut a record ourselves because the record
companies didn't want to have anything to
do with us.
"Just before the record
was recorded our bass player left in high-
ly scandalous circumstances and Kim Brad-
shaw joined the band.He's the first fourth
member who's been enthusiastic about our
stuff".
If you want the record
send 90p :ETERNAL PRODUCTIONS,
20 LAWSON STREET,
OXLEY 4075,
QUEENSLAND,AUSTRALIA.

KIM.

IVOR.

CHRIS.

ED.

DOCTORS →

DR.FEELGOOD-STUPIDITY(United Artists-album).

The Feelgoods(Lee Brilleaux-lead vocals,harp,slide-guitar.John B.Sparks-bass guitar.Wilko Johnson-lead guitar,vocals. The Big Figure-drums,vocals).have always been just that bit better'live'than on their recorded stuff.With this album they've secured a place in the live album'hall of fame',it's pure unadalterated energy all the way with no let-up at any point.Those of you who've seen the band will,no doubt,know what to expect but one thing I wasn't expecting was the sound clarity of the album-it's superb.

You can tell when Wilko does one of his"walks"(for want of a better ward) by the audiences'roar of approval.There are no long monologues in between songs,maybe a brief"thank you"that's all.These guys are here to play and they play bloody well,not flash,nothing technical,just good clean rock 'n'roll.Take Wilko's,all too brief,solo in 'All Through the City',it's so short and simple,it's beautiful.'I'm a Man'features full audience participation and'Walking the Dog' has an ace Wilko riff plus a nifty solo not a million miles removed from'Because You're Mine'(from'Malpractice').

Side two goes off at full throttle with'Going Back Home'and the pace is carried through the whole side,coming to a great end with yer'actual'Roxette'.This is the way rock should be;clean,hard,uncompromising and great to annoy neighbours with.

If this is stupidity give me a blow on the head,now!Right punks!

Tracks: Talking About You/20 Yards Behind/ Stupidity/All Through the City/I'm a Man/ Walking the Dog/She Does It Right/Going Back Home/I Don't Mind/Back In the Night/I'm a Hog For You Baby/Checking Up On My Baby/Roxette.

Rick Brown.

(Sorry...the silly bastard forgot to mention that a free single was given away with the first 20,000'Stupidity's featuring,'Riot In Cell Block No.9'and'Johnny B.Goode'.Also there's a single taken from the album-'Roxette'.On the flip there's a great live version of'Keep It Out Of Sight'which ain't on the album.Right,anything else?No?Right then... I'll naff-off-Ed).

ROCKY SHARPE & THE RAZORS(Chiswick-EP).

I wouldn't review this really but it is on Chiswick ain't it,so it's pretty important.Basically it's do-wop/rock'n'roll and it sounds alright but I don't know a fuck about rock'n'roll do I?

I used to go and see this band (they broke up)and it brings back memorys, wah!If you,like the music(do-wop)get it...

Tracks:Drip Drop/What's Your Name/So Hard To Laugh/That's My Desire.

LEW LEWIS-BOOGIE ON THE STREET(Stiff).

Yet another killer from Stiff. Lew Lewis is the guy who used to play harp as Lew Davies in Eddie and the Hot Rods, you know,those great harp-riffs on'Writing On the Wall'and'Horseplay'.All his Southend mates help him out on this tasty slice of Oil City R&B,including a couple of Docs (see over there ←).

Lew's harp is everywhere at once,it's got a great sound,weaving in and out of the guitars.His voice ain't bad either,it handles the sparse lyrics with ease.B-side is a nice one too-'Caravan Man'.

It's fantastic to see Lew doing something at last(I usually see him drunk and crackers)it's be great to see him live.

PINK FAIRIES-BETWEEN THE LINES(Stiff).

Yes,another Stiff.Their only non-killer so far.The Fairies are a great bunch of guys but for me they'll always be a'hippy'band and nothing else.Both sides of this single are a bit unmemorable.The B-side,'Spoiling For a Fight'nearly makes it but for me it's a single to forget.

DAMNED-NEW ROSE(Stiff).

At last,a real'punk'single. The Damned,one of the hardest bands around,have come up with a killer.Produced by Nick Lowe,this single carries everything the Damned have to offer.The energy on 'New Rose'is frightening,listen to this and realise what it's all about.Everyone, old musicians,old'stars',the British record-buying public-find out how rock should sound on record.By this thing or be very boring!

B side is'Help'.

ALL ABOARD WITH ROOGALATOR(Stiff-EP).

At last it's out.Was it worth waiting for?Well yes,it takes a few listens but after a while it gets yer.Roogalator are,what you call,classy.

It was recorded on the John Peel Show and the sound is real soft.'All Aboard'on the first side cruisies along beautifully.Danny Alder(vocals,guitar)is great,very laid-back,but he's good at singing at this pace.Side two is'Cincinatti Fat Back'and it's funky.Again Alder is perfect,singing a'chatty'type lyric.

Not the sort of single/EP that knocks yer head off(like the Damneds)but with both sides being over 5 minutes it's a nice one.

9

← RAZORS.

SG PIN-UP No2. FEELGOODS

SPARKO. + FRIENDS

BIG FIG.

WILKO, LEE,

FRIENDS →

SNIFFIN' GLUE...

AND OTHER ROCK'N'ROLL HABITS, FOR A BUNCH OF BLEEDIN' IDIOTS! NOVEMBER '76.

If you actually like is rag you must be one of the idiots we write it for. Price:

EDDIE AND THE HOT RODS
LIVE AND ALBUM REVIEWS.

THE SUBWAY SECT PLUS CHELSEA

No DOUBT ABOUT IT... IT's S.G. ⑤

MARK P.
Pisses on the lot of 'em!

Over the past month I've noticed how every Tom,Dick and Harry writer takes hold of"punk-rock"and gives it his or her expert opinion.Even the ones I used to trust are jumpin'on the bandwagon and fighting over the exclusive interviews.That's nothing to do with what's happening at the moment.

I hope that with the new young music will come new writers who have got the right to vent their ideas and opinions.Certain writers in the established rags are latching on to the new bands in the same way that they change the fashion of their clothes.Writing about"punk-rock"is the thing to do at the moment.I hope the"fashion"soon dies out,then you'll be able to find out who really believed in the bands!

Half of'em have been to the good ol'college.They've all passed their Eng Lit and all them crappy exams.I used to enjoy reading about the Pistols,the Clash and the other bands in SOUNDS etc.but not anymore.SOUNDS,NME,MELODY MAKER & the new crap-ROCKSTAR should stick to writing about the established artists.Leave our music to us,if anything needs to be written,us kids will do it.We don't need any boring old fart to do it for us!

I might put down all the established writers but I also want to say something else.All you kids out there who read'SG',don't be satisfied with what we write.Go out and start your own fanzines or send reviews to the established papers.Let's really get on their nerves,flood the market with punk-writing!Before you rush out,here's what's in this issue:

There's a Eddie & the Hot Rods live review by Steve Mick while I review their album.Two pretty new bands are also featured- Subway Sect and Chelsea-done by Steve Mick and me respectively.Up towards the back there's also a fanzine review and and news of a new punk-club.Another classic or a load of cobblers?It's not a bad ish'I suppose...could be better though.

All the music papers had better give us a good write-up otherwise we'll lock all their glue away in a cupboard and throw the key amongst a Sex Pistols'mob! So there....(Piss off,Pee!-Steve Mick)

Sorry,Mark P.

SG Competition: Why don't you like SG?

Send in your answers and you could win something that's worth a great deal of money.Winning entry picked by the Damned bassist,Captain Sensible.Cmp closes: 10/12/76.

2

WHAT WE GOT IN THE LUMP OF BOG?...oh shit!

Start again:

WHAT WE GOT IN THE OL'LUMP OF BOG-PAPER THIS WEEK?

Front cover: Barrie Masters of the Rods at the Dentists.Photo taken by Dr.Michael Beal.

Page 3&4: EDDIE & THE HOT RODS-live & LP reviews.

Page 5&6: SUBWAY SECT-a sort of interview.

Page 7: GOSSIP,FANZINES,and any old iron.

Page 8: CHELSEA-bits & pieces.Maybe a live review...I dunno yet.

Page 9: SINGLES-New York stuff plus some good bands. ← PISTOLS

Page 10: Have a look for yourselves...

Page 11: Pin-up of CHELSEA. ↖ FREE MEMBERSHIP TO A CLUB!

'SNIFFIN'GLUE...'personnel:

Mark P: Editor and layout.

Steve Mick: Staff writer and funny clothes.

Also of help were: Michael Beal(Hot Rods' photos),Sheila Rock(Chelsea photos)and the Subway Sect(Subway Sect photos).

Special thanks to anyone who deserves it.

All freebees and new jokes to:

24 ROCHFORT HOUSE, GROVE STREET, DEPTFORD, LONDON,S.E.8. 3LX.

WE HAVE NOW GOT A PHOTOGRAPHER HIS NAME'S HARRY. SEE THE NEXT SG.

All writings in this here mag are under the Sticky Situations Productions banner,so just watch it!

Notice how everyone namedrops'Sniffin'Glue' and Mark P when they decide to write about the new wave.Just shows how easy it is to take people in,these days of apathy...they will fall for any ol'guff!

BACK- ISSUES!
We know that a lot of you guys(and girls)are craving for SG back-issues but we ain't got none.At the moment there's only two of us running the mag so it's a bit hard to think of all the old stuff.We're into thinking ahead, the early issues ain't much good anyway. For chirst's sake don't collect SG for the sake of it.It ain't a stamp collection you know!As I said before-the old issues are a load of crap,forget'em!

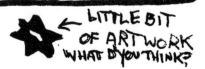

← LITTLE BIT OF ARTWORK WHAT DYOU THINK?

PHOTO: MICHAEL BEAL.

THE HOT RODS HIT WOOLWICH - 5/11/76.

"Hot Rods!...Hot Rods!...Hot Rods!...Hot Rods!".Towards the end of the support band's set the shouts for the Rods increased.

The Rods emerged to a massive welcome."We'd like to play a number called 'Getting Across To You'".You could see that Barrie Masters meant it.

Next number up was'96 Tears'and someone collapses near me in sheer fuckin' joy.He doesn't care.What are a few scratches and bruises when it's the Rods?Who cares if you rip and dirty your clothes,enjoy yourself!Up he gets with a little help and he's back into boppin'like everyone else.

"This is a number called'Keep On Keepin'On'".Barrie claps,everyone claps! 'All I Need Is Money'and'Show Me'from their new album followed.All of us moved to the beat as if we've known the Rods all our life. The audience is part of the band,what can I say?Fuckin'ell,it's all been said before but it's true.You've got to have been to a Rods' gig to know what it's like-it's incredible!

There's some crazy boppin'every where after Barrie announces-"You all better remember this one when you go out tonight. It's called'Teenage Depression'!".

Some older people are astonished to see the affect of the band on us but who cares.We're enjoying ourselves like never before.

"School teacher buggin'me,
 It's the same old thing,
 Get out of my way,
 I need another shot of gin!"

(Teenage Depression-Dave Higgs)

HOT RODS

Wham!Next up-'The Kids Are Alright'.I almost don't believe it,the atmosphere.It's like everyone is part of what' is going on up on the stage,all us kids can relate to it.The stage is alive.The hall is packed with kids bursting with energy but there's still room to really move.'It's Been So Long'follows.

"Put your hands up!".Everywhere there's hands.Hands waving and clapping in the air to the fast,pounding rhythm.Steve Nicol may not be a spectacular showman but he fuckin'knows how to play.Chirst,he's a powerhouse-what a drummer!

"This one's off the b-side of our first single...".

"CRUISIN'!",came the shouts.

"Ha,that fooled ya!It came out of the sky babe!It came out of the sky!"

The hall's packed solid with Rods'fans now-the fans that would go anywhere to see their band.

Someone throws a scarf at Barrie during'Why Can't It Be?',he wraps it around his neck.Still shakin'hands with some of us and singing like mad

"Wanna shout then?Right,come on!"

Yati-yati-yati!

"Wooly Bully"-acrobats galore. Barrie summersaults across the stage, straight into'Horseplay'with Dave Higgs ramming his riffs home.He's standing still in shades,half naked then suddenly he walks out to and fro still strumming while Steve beats the shit out of his kit!Soon after,the applause starts building up.The next goodie-'Hard Drivin!Man' belches out from the band.

The Rods reflect their fans' lifestyles.I dunno,most of the Pistols and Clash fans seem to be on the dole or at art college.They like dressing up, looking bored and posing.I doubt if many of the kids who go to see the Rods are out of work.You kind of expect them to be still at school or brickies,labourers, something like that.They come home after an hard days work and go out to see a group like the Hot Rods to just enjoy themselves and nothing else.They were certainly enjoying it tonight!

We get'On the Run'next,naturally-it's brilliant.They bring music back to us kids.The band are not removed from us by big auditoriums seperated by fierce security guards.The band are part of the audience and they know what it's like.They've queued for hours,before now,to get in to see shows.

3

The band are kids of our age and us kids-clappin'and jeerin',boppin'and yellin'-are just as important as them.They're playing for us.They reflect the way we live, our whole lifestyles.

Dave kneels beside his amp as if he's going to head it.His hand flickers real fast across the strings.Meanwhile,Steve on drums and Paul Gray on bass give him a tough backing beat.Paul,all in black with shades as usual,veers his bass to and fro, swinging at the front of the stage.During this instrumental break Barrie left the stage Suddenly he re-emerges,his head bandaged up like the'Invisible Man'and'On the Run's beat becomes more exciting than ever,but we're not dancing so hard now.Our eyes are firmly fixed on what's going on on-stage.We're expecting something to happen.Barrie,pointing at us,tells us the meaning:

"We're gonna have a right time we're gonna have a good time and that good time is NOW!"

Upside down goes the mic-stand for'Double Checkin'Woman'and it's waved around like a banner.The number gradually ends as if it's in slow-motion with Dave making a blurry sound on the riff as it grinds to a halt.Finally,'Get Out Of Denver'ends the set.

Paul,turned sideways with his head facing towards us,lurches and swings off the stage still pumping on the bass and singing the chorus to himself.Barrie climbs the P.A.and sings from the top.Fuckin'ell,the roof is coming down-the whole place is shakin'in a frenzy!

Barrie summersaults down from the P.A.and Dave clambers on top of his amp. He just stands there,playing while Steve keeps to his seat and pummels the beats from his kit.

Looking around,everyone's cheering and claping for more.Everybody's sweaty and smiling,exhausted but happy.Kids are turning round to their mates in amazment.

The Rods return with'Gloria' and we're all suddenly turned into a sea of boppin'.Everybody's hands are up as the rat-a-tat-tat drumming takes us into'Satisfaction'and we're all hollering back the choruses to the band.After that they come back for another encore-'Writing On the Wall'-thanks to the kids,who were falling over and losing their voices.

The Rods were brilliant-and their fans-kids with so much energy.Energy to let lose so that they dance themselves giddy,fall over,get up and fall over again! As one fan put it:

"I HAVEN'T HAD SO MUCH FUN SINCE I LOST MY VIRGINITY!"

What a great night!

Steve Mick.

EDDIE + THE HOT RODS' ALBUM.

TEENAGE DEPRESSION(Island-album).

Side one: Get Across To You/Why Can't It Be?/Show Me/All I Need Is Money/Double Checkin' Woman/The Kids Are Alright*.

Side two: Teenage Depression/Horseplay/Been So Long*/Shake/On the Run.

You know,when you go and see the Hot Rods.You have a few drinks and end up jumping about,they're a band that you can get excited about.I mean,Steve Mick's review of their Woolwich gig couldn't be moreexciting-it almost jumps off of the page at yer.They're a live band but this isn't a live album is it?That's why I don't like it.

Live,the Rods are perfect but on record they're still yet to find their feet.Without Lew Davies'harp,which laced the early recordings-'Writing On the Wall', 'Cruisin'',and'Horseplay'-they've got a flat sound in the studio.There's no"feel" to their stuff,no distinctive sound to build on.A live album would have been better-that would have been an instant classic,no questions asked.Instead,I have to listen to this,a sort of souvenir of HR's currant success.Really,it's a poor imitation of the real-live-thing.

A couple of tracks just stand out-'Teenage Depression',slightly better than the single version'cause of the uncensored lyrics,'BeenSo Long',recorded live at the Marquee and'On the Run',which is quite interesting for it's lyrics-it's a sort of modern day'Satisfaction'.As the track's fading in a psychedelic mess Dave Higgs mumbles:

"Is there anybody there?Am I all alone in this place?What d'you mean?Is this real?A number?I'm not a number..."

Perhaps'On the Run'holds the key to the future?I hope so'cause at the moment I'm gonna stick to seeing the band live.It's the only way to stay liking'em.

Most of the new Rods'fans will love this album.It will probably get into the charts but it don't deserve to.The Rods deserve success but this doesn't,see what I mean?

I well disappointed in it!

Mark P.

I forgot to mention the cover.It uses the 'gun to the kids'head'pic again and it's a sort of a blur of colour-like an Island rasta cover gone barmy!On the back there's a pic of the lads down an alley.It's all designed by Micheal Beal and it's pretty good.Perhaps I can just look at the cover!

THE SUBWAY SECT.
A S.G. INTERVIEW BY STEVE MICK

PHOTO: VIC.

PAUL

PHOTO: PAUL.

VIC

The Subway Sect are: Vic Godard-lead vocals,Robert Miller-guitar,Paul Myers-bass and Paul Smith-drums.I asked them all to come along for a chat in the Wimpey at Leicester Square.Only Vic and Paul Myers came 'cause the others were off somewhere else.
The band adopted their name...(Oh!Shut ya mouth.'ere have a bit of the interview-Ed).

SM-What's in the name,Subway Sect?
Paul-Ah?
SM-Err...the name?
Paul-What's in it?Well,we used to go busking down Hammersmith subway and...
Vic-Not busking!
SM-All of ya?
Vic-Na,just three of us...but it wasn't busking so much as we wanted to see what it was like to play to people.Even though they were just walking by...So we weren't really down there to get any money'cause you've gotta join a union to do that really,havn't you?We just played a couple of Velvet Underground numbers down there a couple of times and we evolved from there.
SM-So,who was the other musician?
Vic-No,there's just...I was singing and the guitarist,Rob,was playing and he(Paul)was just standing there.
Paul-Yer,banging a can against the wall most of the time'cause I don't like standing there and doing nothing.
SM-You've been playing for about 4 months?
Vic-Well...practising.
SM-Rob has,hasn't he?
Vic-Well,he's been playing guitar.Paul's been playing bass for about 4 months havn't ya?
Paul-Coming up to 4 months.
Vic-The drummer though,he's only been playing for about 2 months.He's done really well.

Well,that's sorted out who they are and what they do and their short history.Next bit tells about their gigs.

SM-How many gigs have you played now?
Vic-Two...
SM-I thought you played a party or something-a wedding.
Vic-That was good that was.We did Sex Pistols'numbers,a couple of...not the ones they've written,we did"Steppin'Stone'and a couple of ones I'd written then which we don't do now.We did a complete'noise' first,at that party-that's what made everyone walk out-where everyone smashed their guitars around.I just chanted some poetry over it all.
Paul-At the time I wasn't very good on bass and I reckon I got about three notes right in the whole set.I had my back to the audience so they couldn't see what I was doing.
SM-Did they pay you for that?
Paul-No!
Vic-Joking!
Paul-They kicked us....
SM-What did you think of yourselves at the punk fest?
Vic-I thought I wasn't going to like going on stage but when you get up there it's just like you're one of the audience.When we play I always take the attitude that we're just practising in front of a load of people.So it seems to me,we do exactly the same when we're practising as when we play live.There's only one difference-when we practice and we do something wrong we stop but when we play live and we do something wrong we just carry on.
SM-You look bored on stage,is that natural or is it all planned?
Vic-We're not trying to make it an image or anything.
Paul-The reason I don't move is...if I moved I wouldn't be able to play the bass. I'd miss all the notes,so I just stand still.If it is an image I'm glad it's original anyway.

5

Vic-The reason we do it is that those two
can't move'cause they're not good at playing,
so they just stand there and concentrate.It'd
look a bit silly if that lot stood still and
I jumped all over the place.So I stand still
as well.
SM-What do you care about(Getting serious-Ed)
Vic-I care about being involved in society.
SM-You think you're involved enough?
Vic-I'm not saying that my playing is being
involved in society.I'm talkin'about being
involved in doing things that...causes that
you stand up for...things like that.
SM-What sort of causes do you stand up for?
Vic-Well...things like radicting oppression
of workers and things like that,you know?
SM-Are you political through your music?
Vic-None of the rest of the group are political but my songs...some of'em have got political ideas in them.What I meant by"getting
involved"was things like...you know what I
did the other day?I'll tell you what I did.
Everyone else will take the piss out of this!
There's some Californian grape farmers and
they're being oppressed by the Mafia-big business and they're not unionised which means
they really...about 20 quid a week and they
are really worked to the bone.All their grapes
are coming over to England and...I don't know
if you've heard about it-United Farm Workers
Co-operative,you heard of that?All these grapes are coming over to England.Now,they'll be
here from October to March.All the red grapes
you see in England,about 70% of those will be
from California and what they were trying to
do was boycott anyone from eating those red
grapes.I've been round all the local green-
grocers in my area asking them not to stock
red grapes.I know it seems petty but there's
a lot of...what happened was,in 1971 these
red grapes were brought over to England and
all the dockers refused to take'em but now,
with the advant of containers all the grapes
are mixed up so it's gotta be done by the con-
sumers if anything is to be done...
SM-You say you're"political".What do you think of the"anarchy"and that?
Vic-Rather than go around with"ANARCHY"written all over ya self you should do something
like what I did.It's sounds petty but you
should get involved with things.If you're an
anarchist,well...I think all the people that
go about with"anarchy"written over themselves
I don't think they're anarchists.They don't
go around blowing up things!

A Song

Vic-"TAKE SOME SCRAPS,
    TAKE SOME SCRAPS,
    THROW IT ON THE WALL,
    I AM GOING BACK TO MATHS".

    The song's called'Idea-pull'.

NEWSPAPER.

SM-What was that about,the newspaper at
the ICA gig?
Vic-What newspaper?
SM-The newspaper you held in yer hand on
stage?
Vic-What mine?
SM-Yeah,I'm sure it was.
Vic-Oh.That was the words of the songs.We
were doing three songs and I hadn't long
written them so I wasn't sure of the words
of some of'em.
SM-'Cause I thought you was going to suddenly stop the show and read out some
headline.
Vic-Oh no,it wasn't that.
Paul-He had to tell us when to change.
Vic-That's right,yeah.You mean when I
kept putting it up?That was when they
changed chords.
Paul-We kept looking at him when to change.
Vic-'Cause they were new numbers and they
had to look at me when to change'cause
they don't know the words all that well.
When I put my hand up...that means they
change and we go into the chorus or something like that,you know?
Paul-Well,we couldn't hear what he was
singing so it didn't matter anyway.

Subway Sect photos by the Subway Sect.

Don't forget to check'em out'cause they're
a fuckin'amazing band...
                              Steve Mick.

ROBERT MILLER.

6

KNIFE IN THE BACK

QUOTE OF THE MONTH: From Vic Godard of the Sect- "I'd sort of like to describe myself as a kid really,I don't wanna grow old.I hate the thought of being old.I always wanna be a teenager and when I'm old I'm not gonna act as an adult.I mean it when people say "you're childish"at the age of 25.WhenI'm 25 I'm still gonna do things like...er...dribble".

WHAT WE GONNA CALL IT? (Oh,this is dopey!) Ron Watts(100 Club booker)saw the Jam smash some gear at Upstairs At Ronnies.Think Ron will book'em after seeing that?It was the best Steve Mick's seen'em play..."Britain's burning,dial 999!"-Ingham is very hip.Get well soon,Jonh...Even though Johnny Moped is so cool that every body thought he was dead, he's managed to contact a girl called Shann who is gonna be his bassist...it seems that the original Louise's crowd have come out in to the open(they were Subterreans)as NME writers.Just ask Julie Birchell or better st- ill read her articles on women rockers.Don't you think you went slightly over the top in your Patti Smith reviews,Julie?...and talking "going over the top"-the Pistols''Anarchy In the UK'is gonna kill everybody...and we mean EVERYBODY!It's gonna be the greatest hit si- nce'Rule Brittania'...all you bleedin'letter writers.We're not gonna print any just'cause some of you cunts want to see your name in print.If you wanna air your views start yer own mag,like...Adrian of 27 Rivermill,Harlow and it's"Essex's only punk fanzine!".He told us it costs him 15p to print and he don't wanna make any money out of it.So send off for it now.Chuck in about 30p'cause he's had the guts to start it,not like you!...you may have read in the MM that"we hate our readers" Well,it's true.Just like we hate Led Zeppelin fans,disco fans and other'fans!If you're a fan it means that you're satisfied.We at SG are never satisfied and never contented-

THE FANZINE'S CALLED '48 THRILLS'.

'ANARCHY IN THE RAGS!'"

Continued from over there →

RIPPED & TORN-the best fanzine around at the moment.It's run by a couple of nut- cases in Scotland and it's captures the atmosphere of punk perfectly.The editors name is Tony D(Drayton) and he's helped by a right loony-bin job called the Skid Kid.Even better than 'Sniffin'Glue'.My god,it must be a goodie!The address is: 19 Glen View, Kildrum,Cumbernauld,GLASGOW,G67 2DT. They didn't say what they price was.

SHOULD BE IN THE USUAL GOOD PLACES SOON FOR 30p.

So that's about it.Oh,yeah,I mean,if those couple of sods up in Scotland can do it,why can't you?So,everybody start a punk fanzine and flood the market.Let's des- troy all the established mags!
                                        Mark P.

FANZINES

Like,sometimes when I'm han- ging about at a gig or something people stroll up and ask what I do.I,of course, tell'em to"piss-off".They at once realise who they're are talkin'to and then they say something like,"Oh,your the guy who runs the'Sniffin'Glue'...err...thingy".

You see,most of the boring old cunts don't know what a fanzine is cos they're not really fans...most of'em are layabouts who think"punks"are the"in-thing". That's why every publication from the Airfix Model Magazine to the History Of the Second World War is gonna have an ar- ticle on'punk-rock'.You just wait and see!

This was supposed to be a review of all the other fanzines but I've already waffled on for a couple of para- graphs about crap.It's easy being a writer ain't it?Well,wether it's easy or not,here's a run down of all the established fanzines:

THE SG GUIDE TO THE REST OF'EM!

From the UK:

ZIGZAG- not really a fanzine anymore but trys very hard.Flick through it and find punk stuff by Kris Needs. If there ain't anything spit in- between the pages so that the hippy that buys it is digusted!

HOT WACKS/LIQUORICE- Zig Zag take offs,so you can imagine how bad they are. Don't bother looking...just spit!

O.D- bunch of girls.

BAM BALAM/PENETRATION/DARK STAR/OMAHA
                                     RAINBOW-
        All special fanzines concentrating on Sixties Rock/Heavy Metal/USA- West Coast/Country Rock respectively.

From the States:

WHO BUT THE BOMP- very glossy.It's run by Groovies'manager,Greg Shaw.Get the idea?Yes,record listings(only for collectors),"rock history and tri- via" and who wants history.I only care about the future,boy!

TROUSER PRESS- "America's only British rock magazine".Wow...extra large green gob in the pages of this crap.

PUNK-   This has got nothing to do with anything.It's a kiddy's comic.This crap's actually selling well,it just shows you how dumb people are! 65p as well...fuckin'crap.

Now the good mags:

HONEY,THAT AIN'T NO ROMANCE-THis is great! Iggy Pop special-rough and tacky.

CONTINUED OVER THERE ⟶

Chelsea

"VIOLENCE AIN'T OUR STANCE" (from 'Your Generation' by Tony James)

Photo: SHEILA ROCK

L+R: BILLY IDOL, A LIGGER-WHO GOES BY THE NAME OF MARK P. + TONY JAMES.

I got a great feeling when seeing Chelsea for the first time. Before the gig (at Manchester's Electric Circus) I expected to see another bunch of Pistol, Clash imitators but of course I was wrong. They've got a whole differant approach to their audience than most of the new-wave. Agression is definitely not the key word for the Chelsea guys. They want to play their music and they hope that people get something out of it. As musicians they are competent and as songwriters they are thoughtful. I seen'em three times now and I reckon they're definitely gonna break new ground, if only for their non-aggressive approach.

The original band was—Jean October:lead vocals, Billy Idol:guitar, Tony James:bass and John Towe:drums. A few days ago I was informed that Jean October had left and Billy Idol would take over lead vocals. Of the split Jean said,"There were no personnel feelings involved. I wish the lads good luck, I think they're great". Jean reckons that he'll "bounce back". I hope so 'cause the guy's a strong singer and a hard worker.

Meanwhile, Chelsea are gonna get stronger and stronger. On lead vocals, Billy will be great. Offstage he's calm but infront of anaudience he turns into a hero. He dresses sharp, no pins or painted strips. The cut of his gear is immaculate, his roots are the'cause of this. He was one of the Bromley contingent but although he really likes the Pistols he has got a complete style of his own.

Tony James, the bassist, has also been around the seene for some time. He was part of the'London SS'group that never got off the ground(the group also featured the Clash's Mick Jones and the Damned's Brian James). People have said that he's got the"New York look"about him. Yeah, maybe, but who the hell cares. He's a great bassist and songwriter—that's all that matters.

Drummer, John Towe is less of a"character"than Billy and Tony. He is a quiet bloke but his playing full of energy. The kit he uses is large but it's used to the full in the band's well arranged songs.

This group are important. They are something new, young and exciting. They're fuckin'great!

Mark P.

8

'ANARCHY IN THE SINGLES!"

SINGLES REVIEWED BY MARK P.

SEX PISTOLS-ANARCHY IN THE U.K.(EMI).
"DESTROY!",Johnny Rotten screams at the end of this record.That's what it's all about.This single destroys all the rock'n'roll laws.Just by getting this thing released the Pistols have kicked the establishment right in the balls!

I'm not fuckin'joking when I say that this is the most important record that's ever been released.No question about it this is the real thing.It's what all this new wave scene is about.Go out and buy this and play it everywhere.Gatecrash discos and shove 'Anarchy'on the turntable.That'll give the apathetic bastards something to dance about. Fuckin''ANARCHY!'.Don't anybody understand that anarchy's the only thing left to happen?

You see,the Pistols have smashed'em all.This is the best record I've every heard.Go out and buy it'cause if you don't you're an idiot!

The B-side is'I Wanna Be Me'.

"Many ways to get what you want,   BIT OF
 I use the best,I use the rest,   ← 'ANARCHY'
 I use the NME,I use...ANARCHY!"
                    (Sex Pistols'76).
So,all you kids.Go and get what you want with the sound of'Anarchy'ringing in yer ears!

Oh,fuckin'ell...how can anything follow that? I'll try...
RAMONES-I WANNA BE YOUR BOYFRIEND(Sire).
The A-side's alright but it's the weakest track off the album.Who cares... don't play it.Chuck on the flip'cause it's a fuckin'killer!

Yeah,a live recording of 'California Sun'(not on their album),'I Don't Wanna Walk Around With You'and the intro to 'Today Your Love,Tomorrow the World'.Needless to say really,it's fantastic.If only they'd made it a live EP with a couple more live'ns on the A-side.Even with that slight moan it's still much better than the crapy:

BLONDIE-X OFFENDER(Private Stock).
At last I get to hear the chick that I've been wan...err...you know what I mean?Those pics of her in PUNK were pretty foxy and after hearing this crap I think I'd prefer to just look at the pics.I mean,it's so old fashioned.

The A-side draws from the Shangri-Las and the B-side-'In the Sun'-from surf music.It adds up to one big drag.It's not helped by the production either,you know, one of those"Phil Spector was my hero"over the top jobs.Perhaps she's better live...if she stripped off it'd be great!Then again,I'm not supposed to like sex,am I?

WAYNE COUNTY & THE BACKSTREET BOYS-
MAX'S,KANSAS CITY'76(Max).
This as got a nice riff and the band are OK.Wayne is great,putting on his Lou Reed type pout.On the flip there's Part 2 and it's in a dopey picture cover with Wayne dressed up as a waitress.What more do you want?

Oh yer-"You better not forget to bring your masquerade mask and your ego-trip'cause you're gonna need it when you go down to Max's,Kansas City... baby!"

RICHARD HELL(Stiff-LTD.ED: 5,000).
First recording of Hell's new band-Voidoids.This single's not bad. The great'Blank Generation'is included so it survives from being a"miss".The other two songs-'Another World'and'You Gotta Lose'-are both dead.I just don't get carried away with the sound of the band and there's too much guitar soloing.Perhaps he should fix himself up with more interesting sidemen.

I wished I'd had heard him with Television or the Heartbreakers. I hear he's recording an album and it's a lot better than this single.Hope so...

LITTLE BOB STORY(Chiswick EP).
Tracks: I'm Crying/Come On Home/I Need Money/Baby Don't Cry.
This French band is gigging around at the moment led by the tubby little singer,Robert Piazza.On stage I've never really liked'em much but this is a bloody good record.It's easily Roger Armstrong's best production job to date.

Bung up the ol'volume and a great slice of rock'n'roll leaps out at yer.Pub-rock is definitely still with us and I'm glad Chiswick knows it.

Oh yer,before I get loads of abuse.Of course this single don't mean anything next to the new-wave,mannn...but I happen to dig small record companies like this who put out what they believe in!

EATER - LIVE AT THE HOPE + ANCHOR WEDNESDAY ISTDEC.

9

✻ **FREE WITH THIS ISSUE!** ✻

MEMBERSHIP TO LONDON'S ONLY
LATE CLUB.
OPENING VERY SOON.
PLAYING LIVE 1977 SOUNDS
(YEAH, ALRIGHT. CALL IT "PUNK" IF
YA WANT).

JUST SEND THIS BELOW TO THE
'SNIFFIN' GLUE...' H.Q.

COLLECT YOUR MEMBERSHIP AT THE DOOR ON OPENING NIGHT.
_ _ _ _ RIP HERE → _ _ _ _ _ _ _ _ _ _ _ _ _ _ _ _ _
ROXY CLUB, 41-43 NEAL STREET, WC2 (SEND FORM TO SG)

NAME - _ _ _ _ _ _ _ _ _ _ _ _ _ _ _ _ _ _

ADDRESS - _ _ _ _ _ _ _ _ _ _ _ _ _ _ _ _

DATE - _ _ _ _ _ _ _ _ AGE (YOU MUST BE OVER 18) - _ _ _ _

SG PIN-UP- CHELSEA. (ALREADY OUT OF DATE BUT STILL A GOOD PHOTO).

TOP ROW — TONY JAMES, BILLY IDOL + JOHN TOWE, BOTTOM — EX. VOCALIST, SEAN OCTOBER.

PHOTO BY SHEILA ROCK

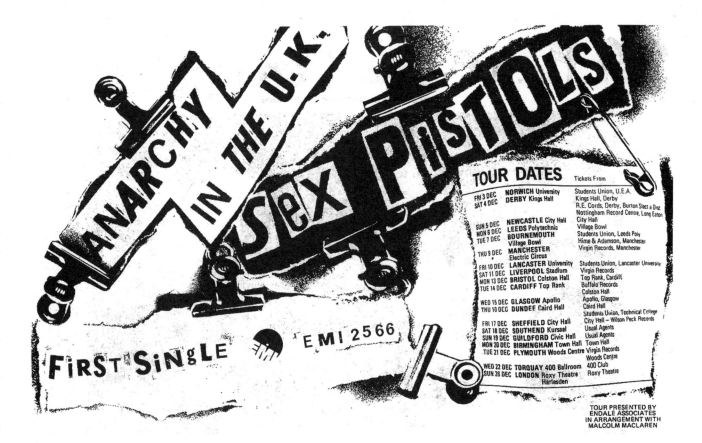

ANARCHY IN THE U.K.

Sex Pistols

FIRST SINGLE EMI 2566

TOUR DATES		Tickets From
FRI 3 DEC	**NORWICH** University	Students Union, U.E.A.
SAT 4 DEC	**DERBY** Kings Hall	Kings Hall, Derby
		R.E. Cords, Derby, Burton Slect a Disc
		Nottingham Record Centre, Long Eaton
SUN 5 DEC	**NEWCASTLE** City Hall	City Hall
MON 6 DEC	**LEEDS** Polytechnic	Village Bowl
TUE 7 DEC	**BOURNEMOUTH** Village Bowl	Students Union, Leeds Poly
		Hime & Adamson, Manchester
THU 9 DEC	**MANCHESTER** Electric Circus	Virgin Records, Manchester
FRI 10 DEC	**LANCASTER** University	Students Union, Lancaster University
SAT 11 DEC	**LIVERPOOL** Stadium	Virgin Records
MON 13 DEC	**BRISTOL** Colston Hall	Top Rank, Cardiff
TUE 14 DEC	**CARDIFF** Top Rank	Buffalo Records
		Colston Hall
WED 15 DEC	**GLASGOW** Apollo	Apollo, Glasgow
THU 10 DEC	**DUNDEE** Caird Hall	Caird Hall
		Students Union, Technical College
FRI 17 DEC	**SHEFFIELD** City Hall	City Hall – Wilson Peck Records
SAT 18 DEC	**SOUTHEND** Kursaal	Usual Agents
SUN 19 DEC	**GUILDFORD** Civic Hall	Usual Agents
MON 20 DEC	**BIRMINGHAM** Town Hall	Town Hall
TUE 21 DEC	**PLYMOUTH** Woods Centre	Virgin Records
		Woods Centre
WED 22 DEC	**TORQUAY** 400 Ballroom	400 Club
SUN 26 DEC	**LONDON** Roxy Theatre Harlesden	Roxy Theatre

TOUR PRESENTED BY
ENDALE ASSOCIATES
IN ARRANGEMENT WITH
MALCOLM MACLAREN

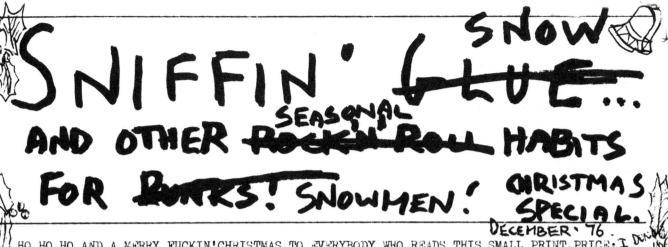

SNIFFIN' ~~GLUE~~ SNOW...

AND OTHER ~~ROCK'N'ROLL~~ SEASONAL HABITS

FOR ~~PUNKS!~~ SNOWMEN!

CHRISTMAS SPECIAL.

DECEMBER '76.

HO,HO,HO AND A MERRY FUCKIN'CHRISTMAS TO EVERYBODY WHO READS THIS SMALL PRINT.PRICE:I DUNNO
THIS IS A THREE PAGE SG CHRISTMAS SPECIAL,BROUGHT OUT BY POPULAR DEMAND.IT'S WAS PHIL'S IDEA.

WE COULDN'T REALLY AFFORD TO GET THIS MINI-ISSUE PRINTED SO WE DIDN'T USE PHOTOS.THAT'S
WHY WE'VE USED A DRAWING.IT'S BY A PUNK CALLED-Zizz.I CAN'T STAND"ART"MYSELF BUT YOU'LL
PROBABLEY LIKE IT.

← JOHNNY ROTTEN

↓

SEX PISTOLS

LONDON'S BURNIN' WITH GROUPS!

I thought that 'cause it's the end of the year we'd have a run down of all the important artists:

<u>The Sex Pistols</u>: Obviously the Pistols are the most important group on the scene.They've done what no other bands have dared to do.They've broken the rules,not just the establishment rules but all the rock'n'roll laws.They hate and despise everything,because of that they're able to think only of <u>their</u> music.Live, they are a phenomenon.Only the Clash match'em for their stage show.Rotten is the scene's Face,'Anarchy In the UK'is the best single ever and they are simply the best group in the world!

<u>The Clash</u>:As Jonh once said-"like a million hammers pummeling on corregated iron!".What that means,I don't know but I think you'll get the point.The Clash are tough,serious and chaotic.Mick Jones'is the best guitarist on the scene.Joe Strummer and Paul Simenon play like maniacs.You can't even describe their sound,it's like a wall of sheet-metal.Nothing will break'em.They need more gigs,like all the other punks.The best thing they can do is get a record deal and put'White Riot', '1977','Janie Jones'and'Career Opportunities' out as an EP.

<u>The Damned</u>:Don't say much in their lyrics but their sheer force on stage says it all for'em. They are a fuckin'racket.Like a cross between the Stooges and MC5.Their single-'New Rose'- is a killer.Rat Scabies is a <u>real</u> drummer,the best there is.If they can keep up their power for their album it will be a public menace. Just don't stand too near the speakers.

<u>Buzzcocks</u>:Don't play many gigs but they are important.They're from Manchester,they've got weird problems.Howard Devoto writes nasty little songs,Pete Shelley plays a nasty,raspin littleguitar.They look dopey,sometimes play without enough power but they're good and honest.They should come down to London and play the Roxy.

<u>Generation X</u>:Newest group on the scene but easily one of the strongest.They changed their name from Chelsea and they've got a fuckin' amazing line-up.New guitarist Bob Andrews is a fuckin'real player.I mean,after only 3 gigs he was playing like a bleedin'demon.Blond haired Billy Idol is a nice singer.Some of their songs would be great singles-'Ready, Steady,Go!','New Orders','Youth,Youth,Youth' and'Your Generation'.

<u>SUBWAY SECT</u>:This band are real punks.Vic Godard wants to still dribble when he's 25.Their music is very simple,usually using just 2 or 3 chords but the strength of the band's personality as a whole makesup for lack expertise.They deserve more gigs,more chances to show how much they're worth.Rumour has it that a small record company called WARM are interested in'em.A band like this needs to be heard. They're a example to every kid who wants to do something positive.

<u>EDDIE & THE HOT RODS</u>:Not considered to be "new-wave"but no one can deny their strengh on stage.They're for the kids who just wanna jump about.They're all good blokes and competant musicians.Three singles- 'Writing On the Wall','Wooly Bully'and 'Teenage Depression'-1 EP-'Live at the Marquee'and 1 LP-'Teenage Depression'.All on the Island label.

<u>EATER</u>:Youngest band on the scene and also the hardest to pin down.They're are young so I don't even know if their reasons for playing"punk"are justified.They're a right bunch of'olligans and a lot of fun to watch. Ian Woodcock is a great bassist and Dee Generate is a crazy drummer(probably'cause he was taught by Rat Scabies).They've gone through buisness troubles lately,I hope they come out of it with a bit more ex- perience.A record may be released in the new year-'You'.

Other groups around: The Jam,the Gorillas, the Stranglers,the Vibrators,the Slits,the Wet Lepers,Siouxsie and the Banshies,the Count Bishops and Slaughter and the Dogs. Of these other groups a few might do some good things in the future.A few of'em ain't worth a light.Time will tell.

Mark P.

See you all in the year-1977.

SG WILL NEVER JOIN THE ESTABLISHMENT SO STICK WITH US!

1977 HAD BETTER BE A GOOD'N.

MERRY FUCKIN' XMAS.

Right, here's a list of all the'76 good things: the Sex Pistols, the Clash, the Ramones, the Buzzcocks, Subway Sect, Hot Rods, Stiff, Patti Smith, glue, Rock On(Roger, Phil, Stan, Ted, Sue and everybody else who I forgot), the Damned, "Little Johnny Jewel", Jonh Ingham, Stewart Joseph and Rough Trade mob, Caroline Coon, Bizarre(Larry, Tim, Derek), Andy "Andy"Czezowski, Generation X, Jean October, Mary Harron, Sheila Rock, Michael Beal, Louise, Sean(Bondage), Gil, Adrian(48 Thrills), Tony D (Ripped & Torn), Terry Chimes, Siouxsie & the Banshies, Marc Zermati, Kris Needs, Airfix, Sid Vicious and Steve Walsh, Erika, Nora, BTM, the Slits, Rocco, Disease, the Wet Lepers, Ed Hollis, Howard, Asward, Can, Stephen Lavers, Jake, Nick Lowe, Stranglers, Phylis, Chiswick, Judy Nylon, Bruce, the Adverts, Eyes, H.T's mum & dad, Father Chirstmas, Alice, Nick Kent, Fredda(the dog), Chi, Debb-ie, Jill, Benard(Clash), Malcolm(SP), Sharon, Lemmy, Sonja, Heartbreakers, Lenny, Iggy, Giovanni, Bill Grundy(good for a laugh), John Rowe, John J, Mick B, M R, Ron Watts, Rick Brown, Eater, Richard Hell, Patti and Lenny K, Vivian, Lew, Flea, Charlotte, Tyrone, Shann, Johnny Moped, Anette, Cimarons, C.Chaos, Chaotic Bass, WARM, Wire, Keith Levine, the Saints, MX-80 Sound, the Gorillas, Tapper Zukie, Danny Fields, John Holstrom, Jon Savage(London's Outrage), Zizz, J. Barnett, ICA, The Roxy, Squeeze, Big Youth, Angie, Ray S, Si, The S.E.London Mercury, Rosko G, Not Just a Phase(great fanzine), Susie, Quick Spurts, the Jam, Dr.Feelgood, Blondie's body, Nick at Compendium, NME(for not jumpin'on the bandwagon), Dust On the Needle, Hope & Anchor, the Nashville, Dead Fred and Celia

If you think you've been left out, we don't care a shit.You'll have to wait until next year.

Yeah, it's been a pretty good year. The London punk scene is going along fine and we've had some visits from some good New York bands.'Anarchy In the UK' is the best single <u>ever</u>.'Sniffin'Glue...'as became a bore but it might pick up in the new year. What do I mean—"might". Of course it's gonna get better. With all these good bands around it can't do much else. We've now got a photographer—H.T.Murlowski.He'll be zapping around at all the best gigs sticking his lens in yer mushes. The best bet is to make out he's not there so you can look really cool.I'm not gonna ramble on anymore, just send all presents to:

24 ROCHFORT HSE.,
GROVE ST.,
LONDON,S.E.8 3LX.

SG 6 should have bits on the Jam, Eater, Generation X and the Pistols/Grundy/EMI thing.

Mark P.

PS I CAN'T STEVE MICK TODAY SO THAT'S WHY HE DIDN'T WRYTE IN THIS ISSUE.

JOEY RAMONE
BY ZIZZ.

'Cause we've became established and all soppy here's the

'SNIFFIN'GLUE...'READERS POLL.

Best UK group:

Best NYC group:

Singer:

Guitarist:

Bassist:

Drummer:

Single:

Album:

Person:

Writer(if you don't put Steve Mick you can't read):

Mag(other than SG):

Record shop:

Think up any other catogories if you want. The Poll will be printed again in SG 6,so take yer time.

SNIFFIN' GLUE...
AND OTHER ROCK'N'ROLL HABITS, FOR ANYBODY WHO CARES ABOUT ⑥ JAN'77. 1977!

THE CLASH PHOTO(BELOW)BY SHEILA ROCK.THERE'S NOTHING ABOUT'EM IN THIS ISSUE BUT...WHO CARES!

IN THIS ISSUE:
SEX PISTOLS
+
EATER
+
GENERATION X
AND
CHELSEA
PLUS

THIS ISSUE IS FOR JOHN COLLIS. R.I.P. PHYLLIS

MARK P's BIT.

Fuckin'ell,I'm the bleedin Editor and the layout geezer yet I still end up with only half-a-page col/umn.Anyway,this issue has been a long time coming.I think it's been worth the wait'cause there's so much in this one.

The Pistols piece is the Time Out balls-up in it's fullness.John Collis hacked it to bits when he edited it for the crappy TO.He can't touch it in SG,that's why it's here!The Generation X,Chelsea and Eater pieces are all young,fresh and virile.I've even allowed a female to write in this ish. Phyllis is a gas,that's why she's here.I do hope all you men don't mind...like fuck do I mind!

I saw the Gorillas the other week and they were great,they'll probably be something on'em in the future.One band I am fuckin'mad about is the Heartbreakers.I saw 'em four times when they were over and every gig was a killer.They're coming back in Feb. so we'll interview'em and get some exclusive photos.Oh,yeah...the Chiswick label have re-leased the new Gorillas'single-'Gatecrasher' although I havn't got a copy yet the live version was bouncy and very like'She's My Gal'.

All this crap about the Pistols/ EMI/Grundy is completely killing me.I could go on about how Grundy's a nurd and EMI are ol'farts etc but I've read it so many times. You know,what the fuck...let's just see what happens.I hope it works out,see yer-MARK P.

x

x

S.G. No. 6

IT'S THE CONTENTS AIN'T IT?

Staff:

MARK P: Editor and layout.

HARRY T.MURLOWSKI: Photographer and any business hassles.

Contributing writer: STEVE MICK.

Thanks to: Sheila Rock(Clash photo),Erica Echenberg(Brian Chevette photo),Jill Fur-manovsky(H.T.Murlowski photo)and Phyllis.

Also: Stewart Joseph(printing),Rough Trade (comfort),Rock On(Gorillas)and Bizarre(for support).

New address:
'SNIFFIN'GLUE...',
c/o ROUGH TRADE,
202 KENSINGTON PARK ROAD,
LONDON,W 11.

A LIVIN' LEGEND - HARRY T. MURLOWSKI

How does this bleedin' thing work ??

PHOTO BY JILL FURMANOVSKY

2

THE SEX PISTOLS FOR TIME OUT

A GREAT BRITISH INSTITUTION ←

Right,here's a little story.I had a piece printed in Time Out No.352.It was about the Sex Pistols.Originally they asked me to write 2,000 words,I wrote just over a 1,000 so they wouldn't cut it down. They still cut it down.I was fucked off by that so here's the piece in it's entirety.

THE START: No way are the Pistols gonna be filed under: Pop Groups.EMI will have to think up a new one'cause this is the time for change.The Sex Pistols are gonna break all the rules.They'll bring about a change that will make the outlook for British rock music very exciting.Rock's been a"light entertainment"for too long,it's all too safe and it's not scaring parents.The Pistols are gonna scare more than just parents.They'll scare all the apathetic rock fans who've been satisfied with shit for so long.

The Pistols are the most important rock group in Britain at the moment. Not because they're playing 5 nights at Wembley or releasing a"Best of..."triple set but because they've chucked out the most relevant rock single since'My Generation'.'Anarchy In the UK'is the title,and when it gets heard it will startle,suprise and shock. With the tour as well the group will get to almost everyone.They'll bring about a reaction in everybody who sees and hears'em.Good or bad,the reaction will be positive.They're going to give the music scene what it needs-a good kick up the throat.

Most kids have never experienced a feeling of unity between audience and performer.They've never had an idle who was on their level,I mean,how many kids have been to the South Of France?Even the Who, they were once an important group but what does'My Generation'mean now when it's sung by a 30 year old.The audience for the Pistols is waiting-out there in the discos,on the football terraces and living in boring council estates.The Sex Pistols are not a"new fashion craze",they're reality.If people are scared of'em it's their own fault,it's because they don't understand life.Life's about concrete,the sinking pound,apathatic boring people and the highest unemployment figures ever.

The Pistols are helping kids to think.That's why everybody's scared,because there's some kids that are actually thinking.The Pistols reflect life as it is in the council flats,not some fantasy world that most rock artists create.Yes,they will destroy,but it won't be mindless destruction. What they destroy will be replaced by a more honest creation.The likes of Led Zeppelin,

Queen and Pink Floyd need to be chucked in the"classical"music section.Those and bands like them are composers,musicians and artistes.They've got to make way for real people and the Sex Pistols are the first of them!

The original group(Steve Jones,Glenn Matlock and Paul Cook)started out like any other.They used to rehearse in a Hammersmith warehouse.They played just sixties stuff and the future wasn't very interesting.Until they met Malcolm McLaren that is.McLaren ran the Sex boutique in the King's Road and they approached him about helping the group.He'd had experience in rock music before because he used to be manager of the New York Dolls. Johnny Rotten was soon brought in as vocalist after they saw him in the Sex shop, looking bored.The early gigs,in November 1975 were shakey but baked by McLaren's drive they used the non-reactions to their advantage.By April'76 they had a loyal following and were playing regulary at the 100 Club.This soon became the only place they could play after being banned at the Marquee,Nashville and Dingwalls for various incidents.Even with these obsticles they continued to play excellent sets when they were allowed to.July was a peak month when they played Manchester and'Anarchy In the UK'for the first time.Through August and September their audiences grew,there were more and more kids coming from out of town to see'em.The kids were great,they were there not just to enjoy a night out. They were there because they wanted to experience the energy and the honesty.

By this time other bands had formed-the Clash,the Damned,Buzzcocks, Subway Sect and Siouxsie and the Banshees. They all came together for a"festival"at the 100 Club in late September.On the first night,the Monday,the Pistols played great. There was no violence just exciting music. The following night was mared by the throwing of a glass during the Damned's set. It smashed on a pillar and one of the fragments blinded a girl's eye.It could have happened anywhere but the managment put the blame on"punk-rock"so the music was banned. The Sex Pistols now had nowhere to play. The interest from the record companies still grew.They talked with Polydor for two weeks but Polydor were too slow,EMI zapped in and signed them.

Through October they were in the recording studio-Queen were in at the same time,I bet the Pistols annoyed them.

Contd. on next page →

3

On the 12th November they appeared on Nation-wide. A lot of people watched the programme and most of them hated it. It was a positive reaction. On the 15th they played the small Notre Dame Hall in Leicester Place, it was their first London gig for over a month. Some of it was filmed for TV.

The Pistols were great. After a month of recording and rehearsing they were as solid as a rock. A short set was done for the cameras and they came back to play a "real" set for the fans. Rotten was fantastic, he was breaking all the rules. What other guy would just stand stage-centre after the set and clap for an encore with the crowd. He was saying how he wanted rock to be. No rock'n' roll cliches for him. He's the most honest performer around at the moment. Rotten is the FACE, a cult figure, he's saying "up yours" to everyone. You can't helping liking the guy, all that you see of him on stage is the truth Some people love to hate him. It's natural 'cause they're probably scared of him. It's the same with the rest of the group, they don't apologise to an audience like most "small" bands. They'll shove their music down your throat. Glenn Matlock on bass, Paul Cook on drums and Steve Jones on guitar, they're all honest guys. There's not one bullshitter amongst them. This is the reason the group will make it. I'm not talking about the ac-cepted way-i.e:record sales,sell-out concer-ts etc. but on the honest level rock should be. The level that pleases the kids on the street. McLaren knows it-"With the Pistols the kids really bop, that shows you they've made it!"

That's what's bothering kids today. They feel resricted in everything they try to do. All those giant security guards at the big halls to stop them dancing until the encore. Some kids accept that kind of treatment but with the Pistols they get some kind of freedom. In this day and age you've got to learn to spit in authorities' face, otherwise they'll pin you down and you'll be boring like them. All the old creeps want respect because they "fought for you". Well, the youngsters of today ain't gonna fall for that old one. Britain is going downhill and it'll take more than memorys of glory to save it. The Pistols are here because this country's so pathetic, they're a reaction against all the stupid apathy and ignorance. They don't want to be associated with honour and respect. That's nothing to do with change, the Sex Pistols are.

It doesn't even matter if 'Anarchy In the UK' sells well or not. The fact that it's been released proves that the record companies are a load of pathetic bores. The Pistols have won the first battle. From now on they'll move forward and smash every rock'n'roll law there is. Even now that in the recording business they still won't play by the rules. They'll be nasty and mean because that's the only way to get anything positive done.

You wanna thank god they've got their guitars and equipment 'cause other-wise they'd be burning down the record companies. At least they're doing it through music. Now they're on the inside they're gonna eat away at all the crap until there's none of the old stuff left. As McLaren said on Nationwide-"In order to create you must first destroy". Well, everybody better watch out 'cause the Sex Pistols are gonna destroy YOU!   THE END.

As you've probably already sussed out, I wrote the above before the Grundy thing. Even with that fuck up I still believe in everything I said about the Sex Pistols. They're still gonna make it.

I hope that John Collis is forced into retirement. May he rest in peace.

Mark P.

PHOTOS BY H.T.HURLOWSKI.

4

SEX PISTOLS IN MANCHESTER.

PHOTOS BY H.T. MURLOWSKI

Hey ho,let's go!(Bollocks-HT).

ANYTHING - GOSSIP!

Did you read the reports about the Pistols
at Heathrow Airport,leaving for Holland-
i.e:"spitting at each other","being sick in
the airport lounge"and"causing a disturbance
with other passengers".A very reliable source
told SG's H.T Murlowski that the storys were
"complete frabrication".Rotten's right,this
is"1984"...the Gorillas gig at the Nashville
the other week was free.Just like the early
days of the Stranglers.Now you have to pay
over a quid to see'em and then they're most
likely supporting the Climax Blues Band...we
interviewed the Jam the other day but they
blew it.All they did was lark about,that's
why we've not printed it.They played the new
Roxy Club the other day and they were so
laid back I thought it was a demo tape gone
wrong.As Steve Mick says,"The Jam are tight,
but so are Led Zeppelin.The Jam are"doing
something"but so are Led Zeppelin".Yeah,the
Jam should really sort theirselves out...the
Clash have spent a couple of days in the
studio.They got good ol'Terry Chimes back
for the sessions.That's the best thing they
have done for two months.I wish they'd get a
bleedin'record out,I'm to hear'em in my poxy
little flat...Johnny Rotten wants to do some
thing special for SG7.I just hope he acts,I
just hope he acts...Next issue's gonna have
...err,I won't say nuthin'cause I'm always
wrong.

THE ROXY CLUB.

41-43 NEAL ST., LONDON W.C.2

OPEN EVERY NIGHT EXCEPT FRIDAYS DURING JANUARY. FROM FEB 1ST OPEN 7 NIGHTS A WEEK. FREE MEMBERSHIP.

DATES:

MON 17TH JAN - DAMNED/BOYS.

WED 19TH JAN - SLAUGHTER + THE DOGS/ADVERTS.

THURS 20TH JAN - SQUEEZE/ZIPS.

SAT 22ND JAN - STRANGLERS/A PLAY! WITH REAL ACTORS!

THURS 27TH JAN - VIBRATORS/OUTSIDERS.

SAT 29TH JAN - GENERATION X/?

MON 31ST JAN - DAMNED/REJECTS.

ADMISSION FEE VARIES. (NORMALLY - £1).

6 FREE ADMISSION ON NON-GROUP NIGHTS DURING JAN.

GENERATION X "NEW ORDERS"

PHOTOS BY H.T. MURLOWSKI.

JOHN TOWE · BOB ANDREWS · TONY JAMES · BILLY IDOL

I was well pissed off when the original Chelsea split up.I needn't have been'cause GENERATION X are amazing.

After the departure of Gene October from Chelsea,the rest of the group-Billy Idol,Tony James and John Towe-went on to get a new name,guitarist and manager.The name is part of the"tryin'to forget your generation"concept,the guitarist is a great kid called Bob Andrews and the manager is ex-Damned boss,Andy Czezowski-also runs the Roxy Club.

The first Chelsea gigs were good but Generation X have played killers. They sing songs about a new way of life,the way they play'em is takin'the"new-wave"in a fresh direction.Their gig at the Hope and Anchor said it all,they broke through to a crowd who were fed up with the Pistols and the Clash being in Plymouth.The Generation X will move in a direction which can only mean more great gigs and even great records.They will make amazing singles-'Your Generation', 'New Orders','Ready,Steady,Go!','Above Love', 'Youth,Youth,Youth'and the tasty'Tryin'For Kicks'.

Technically,they're the best on the scene.New guitarist,Bob Andrews is a great find.He was playing at some party with his old band when Billy saw him .After a few rehearsals he played a brilliant debut with the band at Central London Art College.His sort,sharp breaks are always worth keeping an ear open for.Without a guitar,Billy is coming along nicely as a flashy lead singer. Most of the lyrics are Tony's but the whole group believe in'em.They care about melody and arrangment.They actually care what the audience hears.Oh don't worry,they're not soft-their music is hard and fast.One number after another digs itself deep inside yer head so you won't forget it.You won't forget their message-Generation X.New orders,new music and a new experience.I wanna have it again and again,the guys have got round me!

For God's sake,don't ignore Generation X'cause they don't tell you to "Fuck off!".They want everyone to listen... right,so listen to'em-Billy Idol:vocals, Bob Andrews:guitar,Tony James:bass and John Towe:drums.

Mark P.

7

TONY   BILLY

"TO DIE WHEN YOU'RE NUTHIN"

I know Gene October said that he would"bounce back"after the original Chelsea split but I never expected him to come up with another group so soon.This new CHELSEA have a completely differant way of thinking than the original mob.Gene's lyrics are hard and political,the songs are like worker's chants-Curfew','Pretty Vacant'(not the Pistol's song),'Right To Work','Gotta Go', 'Government','No Admission','An Atrocity'and 'The Loner'.They all have a bite,Gene's vocals are always on the ball.He has a hard stage presence,sometimes too hard.When he cuts the chat and sings he is great.

The rest of the group are Bob Jessie:bass,Marti Stacey:guitar and Carey Fortune:drums.Two weeks of good,hard slog in the rehearsal rooms payed off,when they played a nice debut supporting the Clash at the Roxy Club.

They played their second and third in one amazing night.The first gig was at the Hope and Anchor.It was being filmed and they were stunning.The sparse audience loved it and everyone was eager to hear the second set.

About five minutes before they were due to go on again,about thirty Teds came in the pub.They caused trouble straight away by knocking a couple of kids with safty pinned jackets about.The police soon arrived but it really put the dampers on the whole gig.Chelsea packed up their gear and we all made our way to the Roxy Club.

Gene was eager to play again. In half-hour they were set up at the Roxy and into their hard,fast set for the second time that evening.Now that's what rock's all about,getting up and playing.Chelsea would gig every night if they could,energy is what they've definitely got.

With the energy comes a nice mixture of experience and new ideas.Carey used to work for the Stranglers,he knows what he's doing.Marti and Bob inject the freshness into the group.Together,they are a great unit.

They've already come under heavy flak from a lot of the bands.Like, as someone pointed out,Gene sings"I don't take drugs,I don't take beer"when we all know that he likes a drink.Of Generation X,he says,"They used to be in Chelsea".All sorts of little things like that make it hard to work Gene out.All I know up to now is that Chelsea are a great little band and Gene October is,perhaps,the best singer on the scene.Time will tell wether their hearts are in it or not.I hope so 'cause I like'em,on and off stage.

The title of this piece came from Gene,perhaps that's what Chelsea are scared of.I hope they make it,the more this group climbs,the more they'll sort theirselves out.I hope the best is yet to come.

Mark P.

CHELSEA CHELSEA

PHOTO BY H.T. MURLOWSKI.

CAREY FORTUNE · MARTI STACEY · BOB JESSIE · GENE OCTOBER

8

EATER

Since the Pistols/Grundy thing exploded all over the nationals, EATER have had a lot of unusual publicity. Like the quotes from Dee Generate's mum and their ex-manager Rob Hallett announcing the group as the band that's going to "take over the Sex Pistols' audience". EATER were going about things the wrong way, it wasn't the lads fault, it was a case of bad management. Now that all that bullshit's over and done with, EATER will really have to <u>work</u>. They'll have start writing some more songs and not over play the fact that they're the youngest band on the scene. I hope that they come through alright.

Anyway, the whole idea of the following piece is to put Eater's point of view over. We was gonna print it as a normal type of interview but we decided get more things across by just printing straight quotes. It was all done in a pub off Picadilly Circus to the sound of a really awlful pub-singer, who was told to "fuck off" by Andy. Now that's not very nice, is it lads...?

EATER are: Andy Blade-lead vocals.
Brian Chevette-guitar.
Ian Woodcock-bass.
Dee Generate-drums.

ANDY BLADE

Photo : H.T. MURLOWSKI.

Andy-I think the Sex Pistols are great 'cause they started this thing off. They ain't gonna go very far 'cause they're breaking up for the likes of us. They've blown it but they're really kind and generous.

Dee-I want loads of kids to come and see us. That's why I wanna get out of the pub circuit. I want kids of my age to come, they'd be dressing up like us and we're their heroes.

Brian-Anyone can come to see us as long as they don't try to change us. All the older people what come always say, "that was really good, but why don't you wear glitter suits".

Ian-I think we should look similar, not totally disimilar. You(pointing at Brian)looked like you came down to read the gas meter, the other night.

Andy-If you ask me, the "blank Generation" is all the old people, like, you know, if you push my grandad over by the fire. The next morning he's still lying there. He's really blank, he is...pretty vacant.

Brian-They're so bloody boring, they make yer sick...all superstars are wankers!

Dee-I like when old granies laugh at me on the tube and we spit on'em. We know what's happening in the world, they don't.

Andy-If we did get on 'Top Of the Pops' it wouldn't be degrading. It means our record's selling well, which means, sort of... we're getting the message over.

Brian-We're the only band that can really relate to the kids, even the Pistols... they're old enough to be our dads.

Dee-If you do a drum solo, it's alright if there's a crowd of drummers out there. People don't come to hear solos, do they? I don't play anything technical, Rat Scabies taught me and he doesn't know any technical stuff. He just plays, sort of, off the cuff.

Ian-I like playing fast music and I can play fast for EATER and that's why I'm playing. I'm not playing for people to look at me.

Andy-I'd really like people to go and blow up schools. Turn on their parents and slash'em up with razor blades.

Brian-Hippies are better than just normal lads arn't they? At least they're something differant.

Brian-I'll never forget the first time I met Mark P. in the toilet at the Nashville. Really good it was, we had a piss together.

Ian-First time I ever saw Eater I thought they were crap.I answered an ad,I had to have an audition.

Brian-The Clash are good but politics is boring.

Andy-Slaughter and the Dogs?I think they're good but they've got nothing to do with what's going on.They're just another rock band.

Ian-Vibraters?I really like'em...fast.

Dee-I don't know anything about"punk".I was just asked to join a band called EATER and I did.I was wearing a ripped up t-shirt at the time.They said,"You must be a punk"and I said,"Oh,yeah".I read about it in the papers so I just joined'em.

Brian-It just comes under the thing of"punk rock".It's more like rebel-rock...it's just aggressive rock!

Compiled by Mark P.

PHOTO : H.T. MURLOWSKI.

IAN WOODCOCK

One band I do like is Eater. They're still the youngest band on the scene even though they've been around for a couple of months now.When they first appeared on stage they took us by storm with a frightening sound and an abusive stance,at that Fincley place-they made us all feel too old at 19!

Now the element of suprise has gone.Now when we go to one of their gigs we know what to except.Dee smashing maniacally away on drums,Ian squeezing the goodie

bass riffs keeping in band on the right route,Brian struggles on guitar-not the easiest of instruments to play when you're young-and Andy hollering down the mike-not a pretty voice.Together,they have a lot of fun with their fans and generate a lot of noise and excitment.No one could criticise Eater as a sloppy band'cos they are still very young and very eager to enjoy learning.Their sound id never very good and it is not often that anyone can hear the vocals,except when Andy's swearing at ya!The important thing is that they do produce a very tense sound which incites feelings in ya to bop and go mad!Eater are controlled madness-just-right through until the drum-kit is obliterated and left smouldéring all over the stage.

The group's songs range from their forthcoming single-"Outside View"-and a few others they've written themselves-"Bedroom Fix","Reflections", "You","Point Of View","Get Raped!",etc-to their versions of golden oldies like, "Queen Bitch","Sweet Jane"and"Waiting For the Man".All said and done,Eater try to reflect the mood of the times-like the more important bands on the scene-but nevertheless,Eater are treated lightly by most audiences.That is not to say that they are laughed at but the plain truth is that they are not taken at all seriously.Eater seem to be more important as every schoolboys dream of what he'd like to fuckin'do on prizeday.For most kids such a dream never hits reality but Eater have got the chance to really get up all the old cunts noses.

Eater may write songs which reflect their lives but they're more of a successful rock formula than one of the serious bands who know what they believe in and that's what it's all about. The band still swear and wear swastikas, more to shock the older generation who fought against it all rather than as a means to make people think.The swastika is a symbol of aggression,that's not what Eater are about.They're about having a laugh,enjoying yourself and sending up the shit.

Up to now they've had it easy,thanks to other groups like the Sex Pistols who paved the way for'em.It all must mean more than just a good night out and a residency at the Hope & Anchor. At the moment it seems the only way the band will change is technically 'cause they've already said all they can and are burning theirselves out in their own self destruction.

Steve Mick.

SINGLES → REVIEWS. MAGS ↓

ALL REVIEWS BY MARK P.

THE SAINTS-(I'M)STRANDED(Power Exchange).
I remember the old days when this was availiable only on Australian import.The Saints are now cult superstars,now they're probabley bombing around the outback in their gold Lincoln.Sheep shearing is in the past,these punks don't wanna wear wool anymore...they're ncw into leather!Yeah,I reckon they're beating all the Abo's up with the ol'baseball bats.Poor bastards...no,now I'm being serious,I don't reckon they've changed at all,I bet they still havn't got a phone.
B-side is'No Time',and the whole thing is fantastic.It's a fuckin'great noise!
(An autographed copy of the original single on the Fatal Record label is up for offers in Rough Trade record shop.All takin's go to 'Sniffin'Glue').

BESERKLEY 6 PACK;

EARTHQUAKE-FRIDAY ON MY MIND/JONATHAN RICHMAN-ROADRUNNER.

RUBINOOS-I THINK WE'RE ALONE NOW/AS LONG AS I'M WITH YOU.

JONATHAN RICHMAN-HERE COME THE MARTIAN MARTIANS/NEW ENGLAND.

GREG KIHN-LOVE'S MADE A FOOL OF YOU/SORRY.

SON OF PETE-SILENT KNIGHT/DISCO PARTY,PT 2.

EARTHQUAKE-KICKS/TRAINRIDE.
This would have been a great Christmas present,trouble is we couldn't get SG 6 out before 1977 so that fucked that up didn't it?
Earthquake-Sound like Deep Purple,but not quite as bad.5 outta 10.
Jonathan Richman-Need I say it?10 outta 10, three of his classic tracks.
Rubinoos-Very poppy,but they're good at it. 'I Think We're Alone Now'would make a great No.1 hit single.7 outta 10 for being simple and nice...bunch of poofs!
Greg Kihn-Like the Rubinoos but he sounds like he's got the heavy mob(i.e:Earthquake) up behind him.'Fool Of You'is a fuckin' nice song,6 outta 10 for it.
Son Of Pete-Fuckin'ell,the clearest production I've ever heard.Eathquake are not on this!10 outta 10 for originality.

SON OF PETE & THE MUFFDIVERS-SAGA OF YUKON PETE(Organ).
From the brainwave that brought us'SilentKnight'comes this HR Crumb take-off on plastic.Nasty little dirty record with a free nasty little dirty booklet.A"version"is on the flip.Stick with'Silent Knight'for definitive Son Of Pete.

12

Right,due to the great response to our last fanzine review here's a bit more.Notice that there's a lot of young whipper-snappers bringing out fanzines.We at SG are proud to be British(!):

Newis-

BONDAGE Fun,fun,fun all the way!Issue No.1 has got Eater,the Jam and a Pistols/Grundy thing.Shane is a real punk!

48 THRILLS A good lot to read,Adrian's a thoughtful guy.Issue 1 had Sex Pistols, Eater,the Clash,the Jame plus reviews and that.Issue 2's out soon. *No.2 OUT NOW!*

NOT JUST A PHASE This my personnel fav.It's written by one of the Subway Sect's mates. Original,loose,funny...it's everything.On the cover-"A magazine for you...but not for you,hippie!"

SIDEBURNS This is a bit too nice plus they like the Stranglers.Stranglers,Hot Rods,Dr. Feelgood plus various reviews.Unoriginal.

LONDON'S OUTRAGE This is a concept mag. It's a collection of ideas,cuttings,bits, photos and it's put together by a guy who has got a bit of the ol'nod'll.Very,very interesting look at the scene.

ANARCHY IN THE U.K Put together by the Sex Pistols office-Glitterbest Ltd.It's about the size of a Sounds and Issue 1 features mostly photos of the Pistols and their fans.Not much yet but the 2nd one'll be out soon with some writing(I think)in it. If this mag was used the right way it could be amazing.

LONDON'S BURNING The entire thing is the brainwave of Jonh Ingham.It trys to sort out what the Clash are all about.A lot of work's gone into it.Lyrics,photos,newspaper combine to give a interesting viewpoint on the Clash.It was well worth all the work'cause it's great.Perhaps it's be-I am a Clash follower(very serious word). Yeah,I believe in the Clash.

Old farts-

RIPPED & TORN No.2 Another amusing issue from the nutters up in Glasgow.No.2's got Sex Pistols'"tour",the Nobodies,various reviews and some contributions from poet Sandy Robertson.Get it...NOW!

PUNK No.7 Blue Oyster Cult,Patti Smith,Hot Rods,Satan(?),Dead Boys and Lou Reed's Rapidograph Drawings.The content's OK but I just can't believe how childish the layout is.I mean,if SG had PUNK's resources... oh fuck,I just don't know how they get away with it.
Write to ROUGH TRADE for magazine list for prices etc.Adress on Page 2.

SG PIN-UP : BRIAN CHEVETTE
OF EATER.
PHOTO BY ERICA ECHENBERG.

PHOTO BY ERICA ECHENBERG.

SNIFFIN' GLUE...

30p

AND OTHER ROCK 'N' ROLL HABITS
FOR PINHEADS AND SURFERS! ⑦ FEB '77

...Black...White...Black...White...Bl......White...Black...White...Black...

ADVERTS - DON LETTS - GORILLAS

GAYE ADVERT
SEZ: THIS ALBUM
TURNS MEN INTO
GIRLS!

BUY IT YOU
WIMPS!
ONLY £3·49

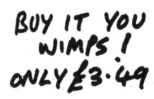

MARK P.

We're really knocking the ol'SG's out now right?Issue 7 already and issue 8 should be out in about 5 weeks.The first few weeks of'77 have been so busy I reckon we could have put out SG every two weeks and still keep it interesting.Every 5 weeks is the best we can do'cause we've got a lot of money problems.

In this issue I've done a couple of interviews with people I really believe in.The Adverts are a new band who are already one of my favourites.They've got an interesting approach to their music. Lead singer,TV Smith and bassist,Gaye Advert both come from Devon.There must be loads more frustrated kids in places like Devon and that. It's a pity they can't become involved in the new music that's being played here in London at the moment.

The interview with Roxy Club"DJ",Don'Dread'Letts was supposed to be a reggae piece but it turned into an interesting look on the scene.I reckon the crititisms that Don makes are very relevent.I hope that everybody understands why we put it in SG.If you don't,hard luck.

Also in this issue is a review of the great Gorillas by Steve Mick. It's another of Steve's boppin'live reports.

H.T.has more of his good pics scattered around and Erica chose the Damned for her Hang-Up'cause their album's released this month.I would have reviewed it but I couldn't get a copy in time.

See yer,Mark P.

S.G. 7

CONTENTS

MARK P: Editor and layout.

HARRY T.MURLOWSKI: Photographer and even more serious business hassles.

STEVE MICK: Contributing writer.

ERICA ECHENBERG: Hang-ups.

Address:

'Sniffin'Glue...'
c/o Rough Trade,
202 Kensington Park Road,
LONDON,W11.

This issue is dedicated to all the"pinheads" from New York and all the"surfers"from the West Coast of America who now read SG,oh yeah it's also for Genesis P-Orridge and Throbbing Gristle.

MAIL-ORDER

Sorry about the fucked up prices we charged for the mail-order in SG6.Here's what we should have printed:

(prices include P&P).

35p for the UK and Eire.

50p for Europe and seamail to rest of the world.

65p for airmail outside Europe.

The maximum subscription you can have is 4 issues,which is 4 times the price of one issue.

MAIL-ORDER

← DAVE VANIAN OF THE DAMNED AT THE ROXY CLUB, 31/1/77 (PHOTO - H.T).

2

THE ADVERTS.

L to R- GAYE, T.V. HOWARD + LAURIE.

What is it-Interview.
Subject-New group called the ADVERTS.
Members present-TV Smith-lead vocals.
   Gaye Advert-bass.
   Howard-guitar.
Not present-Laurie Driver-drums.
Details-At the time of this chat the Adverts
had only played 3 gigs-Support at the Roxy
Club on 15th Jan and 19th Jan plus support
to the Stranglers at the Royal College Of·
Art on 21st Jan.They sound like nothing else
around at the moment.TV's songs are'One Chord
Wonders','Newboys','The Quickstep','On the
Roof','New Day Dawning','We Who Wait','Bomb-
site Boy'and'Bored Teenagers'.There's more
but that's what was played the first time I
saw'em.I was suprised when I saw'em,they hit
me hard.They played fast but it didn't mess
'em up.The strong songs came through,the message if you like,was seen.I couldn't take my
eyes off Gaye at first but then I noticed
that she was playing great bass lines.On
guitar-Howard,Gaye reckons he looks like a
very famous film monster.He doesn't play
like one,he's good.His breaks are unusual.
Laurie Driver is a drummer.A drummer-solid.
TV Smith,the singer,is always unhappy but it
makes some great music.His songs mean alot
to him,you can tell by the way he sings'em.
Really,the Adverts are like one thing and
that thing is the Adverts:

TV: This band's got about 2 months history.
Gaye's been learning to play bass for about
6 months.We've had a guitarist about 2 months and the drummer about a month.

MP: When did you first think of forming a
band?

TV: I've been doing it since I was at school.
I've always been doing me own stuff.I had a
couple of school bands.None of us could play
'cept in that time it used to be heavy make
up and all that sort of stuff,you know,in
the lunch hours.Doing the maths lesson with
glitter all over me face'cause I couldn't
get it all off.I did a year at college-
'cause I didn't know what to do-and I had
another band then.It wern't really regular
'cause this was in...well,the school band
was in a village in the middle of Devon.
The college was also in Devon so we got
about 4 gigs in 4 months.

MP: How did you get up to London?

TV: We came up to get a band,it's the only
place anything's happening.Devon's great
for learning to get bored.You've got to
have something like a band or you go insane.

Gaye: The two of us were doing fine,you
know,practising in my parent's house.You
see,we've known each other for two years.
Yeah,we could practise but that's as far as
we could go.

TV: One day she said that she'd like to play
bass,so we learnt.

Gaye: I don't know why I decided on bass.
There was loads of lead guitars for sale in
Devon but hardly any basses.We spent ages
trying to find a bass.It cost £35.

TV- Yeah,that's the beginning of this band.
That little poxy amplifier sitting in a bedroom with this and that(pointing at two
cheap guitars)and thinking what great hei-
ghts we'd reach.

Gaye: Yeah,I got that amp and the Stooges'
first album for a tenner.

NEW SUBJECT.

TV: My old band chucked me out.They wanted
to do Jimi Hendrix numbers.We was doing my
stuff which was a step back from what we do
now.I've always been doing my own stuff,
even when I was at school.So I havn't actually had very good reactions to it,most
of the time.People can't sing along to it
'cause they don't know what's happening.
It's good that the Roxy's there'cause we
probably still wouldn't have a chance to
do it otherwise.I think the Roxy's great.
The fact that it gives people the chance to
do a gig without even hearing them.It means
anyone can have at least one try.I hope it
don't get closed down.

Gaye: Yeah,when we played the RCA the atmosphere wasn't as good.To me,it was like
rehearsing'cause we didn't make any mis-
takes.I still prefer the Roxy.

3

GOOD OL'"PUNK ROCK"

TV: I hope nobody defines it'cause then people won't think about it anymore.

MP: What would you define your material as, where does it come from...your atitude?

TV: I dunno,it's not for me to say.It's for the people who listen I suppose...I just do it.I DON'T THINK ABOUT WHAT I THINK.
        I sit down with the guitar and any ideas I've got...no!It's not even like that really,it could happen anyway.

GAYE.

Gaye: 'Cause,I used to like the Stooges and the New York Dolls.Iggy's been my hero for lots of years now.I've been an Iggy fanatic for about 4 years.Before I even got'Raw Power'I used to borrow somebody else's.I used to take the cover to bed with me and lay in bed with the cover on the pillar.Yeah I was into the Stooges down in Devon.Originally I was into Frank Zappa and things like that.
        The first time I saw the Pistols last Spring they done an Iggy number and I saw'em every week after that.I thought it was amazing.I never believed Johnny Rotten would like us but he said he did.He's a nice guy.
        Before we moved up to London I thought up part of a song'cause I was in this horrible,revolting factory.They had this sign up on the wall saying about,"draw to your attention that we've got mice here and we have got rat inspectors..."and I thought up this song.What was it?Yeah...Look after all the rats and strangle all the fuckin'cats!That's the first part.That's the sort of thing I do,so I thought,I'd better shut my mouth.I'm better off just doing the bass lines.

TV: You'd wanna do an hour of Iggy Pop songs!

MP: What do you think of the audience at the moment?

TV: I think it's in danger of becoming super cool.When we did that first gig,like,-from watching other bands before-if nobody walks out it probably means they like us.If they stand there it's alright,I mean,I don't care what an audience does.If they like it,great, I don't want people clapping after every number.

TV

TV: A lot of bands have started playing since the Pistols and started writing since then and that.Which is good but I've been writing a long time.

Gaye: Do you reckon our guitarist looks like Frankenstein?

4

ENTER...FRANKENSTEIN!
(The interview was at TV and Gaye's flat but now it's in Franke...Howard's flat).

TV: Subway Sect used to busk in Hammersmith subway,didn't they?I did as well...

Howard: I got caught busking in Tottenham Court Road station.London Transport police-"Would you mind moving along,next time we catch you we'll have you!"

TV: I'd be singin',"There's a killer in yer subway...".People didn't give me much money.

Gaye: A policeman suggested that you should get singin'lessons,with the money you'd got but he money got about 10p.

TV: Not only was he a policeman telling me to go away,he was a critical policeman.If you're good-"Accompany me to the station and do a free concert for the lads".

HOWARD.

Howard: When you see people at the front, jumpin'and dancin'along.You know,I don't think about anything else.I don't think about recording studios or big stages.I just like seeing people enjoy themselves and you actually fing yourself playing to 'em.What upsets me a bit is the spotlights and things,always being on stage.You can't see people at the back,you know.
        This band is a good band.TV would probably be playing this sort of music anyway.It just happens to have coincided with,what is,basically new music and new outlook for young people.There's only certain chords you can play on a guitar and there's only certain notes in a scale,right. I mean,the lyrics and yer feeling and the way you develope the music is what is new about it.
        I think there's a sort of elitism developing on the new wave scene. Although,that could be something that's been generated by the press.The Pistols,the Clash,the Damned and now Generation X.

THE ANSWER TO ALL THE PEOPLE WHO RECKON THAT TV SMITH ACTS LIKE JOHNNY ROTTEN ON STAGE.

TV: I'm not aware of it,but so many people have said it to me that it's starting to get into my brain.

Gaye: TV used to have a band in Devon.He was exactly like that then.He used to be even ruder to the audience,he was really object-ionable.Exactly the same as he is now.

TV: As far as I'm concerned I havn't changed from when I did it 2 years ago or when I did it in a school band even.I'm just gonna carry on,I don't really care.I mean,people have to relate to something.People always go to the nearest thing,you know,just a thing in human nature.Like,people wanna call the scene-"punk",you know.They see me perform and they wanna say"it's like Johnny Rotten".There's no need for it,who cares...

Gaye: Yeah,I've had somebody accusing me of copying the bassist of Talking Heads'cause I'm female.Just'cause I'm female!

FIRST LP COVER.

TV- Who cares...we havn't really been giving you positive imformation really.

Howard-The first time you've had a negative interview.

TV- We're Generation -,we are.I wouldn't like to read this shit!

Interview by Mark P.
Photographs by Harry T.Murlowski.

" JUST PUT WHAT YOU WANT..."

As you all already know the CLASH have signed to CBS.The first release will be a single,probably White Riot/1977. They're also playing three nights at the Roxy at the end of February.I was shocked when I heard they were actually doin'somethin' ...Track have been getting involved with the scene recently.They keep telling everybody that the"punk scene must stay independent". Yeah,well I reckon we should stay indepen-dent and forget about record companies that had their glory in the swingin'sixties...ex-cept when they save SG7 from the graveyard by paying out £60 for their page ad...the amazing GENERATION X have split with their manager,Andy Czezowski(he also runs the Roxy Club).Apparently,they're looking for more of a"political direction".Perhaps they'll find it in the two guys who are currantly sniff-in'heavily in their direction-Jonh Ingham of Sounds fame and Stuart Joseph of Rough Trade fame.I hope they don't change music-ally...the Adverts'new song-'The Great Brit-ish Mistake'is destined to become a classic. Stiff were caught talking to'em after their gig at the Roxy recently...After telling Billy Idol to get singin'lessons recently Harry T.Murlowski(that well-known poxy lens-man)then turned to his verbal punchbag,Mark P.and told him to get typing lessons...what did you get in your post,Veedge...we ain't recieved hardly any poll responses,that's why it ain't printed this month.Pull yer fingers out and get the fuckers to us...new U.S.bands: Nerves/Low Numbers/Bizarros/Thun-dertrain/Count Viglione/Gizmos/Venus and the Razorblades/Sneakers/Slickee Boys/Pentagram/ Pictures...if you order anything from us and you pay by cheque or postal-order please leavr payee section blank.'Cause we ain't Paul Getty takeoffs with 10 bank accounts... what ever happened to the SUBWAY SECT.They used to get up on stage and be theirselves, now they're rehearsing like an established band(SM)...fanzines that have come out sin-ce the last issue: Teenage Depression/White Stuff/Kid's Stuff/More-On 2/Zip-vinyl/Side-burns 2/O.D 2/Flicks/Fishnet Tights...
NEXT ISSUE: HEARTBREAKERS
THE JAM , JOHNNY MOPED + DAMNED.

ADS.

"EVERYBODY FORGOT ABOUT DRINKING..."

Things had been getting pretty dead at the Nashville so it was about time that a really good band played there.

The Gorillas are Jesse Hector -guitar,vocals,Al Butler-bass and Matt McIntyre-drums.They've not long come back from France and this was their second London gig.

The Nashville was jam-packed to give'em a welcome and the Gorillas brought with'em,a lot of fun.They definitely proved they're a band for a live audience.The Gorillas gave the impression they are like Slade,everyone of their short,hard rock songs had a powerful hard beat to it.

Straight off the cuff the first number they came up with really held yer attention.It was really catchy and the music stopped every time for the spelt-out chorus-"Yer can't always tell a book by looking at it's cover!"

Yer can't help yourself,you have to bop to their tunes and enjoy yourself.Jesse gets us all going by talking with us all the time in-between numbers but they never slacken the pace.The set speeds along and everything about the 3 piece spells out their promise for success.You can tell that they're a great band but they're nothing new and they don't hide their influences.The Gorillas are just a popular rock band,they are fun for all the family,as the punks,hippies,discos and footballs who turned out to see'em proved.

Nobody takes their eyes off the band for a second and everybody forgot about talking and drinking with each other for a while.The Gorillas are too much fun and they're immediately likeable.

After the next song Jesse asks us,"We want you all to sing along to that one next time!"before taking the breaks off their next number-a nice little singalong version of the Small Faces''All Or Nothing',which didn't sound much differant than the original.The set's getting more and more exciting as they steam on.

The next song was their new single-'Gatecrasher'.

"'Ere,we're gonna keep on playing",screams Jesse and you can see the sweat shining on his beaming face.

"Com'on,babee..."

Their format my be old and well tried but they sound raw and fresh.

'Wild Thing'was something we never expected and they did it complete with feedback.Jesse put on a thick accent and dived and sommersaulted all over the front of the stage like Hendrix.Jesse looks like he's writhing in agony but he looks as if he could do the song standing on his head while Al pulls out the bass riffs, heaving the guitar up and down with all his strength to bring out the right sound.Matt carries on slamming out on drums without a trace of suprise on his face.He looks like he's seen it all before but you can tell that-like the audience-he's having fun.

Jesse crys out to us mob,"I wanna hear yer,wild thing...get over this 'ere thing!",showing us what he means by making all sorts of psychedelic,butterfly fluttering noises on his guitar.

"At the back there,let's hear ya!Com'on,1 wanna see ya!",shouts Jesse, pointing to us all.(Contd.over page).

6

...SHOCK! GASP! HORROR! IT MUST BE THE

GORILLAS

AT THE NASHVILLE!

(ALRIGHT, OVER THE TOP).

L to R: AL BUTLER, JESSE HECTOR, PAUL GRAY (OF THE HOT RODS), + MATT McINTYRE, BACKSTAGE-NASHVILLE.

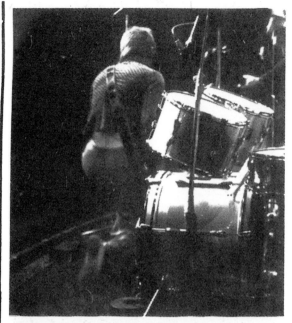

(Contd.from page 6).

   After'Wild Thing'comes Hen-
drix's'Foxy Lady'and even that hippy Jesus
is there with his poxy tambourine.
   Some more chug-a-chug bass
and guitar is stored up in the next song,
'Keep On To Me'which is loud,hard and full
of energy.Then it's all over bar the shouting'cept for some real fanatics who manage
to rouse the band back for an encore.
   The Gorillas are nothing to
do with the new wave except that they're
on the same level-you can talk to'em and
they're not superstars.They're a peoples
band as the variety in the audience proved.
Nothing breathtaking or spectacular-just a
rock band with guts.

          Steve Mick.

← JESSE HECTOR ROLLIN' ABOUT.

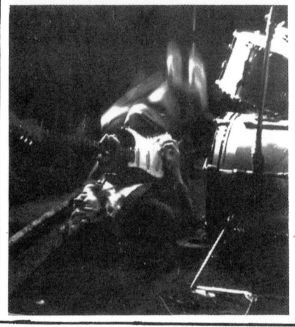
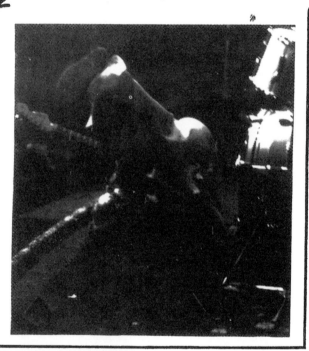

FEBRUARY DATE
SHEET.

ROXY CLUB

41-43 Neal Street London W.C.2. Tel: 836 8811

FEBRUARY DATE
SHEET.

Mon.14th: Damned & Adverts

Wed.16th: Vibrators & G.B.H.

Sat.19th: Cortinas & Bombers.

Sun.20th: Reggae night.

Mon.21st: Damned & Johnny Moped.

Tue.22nd: The Late Eddie Cochran.

Wed.23rd: Slaughter and the Dogs & G.B.H.

Thurs.24th: Jam & Rejects.

Fri.25th: ⎫
Sat.26th: ⎬ Possible biggie —
Sun.27th: ⎭ RING FOR DETAILS

Mon.28th: Damned & Chelsea.

PHONE FOR DETAILS OF OTHER NIGHTS.

7

BLACK - WHITE.
INTERVIEW WITH DON LETTS.

Don is the following things:

Black.
A Rasta.
DJ in the Roxy Club.
Manager(sort of)of the Acme Attractions shop
in the King's Road.
A friend of the Patti Smith Band(he joined
them onstage at Hammersmith Odeon).
A very interesting person.
I reckon his ideas on the punk
scene are very very interesting.That's why
we've got a fuckin'great interview with him.
Fire-

DON: In the DJ box,right?I sit in there and
stare at the kids,and you can see that some
of'em are genuinely interested,right?Then
again,you've got a new set in there which
are like...latent skinheads.They've hung up
their boots,they've cut their hair and come
in...and just come to wreck the place.They
don't give a damn about the music,I reckon
80% of'em are poseurs.They just put on the
clothes...I mean,that chick for instance...
who writes Fishnet Tights?Personally,I think
she's full of shit.To me she's just like a
typical college chick,I'm sure her mum and
dad have got a lot of dough.She don't know
what it is to be fuckin'poor!Were you poor?

MP: No...never.

DON: You never been poor,Mark...you cunt!
You've been workin'class though,right?

MP: Oh yeah,workin'class.

DON: Like,to me,the reggae thing and the
punk thing...it's the same fuckin'thing.Just
the black version and the white version.The
kids are singing about change,they wanna do
away with the establishment.Same thing the
niggers are talkin'about,"Chant down Babylon",it's the same **thing.**Our Babylon is your
establishment,same fuckin'thing.If we beat
it,then you beat it and vise versa.
'Cause like,Johnny Rotten was
telling me the other day.He's walkin'down the
street now and the cops are hittin'on him.
Takin'him in the van,tryin'to bust him for
this and that.'Cause of the way he looks...
it's the same shit we go through.Like,with
me hair and the red,gold and green.Copper
stopped me in me car and tell me I should
walk,cops actually told me I should walk!
'Cause like he said,"People with red,gold
and green nats shouldn't have enough money
to drive flash cars"and all this crap,you
know?
And,like it's fuckin'heavy.
Once you put that hat on your head you're
takin'on a whole lot of shit,you know what I

mean?Same as a punk,right,a punk wears his
clothes.He's makin'an outward sign that
he's rebelling.Same thing we do,right.We
put on the red,gold and green,dread up our
head.We're rebelling and we don't give a
fuck'cause you can't hide this shit,right?
It's all the same battle but
the punk kids don't see that.I heard at one
point them saying,like"Blacks are fucked"
and"black music ain't got nuthin'".Anybody
who says that has gotta be an arsehole,
right.'Cause,you know you've got to owe it
to niggers music wise.That put me off the
punk scene straight away,when I heard that.

MP: What sort of response are you gettin'
for what you play down the Roxy?

DON: It's good.I'm gettin'more askin'me for
reggae than punk.They come in and actually
tell me to take it off,it's true.Joe and
Mick from Clash,even Johnny Rotten...every-
body!At first I wasn't sure wether to play
it or not but then again,there ain't enough
punk material out.Like,they say I'm DJ'ing
at the Roxy...there's no DJ'ing to do!You
got like 10 LP's,right and about 20 singles
and that's it.How the fuck can you DJ?You
just rearrange it everynight.I had to pad
it out with something and I can't stand
soul,the soul right now.The soul now is,
sort of...money inspired.I prefer punk rock
to that shit,I prefer most of the white
music now to most of that soul shit.'Cause
that's money inspired and it ain't coming
from in here(heart)and if music ain't coming
from in here it ain't nuthin'.It's not
inspired right,it's not real. (Contd.over).

8

REGGAE.

DON: I think the majority of the Roxy audience dig it.Quarter of'em really like it, like you really like it.The Clash guys,they all like it.I can talk to'em and tell that they like the music.

You know,you get those other fuckers who say they"dig reggae"'cause it's in to dig reggae now,right?Like Asward,hip to check out Asward now,right?It's a hip thing to dig reggae...for some people.I mean, Caroline Coon and there's one that's worse.I mean,look at that chick...

MP: She used to go down the black clubs in the sixties.

DON:...oh,you see her with her t-shirt carefully ripped between the tits.Punk,my arse. You can tell see dresses up like a punk to go to a punk do and probably puts on a red, gold and green hat to go to a reggae do.I'll tell you who's another one,Janet Street Porter...horsemouth!She's the same kinda thing. I see her do this fifties thing for TV and she wears all fifties clothes and I saw her on the punk rock thing with a t-shirt with 'Punk'across the front.She's fulla shit!You ain't gotta do that.It's like me cutting my hair to go and see a white pop show.You don't have to do that.There's nowhere I don't go lookin'like this,not a place on the earth.I go to white pop shows,I go to fuckin'...I been to church like this,weddings, court,I ain't ashamed.I just speak and when I talk,that gets me by,not how I look.As far as I'm concerned,I'm above clothes.I don't need it no more because all the kids that come into the shop,they put so much importance in clothes.They're building up a force identity.

MP: You say that but you're selling the clothes to'em.

DON: Yeah,I sell the clothes to'em but I don't tell'em the attitude in which they should put it on.Buying clothes and looking far out is cool.As long as you know where it's importance lies,right.As long as you know that clothes are here and you're there and someone says to you,"Well,what are you about?".As long as you can stand there and fuckin'tell the guy.

PUNK ROCK.

DON: There saying it's a new thing,there gonna change this and I say,what are they doing...what is punk rock?How they going about achieving what they're doing,they're fulla shit!They've got the pins in their ears and the clothes ripped up but what they fuckin'doin'?

Punk rock is boring me'cause they're tryin'to tell me it's something new and if it was I'd be right in there with 'em.I'd be right behind'em...I'd be fuckin' up front!But I'm 21 and I can see it already.It's gonna come along,pass and drop. It will pass,unfortunately.

When it all started off I was amazed,I never seen any movement move so quick,right,tremendous potential.All the kids caught on to something,they got on to an idea.They had all this energy in'em, which we've all got...we all feel the same pressures.They felt it and then they got into the clothes-same old fuckin'story-got into the music-same old story-and they said "fuck"and spit on TV or whatever-same old story,Alice Cooper bit off fuckin'snakes' heads,big deal!Then what?Nuthin'right,it's stopped at there."We're gonna change,we're gonna change!",the hippies said,"We're gonna change"-all that peace and love bit-and what did they do?Nuthin'!

DON: If anybody says to me"Where are you at?" I can stand there and tell'em,right.If I can't tell you at least I can fuckin'bullshit you and get by,right.These kids,they can't say nuthin'to yer and it's a drag, you know?They're gettin'dressed up and shit, when they should be gettin'there head together.They've got all this energy and no direction.Like our shop,even our shop.I said to John(Krevine),I said to the people that own the place,why don't we take it a step further and give'em something to read.Even if it's just tellin'em what all these words they're talkin'about mean.I mean,'Anarchy', the fuckers don't know what that means.The kids don't know what they're talkin'about, they just don't know.

(Contd.over).

9

DON: They go on TV.They say"fuck",big storm and they get recognised.That ain't nuthin' new.

Like that chick who said she ripped the heads off her dolls and the punk-ettes in the'News Of the World'throwing the dead pigeons about,right?I mean,that's what all the other pop stars used to do—outrageous things—so the asshole reporter goes"Fuck me" and writes"He does this,does that...",why they gotta do that?Why don't they say something,why don't they say what they think,if they think anything.That's what hurts me so much,it had so much potential so fast.

They're just having fun,if they can just say that I'm more pleased with 'em.It's when some fucker hits on me tryin' to tell me that he's"new wave","new order", "I gonna change this","Reggae ain't doing nuthin'and the hippies ain't doin'nuthin'and Clapton and that lot ain't doin'nuthin'". It's true they ain't but they ain't goin' around,bullshitting,saying they are!

I think,even the skinheads had it together a bit more'cause at least they had some values.The skinheads were pretty together you know'cause,like,they had a be-lief.It may have been a wrong belief but I prefer a"yes"or a"no"to a"don't know".The skinheads had one strong moral and that was out with immigrants.Obviously,I thought it was fuckin'nonsense,right,but the thing is-they had a belief.Like,they'd go round paki-bashing,it might have been a bit un-cool... the thing is,they had a belief and they went about putting it into action,right.I respect that,I respect a guy who hates niggers and goes and knocks'em down as apposed to a guy who says"one of my best friends is a nigger

so..."and all that shit and then his daugh-ter comes in and says,"Dad,look...here's Sammy..."and POW!Know what I mean?The Eng-lish are like that.

The English in general are fucked up.It's not their fault,it's the system.What hurts me is,like,these kids are just perpetuating it.They're helping it flow along.They ain't doing fuck all!

Interview by Mark P.
Photographs by Harry T.Murlowski.

That interview was put in the mag'cause it brought up points about the scene which have needed to be be crit-ised.I mean,safty-pins and all that game is OK but it's getting stupid.We're now getting cunts who rip their jackets,shove a few safty-pins through their cheeks and make out they're doing something creative. This scene,if there is a "scene"anymore,is about movement.It's about constant change, creative change,not fashion changes,no-one's done anything by worrying about clothes.Don said in the interview that he was"above clothes",well,we should all strive for that feeling.

Reggae was also mentioned in the above piece.I was thinking of having reggae reviews in SG'cause I've liked reggae ever since me skinhead days.

There's so much movement in reggae.So much soul and honesty.It's worth checking out,if it only means lis-tening to it down the Roxy Club.If we had room it would definitely be in SG,no Q's asked.

If you can't get down the Roxy,listen to Reggae Time(Radio London, Sunday),read Black Music or read Eric Fuller in National Rockstar(the only thing worth buying it for).

Just fuckin'try to listen to reggae,right!

Jah Mark P.

10

REVIEWS

ALL REVIEWS BY MARK P.

BUZZCOCKS-SPIRAL SCRATCH(New Hormones EP).
Breakdown/Time's Up/Boredom/Friends Of Mine.
                    The first time I played this
thing,it jumped all over the place.I threw
it against the wall and it broke into pieces:

"If I seem a little jittery,
 I can't restrain myself,
 I'm falling into fancy fragments,
 Can't contain myself,
 I gotta breakdown,breakdown yeah

 I can stand austerity,
 But it gets a little much,
 When there's all these livid things,
 That you never get to touch,
 I gotta breakdown,breakdown yeah".
                    I had to buy another one.When
I heard it properly I couldn't believe it.

"Feels my brains'like porridge,
 Coming outta my ears,
 And I was expecting reverie,
 Taken leave of my senses and I'm in arrears,
 My legs buckle over,I'm living on my knees,
 I gotta breakdown,yeah,
 I gotta breakdown,yeah,
 I'm gonna breakdown,yeah-uh-huh".
                    These guys live up in Manches-
ter,that's what makes their music so vital.

"Whatever makes me tick,
 It takes away my concentration,
 Sets my hands trembling,
 Gives me frustration,
 Breakdown yeah.

 I hear that two is company,
 For me it's plenty trouble,
 Though my double thoughts are clearer,
 Now that I am seeing double,
 Breakdown yeah.

 Oh mum can I grow outta,
 What's a little too big for me,
 I'm gonna give up that ghost,
 Before it gives up me,
 I wander loaded as a crowd,
 A nowherewolf of pain,
 Living next to nothing,
 But my nevermind remains,
 I gotta breakdown yeah,I'm gonna breakdown,
 You gimme breakdown yeah".
                    This group is the new-wave.Buy
it,if you don't you shouldn't be reading
this mag.Buzzcocks: Howard Devoto-vocals,
Pete Shelley-guitar,Steve Diggle-bass and
John Maher-drums.(Lyrics-New Hormones c).

If you can't get the Buzzcocks'EP in your
area send £1(plus 10p P&P)to New Hormones,
182 Oxford Road,Manchester 13.

PHOTO BY NIGEL WOODHEAD.

BUZZCOCKS' HOWARD DEVOTO.

STRANGLERS-GRIP(United Artists).
                    The band's boring"let's be
tough"stage stance has long since got on my
wick but this single is great.The Stranglers
are gonna go through life as happy recording
musicians with not one care in the world.
One day it might even be possible that we'll
see Hugh Cornwall wearing a"Fuck"t-shirt at
the Rainbow,the last date of their first
major headlinging tour of the GB.
                    The B-side-'London Lady'is
good but the picture on the cover is silly.

JOHNNY MOPED-STARTING A MOPED(Tape).
Groovy Ruby/Little Queenie/Starting a Moped/
Hard Lovin'Man/Wolf and Dracula/Decision/
3-D Time/Somethin'Else/These Students/Hell-
razor/Assault and Buggery.
                    In case you don't know it,
Moped is a livin'legend.This tape proves it,
30 minutes of real punk rock.
                    Oh yeah,'3-D Time'is a great
song,'Assault and Buggery'is weird and dirty plus the Damned's Captain Sensible plays
guitar and bass throughout.Live,Moped is in-
credible.Try to see'im and buy this tape at
Rock On,Soho Market for a quid.There might
be an interview in the next SG.

11

MORE REVIEWS.

RAMONES LEAVE HOME(Sire LP).
Glad To See You Go/Gimme Gimme Shock Treat-
ment/I Remember You/Oh Oh I Love Her So/Car-
bona Not Glue/Suzy Is a Headbanger/Pinhead/
Now I Wanna Be a Good Boy/Swallow My Pride/
What's Your Game/California Sun/Commando/
You're Gonna Kill That Girl/You Should Never
Have Opened That Door.

"Gabba gabba
We accept you
We accept you
One of us.
I don't wanna be a pinhead no more
I just met a nurse that I could go for.
D-U-M-B
Everyone's accusing me".
　　　　　　　　　('Pinhead'by the Ramones).
　　　　　　The Ramones have done it again.
They've stuck strictly to their old formula
and it's fuckin'great.The production is a
bit more sutle than on'Ramones'but lyricly
they've moved on.I reckon''Pinhead'is their
best song ever.It's 2:42 seconds of Ramones'
power-the best-but it's in the lyrics that
the incredible strength is.Remember when
they came over,every was saying how dumb
they are.Well-to me-in'Pinhead'the Ramones
are saying"So what",they're showing how fuckin'honest they are.
　　　　　　That's one thing this album is
-honest,just like they first one.By putting
out their first album the Ramones inspired
me to start'Sniffin'Glue...'.Well,I reckon
that if it was July'76 again and'Ramones
Leave Home'had been released the same thing
would have happened.
　　　　　　The Ramones-breaking down bar-
riers that have been built by the,so called,
rock establishment.Get back to the fuckin'
real rock sound-guitar,bass,drum,scream-with
the Ramones.
　　　　　　Dumb?Yeah,perhaps...but it's
better than learning how to operate a bleedin'£1,000 synthesizer.

TALKING HEADS-LOVE→BUILDING ON FIRE(Sire).
　　　　　　Less maniac than the Ramones
New York sound.This is very clever,very sop-
histicated pop music.Both the A and B-side-
'New Feelings'-are excellent songs.The playing is superb throughout.The horns sound a
bit out of place at first but even they become a important part of the group after a
few plays.Honest,I really love this group.
David Byrne-guitar and vocals-is the main
part of the group but I'm sure he couldn't
do without the rhythm section of Martina
Weymouth-bass and Chris Frantz-drums.
　　　　　　This band really cook,they're
incredible.The rhythm's Talking Heads play
are great.I'm ready to buy another copy'cause
I've worn this one out.When's the fuckin'
album out?

CRIME-HOT WIRE MY HEART/BABY,YOU'RE SO
　　　　　　　　　　　　　REPULSIVE(Crime)
　　　　　　　　Not availible in Britain yet
but someone's gonna get it over,I think.
　　　　　　　Crime are from the West Coast
and they're very noisey and incompetent.It
is a fuckin'great single though.Both sides
sound like they're record in warehouse,it's
like a really horrible mess.They all dress
in leather and they try to look tough,they
look more like a Fonz imitators.
　　　　　　　I did know all their names
but I lost the press handout that they sent
me.I know that their names I stupid anyhow.
　　　　　　　There's probabley loads of
small States bands putting out this sort of
mess on their own labels.Make sure you get
'em to Britain.
　　　　　　　Oh yeah,one of'em's called
Johnny Strike and another one,Frankie Fix.
Yeah,they're silly right?

CRIME.

PHOTO - ?

GORILLAS-GATECRASHER(Chiswick).
　　　　　　Nice,easy going single which
just fails to capture the atmosphere of
live Gorillas.The production is a lot differant from their last single-'She's My
Gal'.You can hear less of Jesse Hector's
mainiac guitar style and when a guitar break
finally comes the whole thind fades out.A
live EP from this group would be great.
　　　　　　B-side is a bouncy instru-
mental-'Gorillas Got Me'.See Steve Mick's
live review for more enthusiasm.

12

ERICA'S HANG-UP. No.2 : THE DAMNED

PHOTO BY ERICA ECHENBERG.

☆ Dave Vanian ☆ Brian James ☆ Capt. Sensible ☆ Rat Scabies ☆
    VOCALS   GUITAR   BASS   DRUMS

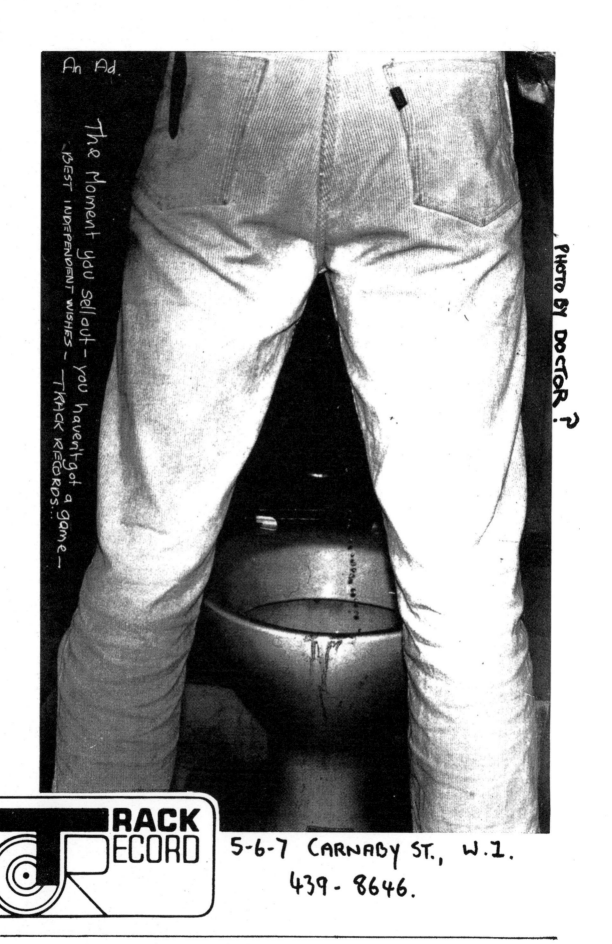

An Ad.

The moment you sell out — you haven't got a game
— BEST INDEPENDENT WISHES — TRACK RECORDS..

PHOTO BY DOCTOR ?

RACK ECORD

5-6-7 CARNABY ST., W.1.
439 - 8646.

SNIFFIN' GLUE...

30p

AND OTHER ROCK 'N' ROLL HABITS FOR PEOPLE WHO THINK IT'S HIP TO READ THE "IN" MAG. MARCH 1977.

In this issue......completely up the wall.There's mistakes everywhere,just like SG 1!

NEW YORK INVASION! HEARTBREAKERS, CHERRY VANILLA, WAYNE COUNTY.

BUZZCOCKS - THE JAM - THE CLASH.

Cream International Artists in association with New Orders presents

John Cale

```
THURS  7th  APRIL: W. RUNTON    Pavilion
SUN   10th  APRIL: LONDON       Roundhouse
MON   11th  APRIL: LONDON       Roundhouse
FRI   15th  APRIL: CAMBRIDGE    Corn Exchange
SAT   16th  APRIL: SOUTHEND     Kursaal
SUN   17th  APRIL: MAIDENHEAD   Skindles
MON   18th  APRIL: PLYMOUTH     Top Rank
TUES  19th  APRIL: BOURNEMOUTH  Winter Gardens
THURS 21st  APRIL: LIVERPOOL    Eric's
FRI   22nd  APRIL: MANCHESTER   Free Trade Hall
SAT   23rd  APRIL: BIRMINGHAM   Barbarella's
SUN   24th  APRIL: LEEDS        University
MON   25th  APRIL: STAFFORD     Top of the World
THURS 28th  APRIL: SWANSEA      Brangwyn Hall
FRI   29th  APRIL: NOTTINGHAM   Trent Polytechnic
SAT   30th  APRIL: CANTERBURY   Odeon
SUN    1st  MAY  : CROYDON      Greyhound
```

Further Information: 01 - 437 - 0712.

...with supporting attractions
(on most dates)

The Count Bishops
The Boys

A 20 YEAR-OLD MARK P.

Welcome to SG8.In this issue we go completely up the wall.

I'm really fed up with the punters on the"scene"at the moment.At the Clash gig in Harlesden there were lots of stupid kids who kept on acting childish by pogoing in front of the stage.They were going completely over the top by punching and kicking each other.It was like being at a fuckin'football match.

Look,am I getting old(I'm 2o now)or something?There's the Clash on stage, trying to say something,and all the kids can do is beat each other up.We've gotta stick together.If you wanna lay into someone wait till it's a government official or a member of a supergroup.They're the cunts to attack, not other kids who are trying to listen to the same groups as you.

I'll admit,there's nothing wrong with jumpin'around to the bands(I've done it myself)but it's gotta be a bit less enthusiastic otherwise new-wave/punk will be banned forever.I may be talking like an old cunt but perhaps I think to much these days. So what,it's still me that's writing this mag and every word I put my fuckin'name to is honest.

Cause like,there's been a few kids having a go at me.So what,I wrote some things for National Rockstar and the Melody Maker.They printed what I wrote.It was still me,I don't change my style for them!

Enjoy this crummy but always honest mag.

Mark P.

Ac BY H.T. MARLOWSKI.

MARK P: Editor,layout and gobing.

HARRY T. MURLOWSKI: Photograher,business manager and worrier.

STEVE MICK: Bump and grind storys plus laziness.

Others: ERICA ECHENBERG(Heartbreakers pics), D(big business)and a office on Oxford Street(?).
+JILL FOURMANOVSKY PHOTOGRAPHIC ADVISOR.
All mail to:

SNIFFIN'GLUE,
c/o ROUGH TRADE RECORD SHOP,
202 KENSINGTON PARK ROAD,
LONDON W.11.

Thanks to Geoff,Steve and all the hangers around at ROUGH TRADE for being so good to us.It's the best record shop in the world. No questions asked,boy!

MAIL-ORDER

35p for the UK and Eire.

50p for Europe and seamail to the rest of the world.

65p for airmail outside Europe.

(prices include P&P).

The maximum subscription you can have is 4 issues.Just send 4 times the price of one issue.

Send order to SG at above address but put "ORDER"on the envelope so we can suss it out quicker.Ta!

MAIL-ORDER.

← THIS IS THE NEW GUY IN THE BUZZCOCKS. HIS NAME IS GARTH. HAPPY BLEEDER AIN'T HE?

THE JAM

Interview with Paul Weller of the Jam.

Paul: A lot of people come to see us, right?They know what we're about,they know what we're heading for.Alright,we play some sixties R&B numbers...so fucking what?So do the Sex Pistols!

SM: What's your ambition?

Paul: To get somewhere so I can...so people can recognise me and respect me and I can get my views across but not force'em on people-which is what you want-the way you're talking.You can't force anything on anybody.

SM: You've got to make people listen to ya.That's what you're up there for in the first place.

Paul: Now and again you have the audience just standing about.How can you communicate like that?Then again,the last time, we had the audience right at the front so we were nearer to'em.They could touch us and we could touch them.

SM: Do you like to do songs to perfection when you're playing?

Paul: Well,you've got to,you've got to!

SM: I don't think you've got to in a sense because it's all been done before. You know,like the Who,Kinks and Small Faces-when their songs were really fresh and original.

Paul: Well,let me tell you.You may think we're professional but compared to a lot of bands we've still got a long way to go and that's another ambition,it's another...

SM: Yeah,I know that but it's not so much as your technicality but your meaning-the feeling behind your songs...

Paul: Yeah,well all I can say is that I respect what you said but we know what we're doing,my songs are all positive and relative to today,right?What can I fuckin'say,you know?I mean,if you don't dig us you don't dig us...that's fair you enough.

SM: You're great musicians but you could do so much more.

Paul: Yeah,well we don't care about the "great musicians"bit,we wanna be a group. A part of the people.

SM: I just can't help feeling that your image is what you think rock should sound like,rather than be yourselves.

Paul:I don't think that at all!On the contrary,I think that a lot of the bands about now have got an image of what a punk band should be-going on stage and singing about how bored you are,shouting and that,standing up and looking bored, you know?A sort of blank look-it's absolute shit!You go on stage and be some-

WELLER.

thing,you jump about,right?Do what you wanna do.Which you can't deny,we don't do.

SM: Well,you did at Ronnie Scott's-that was just incredible!Tell me this,why did you burn'Sniffin'Glue'on stage at the Marquee?

Paul: Because of what you wrote about us. I thought it was a load of shit and I didn't dig that sort of crap,you know?

SM: Why did you think it was a load of shit?

Paul: All this"laid back"bit,you know,and "no direction".All the kids know what direction we're heading and we know where we're heading and if he don't then that's his tough shit.

Harry(hanging around): What direction are heading for?

Paul: For progress,something a bit bigger, something a bit better than the 100 Club and safty pins.Something that can be recognised.I mean,I don't dig hippies but they achieved something in the sixties, right?They brought about a little more liberal thinking,right?

SM: Yeah,well if it wasn't for them we wouldn't be as we are today.

Paul: Yeah,right,that's true.I mean,'cos after everything collapsed there was a lot of apathetical people around.I know the words a bit trendy but that's what happened.A lot of people were scared to try something new again'cause they thought it was gonna throw but nevertheless the hippies did achieve a certain amount

3

of liberal thinking for political parties these days.A little more progress,not much but a little more and that's what we should be trying to do.Something a little more positive,right?We're all standing around saying how bored we are and all this shit,right?But why don't we go and start an action group up,help the community?Now,how many people can you see getting up off their arses-not fucking many!

TOO SERIOUS.
SM: Anyway,the reason we put that in about you being"laid back but tight"is that a member of a great new-wave band(GX)saw you at the Roxy and thought you were so tight that he"might as well give up playing"-which is exactly what it's not all about.I mean,tightness is nothing.
Paul: Don't you think that's great.Next time they're gonna be tighter,it's great. We can get some good tight bands behind us so nobody can say our music's shit.We can say-look we've got some good bands, right?They're as tight as any fucking thing you can turn out.We've got some tight politics,some tight thoughts,right?
SM: Yeah,but it's not just about tightness!
Paul: Course it is!
SM: But ELP and that.Led Zeppelin and the London Philomonic Orchestra are tight!
Paul: Yeah,but I thought we were supposed to be forgetting them.Who cares about how tight they are,fuck that lot! I'm talking about how tight we are!Fuck them,they're nothing to do with us,we don't know'em
SM: Alright,what's the differance?
Paul: 'Cos we are about us now-US-all the kids now and they're about generation,I don't know,second or third above us-they're thirty year olds.I mean,the beourgeois right,you've got your car, your mortage,you've got your three kids right?It's a case of being cool to see Led Zeppelin or Rod Stewart.We don't care about that,let's forget that.
SM: So you say,your tightness is on a different level because it appeals to kids?
Paul: Course we're on a differant level, we're building our own-we're building it up,well...we're not,but we should be.
SM: But what is it building up to?
Paul: I don't know!The scene's progression,it's from walking about looking stupid and that,and people putting you down to getting respected and people saying they've got some ideas...let's listen to'em.
SM: Would you say that by this way it's pretty possible that you're gonna end up exactly like Led Zeppelin?

Paul: Course you are!That is age.That is progression-when I'm thirty I don't want no eight year old kid looking up to me. Go out and start his own thing up,you know,forget about me-which is how it should be-you've gotta have progression in life.You know?I mean,there's a little slogan"solution is evolution",which-I think-sums it up.The only solution we've got is evolution to every problem as time goes on,you know?We've got to forget about the future,forget about the past.At the moment we've got to think about the present.We've got to build up the present and then maybe,we can think about the future...and we'll advance the future.But let's forget it for a while, let's build up now.Let's get something together now,we've got nothing at the moment,nothing at all.

FOXTON.

LIVE JAM!

Nobody could hate the Jam tonight.The Roxy Club wasn't packed but it still had a great atmosphere about it.By the time the Jam jumped on stage we were really ready to give'em a listen.Right from their first number,'Understanding' you could tell it was gonna be a good gig.

The Jam wern't distant tonight,they were with us all the way and we loved'em.They had that early sixties feeling and made it sound raw and fresh.Not one riff or chord seemed laid-back-it was

4

a spontaneous feeling of energy all the way
The Jam are a band of moods.
One night they can be so laid-back that you
fidget almost to sleep,you're so bored and
another night they're so edgy they almost
knock you off your feet.They can make their
songs seem very special when they're on top
form.They throw them-
selves right at ya.The
feeling's so strong it
captivates ya life and
sweeps ya as high as
you're worth.The Jam can
be absolutely brilliant
and tonight they were
fantastic.
      The three
of'em fitted the small
stage perfectly.With
everybody pogoing at the
front.peering from the
back we could see Rick's
white looking face in the
dark staring through his
usual dark shades-like a
Steve Harley lookalike or
something.It's funny to
see him casually watching
us as if he's doing not-
hing with the drums when
all the time he's pumme-
ling his kit with perfect
beats.He plays by instinct
without looking,as though
he was born sitting there.
But even if Rick didn't
look afire,Paul did!
      We're so used
to seeing the Jam in suits that you couldn't
imagine them in anything else-it wouldn't
seem right.Paul is definitely the frontman
of the group and yet there's not much movement from him.Still,the stage is packed with
high-energy and enthusiasm.
      Paul whirls out chords with
meaning and precision but things change.With-
out a moments breather cames'Change My Address'and immediately Paul's shaking so violently to the songs tempo that ne's head's
almost coming off.Madness breaks out both in
the band and with us.The whole stage is shaking and the front erupts.
      It's about time they stopped
spoiling their set with all that tuning up.
Tonight they were getting on with it and this
was the result.They were proving to us their
ideas,they were themselves tonight and we
believed in'em.They wern't lost and the did
not waste time pissing things up for themselves by stopping to tune up.The excitment
wasn't broken up.The enjoyment was continuous
and accumulated bringing a lot of great
climaxes to their set.

"BUCK".

The hot tempo shakes us into a
frenzy during'Slow Down'.But there's room
to breath and enjoy the band at their best.
The positive vitality,the speed,the meaning
and feeling behind the beat is fresh and
invigorating.You just can't stand still,
you just don't want to go away.You know
that this is exactly what
you want from music.You
know it's what you came
for.
   "One,two,three!"-Bruce
joins in vocal strength
for the high-energy beat
of"So you think you've
got it sussed!So you
think you've got it all
worked out!Whatever hap-
pened to the great em-
pire?".
   After the cheering dies
down Paul calls out"We
are gonna take a short
break"but before they
do,'In the City'finish-
es off one of the best
sets the Jam have pla-
yed.
   When they're at their
best this band are a
killer!
   I hope their deal
with Polydor works out
'cause it would be
great to be able to
play some of their
songs at home in my
house.
      I forgot,that the bands names
are Paul Weller-guitar,Bruce Foxton-bass
and Rick Buckler-drums.
            Steve Mick.

5

BUZZCOCKS BREAKDOWN

"I bin waiting at the supermarket,
 Standing in line with the beans(cash up),
 I bin waiting at the post office,
 For sticky pictures of the queen
                          (stick up),

Now I'm waiting for you,
To get yourself ready(make up),
Thinking to myself:
Is this what they mean by going steady?
                          (break up),

I bin waiting in the waiting room,
I bin sitting in the sitting room,
Now I'm whining in the dining room,
Gonna forget what I came for here
                          real soon,

I said-
Time's up and me too,
I out on account of you".

                          ('Time's Up').

Howard Devoto-"I just hate physically
waiting.I'm very undisciplined in that
way.I wrote the first line at Safeways
when I wanted to buy just one item and
I had to wait ages to pay for it at the
cash register.It wasn't beans,actually
it was bananas.Then I went to the post
office.Then I imagined I was going to my
girlfriends and I would have to wait for
her too.I kept thinking,there isn't all
this time to waste,there's stuff to be
done.I made up the second verse completely but it might as well be true.That
stuff about"Time's up and me too"was

going to be about,like,when you've been
waiting for really ages like a Buddist
waiting 20 years for nirvana at an ex-
treme.Maybe that's not exactly waiting.
Maybe they don't wait.Anyhow,you lose
the idea of time,so I wanted the idea of
the suspension of time in the command-
"Time's Up"and the suspension of belief
in self.But it never worked out,so basically it's just a song about being pissed
off at spending so much time waiting".

     Even though Howard Devoto
always struck me as being a weird guy,I
must admit to being shocked when I heard
that he'd left the Buzzcocks.It seemed
to me that Devoto needed some form of
expression.With the release of their EP-
'Spiral Scratch'and heavy interest from
a couple of major record companies the
Buzzcocks have got the chance to break
into bigger things which means bigger
audiences,bigger responses etc.
     The band are already sor-
ted out.Lead guitarist-Pete Shelly is
now singing lead vocals,Steve Diggle has
switched from bass to rhythm guitar,John
Maher is still on drums and there's a
new guy-Garth-on bass.
     Their first gig-at Harles-
den last week-was really good.Vocally
they were slightly weak but the music
made up for it.With Diggle on guitar,
Shelly had time to play some really neat
solos.The numbers they played were'Time's
Up','Breakdown','Friends Of Mine','Boredom'(all from the EP),'Orgasm Addict',
'You Tear Me Up','Get On Our Own','Love
Battery'and four new numbers-'No Reply',
'What Do I Get','16 Again'and'Fast Cars'.
     I'm sure the band wont miss
Devoto and I can't help thinking that he
made a mistake.He said in a statement
that he"don't like most of this new-wave
music.I don't like music.I don't like
movements".So why didn't he try to change
it all.The Buzzcocks are one of the most
important bands in the new-wave,they've
always been out on their own.
     The EP will always be great
to remember Devoto with but I hope the
new Buzzcocks get better and better.We've
got to think of the future.

                          Mark P.

"Now there's nothing behind me,
 And I'm already a has-been,
 My future ain't what it was,
 I think I know the words that I mean,

You know me-I'm acting dumb,
You know the scene-very humdrum,
Boredom-boredom-boredom".

                          ('Boredom').

All lyrics © New Hormones.

6

PIC. BY ERICA ECHENBERG.

HEARTBREAKERS: WALTER, BILLY, JOHNNY + JERRY.

NEW YORK INVASION

Even though the New York new-wave/punk acts are a lot lighter than ours; no one can deny that they've brought a lot of fun into a scene that was becoming slightly to serious with itself.With the New Yorkers you know what you're getting-good ol'rock'n'roll at it's best.No hang-ups,no political overtones just energetic rock music.
        The first NYC club act to make a mark over here were the RAMONES. They came over for a couple of really excitinggigs and then pissed off back to the States.With their fantastic LP as well they influenced a lot of the UK new-wave bands.It's a pity they hadn't have because I'm sure that thefanatic UK kids would make better audiences for them.Instead of kids bopping to'em they probably have to put up with a bunch of New York poseurs.
        With the HEARTBREAKERS it's been different.They came over for the'Anarchy In the UK'tour in December and have been here ever since.They settled nicely into the new-wave circuit and the signing with Track must certainly mean that they're here to stay.
        I not gonna go on about the history of the band.Everyone knows the Dolls/Television conections,so why should I rabbit on about it.It's not important'cause this is 1977 and right now the HEARTBREAKERS are fantastic.The excitment they produce on stage is electric.Johnny Thunders,strutting about the stage ringing out frantic guitar solos. Just power-you know?
        All the songs are good,some are classics-'Chinese Rock', 'Pirate Love', 'Goin'Steady','Born Too Loose'.Hard rock. Thunders,along with drummer Jerry Nolan, done it in the New York Dolls.They'll just keep on rocking.They couldn't do anything else-no way.They'll be sucessful-'Chinese Rock'is gonna be their first single for Track.If it gets played they're gonna make it,they're what rock'n'roll's all about.
        The bass and rythmn guitars are played by Billy Rath and Walter Lure respectively.They're always tight-on a small stage like the Roxy Club or at the halls on the'Anarchy'tour.Nolan is the best drummer on the new-wave circuit,they can't help being tight.
        The HEARTBREAKERS may not tell us to go out and change society but we know what they're all about and they know what they're all about and that's all that matters.If you don't like'em you must be a right lemon.

7

VANILLA→

Next over was CHERRY
VANILLA accompanied by her keyboard
player Zecca and guitarist Louie.They
joined by with Stewart Copeland(drums)
and Sting(bass)who go under the name of
the POLICE(The Police usually play a
support set with guitarist Henry Pa -
ovani).Vanilla's an ex-groupie,ex-pub-
licity girl for David Bowie and a great
rock'n'roller.

Vanilla's songs are lighthearted but tough.Her band are excellent
especially piano player-Zecca,who used
to be a member of the Jimmy Castor Bunch and Louie,who plays really great all
through the set.'Punk'would make a great
single,along with'I Know How To Hook',
'Tulsa'and the opener,'Shake Some Ashes'.

All the females are jea-
lous of Cherry especially all the dyke
Patti Smith fans.They sit there passing
their bitchy comments in her direction
but she don't care a shit.She's great-
a bird that's honest.I can't help ad-
miring her and that's something from me
'cause I normally can't stand women roc-
kers.Don't fuckin'go see her and start
with all that"not relavent to this scene"crap.She's in it for fun so that's
why you watch her-for fun.She sold her
whole apartment to visit London.So don't
forget it-dig her!...and her ↘

WAYNE COUNTY AS PATTI SMITH!

WAYNE COUNTY has been over
here for about a month now,along with his
guitarist,Gregg van Cook.Normally WAYNE
creeps about in jeans,jumper and wooly
hat but as soon as he gets on stage it's
no holds barred.On go the trashy dresses
and ripped tights-it's great.

For years I've read about
him,then I heard some tapes-'Are You Man
Enough To Be a Woman','Are You a Boy Or
Are You a Girl?','Wonderwoman'etc.They
were great.Then the single-'Max's Kansas
City'76'.Really good stuff.

The good thing about Wayne
is that it's not just some drag-queen
fuckin'about on stage'cause the music is
great.It's heavier than both the Heartbreakers and Vanilla.

'If You Don't Wanna Fuck Me,
Fuck Off'Wayne sings but he also gives the
message-if you don't like me,fuck off!
Anyone who tries anything gets it back
whether it's a gob or a punch.Wayne can
definitely handle himself.

Wayne reeks of rock'n'roll.
Ok,so he dresses as a woman but so what.
He's got a great voice,great band and
great songs.

Wayne County-trashy dresses
fishnet tights,enormous wigs,Patti Smith
impersonations,beautiful body-I love
everything about him.

8 WAYNE

NEW YORK

Ok,we've all realised that
New York rock ain't gonna save the world
but what I like about is it's honesty.
Let's face it,they don't wanna do anything but get out there and rock.Let'em
get on with it and go and enjoy it.We're
living in pretty bad times at the moment
and it's great that we've got the chance
to see some good time stuff-the New York
acts-and the heavy message crew-the Clash,
Chelsea,Buzzcocks etc.

The new-wave scene in Lon-
don at the moment is the best in the
world and I welcome the HEARTBREAKERS,
CHERRY VANILLA and WAYNE COUNTY to it.

Mark P.

Heartbreakers pics by Erica Echenberg and
Wayne/Vanilla pics by JILL FURMANOVSKY

WAYNE COUNTY AT DINGWALLS.

JOHNNY THUNDERS- HEARTBREAKERS.

SNIFFIN'GLUE Still needs good quality
camera,35mm SLR-Pentax or something.As
cheap as possible,Zenith E in exchange.
Ring Harry-858 4485 or write to SG with
details.

Guitarist wanted for new-wave band.Hope
to play gigs soon.Phone Derek-743 0609.

gonna be'No Future'?...I couldn't believe it
when I heard TELEVISION's album'Marquee Moon'
I havn't even bothered to review it'cause
it's got nothing to do with the'new-wave'.I
can't be blinded by weird guitar runs of off-
beat bass runs,no way...the BEASTLY CADS are
now called the MODELS.We was going to have
an article on them in this ish but were waiting till we've got more space for an in-
terview.Same goes for the CORTINAS.Both bands
are excellent...SG7½ was about the four-band
gig in Harlesden the other week.It's in a
limited edition of 50(London only)...look
out for ALTERNATIVE T T.V....oh yeah,SUBWAY
SECT's set at Harlesden showed that a lot of
rehearsing hasn't changed them.They'll still

THINGS

one of the most important bands around...the
new HOT RODS single-'Might Be Lying'-is
really good.It's out on April Ist...The
BOMP NEWSLETTER says absolutely nothing to
me atall.I refuse to became involved with
it...mentions to all the good things in the
past month-BOYS(Roxy),HOT RODS(Rainbow),
DOCTORS OF MADNESS(Tunbridge Wells/Marquee),
TOM PETTY(Album & live tape),THROBBING
GRISTLE & GENESIS(fun)and SUE CATWOMAN(love)
all the other interesting things can be
found elsewhere in this here bit of mag...
A message from HARRY-"This is my answer to
all the wimps who've said to me-and the
rumours I've heard-about SG selling out
and going commercial.SG is not just a poxy
little fanzine which is knocked together
after work or college.It is a full time job.
It's our life.We've got to live,and to live
you've got to make some money.Some people
have also bitched about SG carrying ads.
Well,ads are a necessity if you want SG to
survive.Don't ever forget that we're doing
it for you and the music."

9

1977 / WHITE RIOT (CBS)

CLASH-WHITE RIOT/1977(CBS Single).

"White Riot,I wanna riot!White Riot,a riot of me own!".

Yeah,I've been waiting months for this band to release a record.I can't describe the feeling I get from listening to this single.It's so incredible that I honestly believe that it could change the direction of rock music.This single brings rock back to where it should be.Back in the hands of the kids.Kids who have to live in the poxy council estates and grow up into a life of security-a steady job,family and car.

The country's so fucked up at the moment that there's no way out but to start all over again:

"In 1977,
I hope I go to heaven,
Been too long on the dole,
Now I can't work at all,
Danger stranger,
You better paint your face,
No Elvis,Beatles or the Rolling Stones,

In 1977,
Knives in W.11,
Ain't so lucky to be rich,
Sten guns in Knightsbridge,
Danger stranger,
You better paint your face,
No Elvis,Beatles or the Rolling Stones,

In 1977,
You're on the never-never,
You think it can't go on for ever,
But the papers say it's better,
I don't care,
Cos I'm not all there,
No Elvis,Beatles or the Rolling Stones,
In 1977,in 1978,in 1979,in 1980,in 1981,in
1982,in 1983,in 1984!"

('1977'-Strummer/Jones).

Mick Jones + Joe Strummer.

I hope that every kid who buys this single <u>listens</u> to it.Realise that we have got to act <u>now</u>.1977 is the Queen's jubilee year,well let's make it <u>our</u> year as well.Let's get out and do something. Chuck away the fucking stupid safety-pins, think about people's ideas instead of their clothes.This"scene"is not just a thing to do in the evening.It's the only thing around that's honest and on our level!

SG have been having a go at the Clash recently.Well,I admit that they're the most important group in the world at the moment.I believe in them completely, all I said about them in the past is crap. With this single they've proved that they <u>have</u> been working.Nothing but hard work could produce a sound like they've got.

I can't wait to get the album. It's gonna have 14 tracks and that dosen't included'White Riot'and'1977'.

Just go out and create.

Mark P.

ALL CLASH PICS BY H.T. MURLOWSKI.

THE **CLASH**

10

Get up go to work clock on clock off go home watch TV go to bed get up go to work clock on

Get up go to work clock on clock off go home watch TV go to bed get up go to work clock on clock off
go home watch TV go to bed get up have your breakfast go to work clock on clock off go home...

UNEMPLOYMENT

**FOLLOW NO ONE
LEAD YOURSELF!**

Do not change your masters: become your own master

Let the politicians do their own dirty work

REVIEWS

ALL REVIEWS BY MARK P.

EATER-OUTSIDE VIEW/YOU(The Label single).
Sorry lads but this single is crap.It's not even good crap,it's just a waste of time.The reason why it's crap is that it was recorded last November when the band wern't very good.The have improved a lot since then and I know that they didn't want this crap released.

Eater need freedom.They should not be tied down to a company like'The Label' who don't know a thing about the new music, although the producer-Dave Goodman-done a lot of good work for the Pistols.I can't think why he let this single be released.

'The Label'contract ends in November,I think,so the best Eater can do is just keep on playing.If another single has to be released don't let it be'No Brains'- which I know has been recorded-but make it a live E.P.That would at least show the band at their best.

I'll probably get slashed by Andy with a razor-blade now.

TYLA GANG-SUICIDE JOCKEY/CANNONS OF THE
               BOOGIE NIGHT (skydog single)
Sean Tyla's alright really if you don't look at him.This singles a meaty boogie special.Both sides are really heavy.

Live,Sean does some great stero guitar chopping so that the riff goes from side to side of the P.A.but on record it doesn't do it.Which is basically all I can say about this"OK"record.

Don't let people get you down, mate.

LEW LEWIS. PIC-W.T. MORLOWSKI.

LEW LEWIS BAND-OUT FOR A LARK/WATCH
                    YOURSELF(UA single)
Lew is a killer live and this single fails to capture the real Lew excitment.On the A-side the band are OK, Lew's harp is OK but the vocals are right out the window.The song is ten times better live.

'Watch Yourself'is a lot better.If he could get this bluesy feel in his own songs Lew would be playing bigger places than the Hope & Anchor.Then again, he's only out for a lark ain't he?
This guy will rock forever.

BOYS-I DON'T CARE (NEMS single).
I totally ignored the Boys for about three months and then happened to see'em at the Roxy a few weeks back.I thought that they were great,especially bassist and vocalist Kid Reed who is a great guy.I piano seems a bit pointless but over all this band are just right.

The singles gonna be out in April.The B-side-which I've only heard live -mentions SG in the lyrics.
I hope you like the picture Duncan.

THE
BOYS.

KID REED OF THE BOYS. PIC BY W.T.

AMNED,DAMNED,DAMNED (STIFF album).

Side one: Neat Neat Neat/Fan Club/I Fall/
Born To Kill/Stab Your Back/Feel the Pain.

Side two: New Rose/Fish/See Her Tonite/1 Of
the 2/So Messed Up/I Feel Alright.

In the first issue of SG I
said that the Damned were great.With this
fuckin'album they've made it all worthwhile.
All that mucking around,all that honesty.The
Damned have made a great album.
        The first side is mostly fast
stormers.'Feel the Pain'is a little slower
but the power of the band still manages to
suprise.Best song on side one is'Fan Club',
the lyrics are the best on the album.
        'Stab Your Back'is Rat Scabies
quickie.There's a"singalong"version on the
back of the single-'Neat Neat Neat'.
        Side two is all fast,not let-
ting up for one moment.'So Messed Up'has the
dummy ending,it's just like it is on stage.
The whole noise ends with the Iggy song.It's
the most enjoyable"noise"in the world.
        The mob are supporting T.Rex
on tour around the country.I reckon that'll
be good'cause I really like Bolan.It should
be a right laugh.
        The Damned will be sucessful,
I wonder if they're pleased?

ULTRAVOX (ISLAND album).

Side one: Satday Night/Life At Rainbow's End/
Slip Away/I Want To Be A Machine.

Side two: Wide Boys/Dangerous Rhythm/The
Lonely Hunter/The Wild,the Beautiful and the
Damned/My Sex.

        This lot are young but I rec-
kon that they're a bit too serious about the
music.They're like a cross between the Doctors Of Madness and Roxy Music(not helped by
the very Roxy-ish cover).The songs are OK
but the music tends to get a bit too weird,
probably the violin.
        I like this album but I wis-
hed I like it more.They're hitting their
heads against a brick wall.

BRIAN JAMES- DAMNED.

PIC BY U.T. HURLOWSKI.

SEX PISTOLS

After signing to A&M the other week the
SEX PISTOLS left A&M the other week.They
copped £75,000 for doing absolutely no-
thing.After being dismissed by the company they celebrated in their offices in
Oxford St. by swigging lager and chucking
lager at a NBC film crew who were hanging
around.20,000 copies of'No Future'/'No
Feelings'-the first A&M single-are sitting in some boring pressing plant doing
nothing.The SEX PISTOLS have got one
copy-a white label-and it is brilliant.
From the"God save the queen"intro to the
"No future for me/you"ending it is fan-
tastic.I just hope the find some way of
releasing it.

13

ROXY CLUB
41-43 NEAL ST., COVENT GDN,
LONDON W.C.2

MARCH - TUES 22ND : JAM/REJECTS
        WED 23RD : EATER/SHAM 69
        THURS 24TH : BOYS/WUBIE & THE
                                    RATS
        FRI 25TH : CHELSEA/ADVERTS
        TUES 27TH : STRANGLERS
FOR OTHER DETAILS - 836 8811

PIN-UP; SEX PISTOLS

GOD SAVE THE QUEEN

SHE AIN'T NO HUMAN BEING

PHOTO: "STEVENSON"

NO FUTURE

Maximum Penalty £5

SEX PISTOLS

SNIFFIN' GLUE...

30p

AND OTHER ROCK 'N' ROLL HABITS
... AND ANYTHING TO CAUSE AN UPROAR!

9

APRIL/MAY 1977.

WHAT THE FUCK'S HAPPENING TO THIS MAG? OH NO, STEVE MICK'S NOT EDITING THIS ISSUE?!?!

PIC BY ERICA ECHENBERG.

CORTINAS - DAMNED - MODELS

VILE

GLAMOUR ISSUE

中國 72

...THEY CUT OUT HIS HEART...

M.C.5·Borderline/Lookin at You-£1·15

Motorhead·Leavin here/White Line Fever-£1·15

Groovies·I can't Explain/Little Queenie-£1·15

Heartbreakers·Chinese Rocks/Born to Loose-70p

The STEVE MICK bulletin

S.G. 9

Contrary to rumour and gossip Mark p has not left S.G. What's happening is he's takin' a break for a couple of months and I'm doing the editing.But as you can see in this ish, he's still around.

So you nurds can all stop whimpering and enjoy the mag cos your 'Prophet's just aiming to concentrate for a while on his work as a frustrated musician playing for his own band Alternative T.V. and Throbbing Gristle.

I'm not surprised he's given up editing for a while, what with all you cynical whimps moaning he's sold out ever since we started selling more than 50 copies a month. Fuckin' I'll moan - it's more bleedin' stappling to do.

GIGS

I get the impression that outside forces with a lot of money are trying to get our club The Roxy closed, or at least squeeze the NEW WAVE out.But even if the NEW WAVE is slowly being phased out, Andy says that for now, NEW WAVE acts are still gonna be staged, so listen out for whats on.

The Gertrude 's closed for a while. What we need now is a bigger club to open up soon for the Summer. The Gertrud' will be opening up again. But what we need is a club which all the shit-hot New Wave bands can get on stage and play to us every night.

Fuckin' ell I don't know a band that isn't suffering from a gig shortage. More and more kids wanna see these bands and the opportunities are getting less and less... it's stupid.

Common' let's have some more clubs, and not just in London. Kids wanna see bands like Johnny Moped, Chelsea, The Adverts, Pistols, Subway sect, Models, Eater, Damned, Clash, Cortinas and Buzzcocks and dozens more all over the country.

It's too big to ignore.

CONTENTS

STEVE MICK: EDITOR AND LAYOUT, AND NO MONEY.

HARRY T. MURLOWSKI. PHOTOGRAGHER, BUSSINESS HASSLER AND PRUSSIAN.

MARK P: CONTRIBUTING WRITER HELP AND INTERFERERENCE NICE LETTERING and funny legs.

DANNY BAPER: CONTRIBUTING WRITER what else he done? Well 'e thinks he'Sthe Archbishop of Canterbury (nutter)

...also, a big hand to, CAROLINE COON, JILL Furmanovsky, Erica Echenberg, Nick Jones for abuse, Roger and Phil (ROCK ON), Larry and Tim (Bizarre) and all those people who buy us drinks and give us records, AN ALL AT ROUGH TRADE

Address: 'SNIFFIN'GLUE...', c/o ROUGH TRADE, 202 KENSINGTON PARK ROAD, LONDON,W11.

Pic by MARK P.

MAIL ORDER.

Prices per mag(including P&P):

35p for the UK and Eire.

50p for Europe and seamail to rest of the world.

65p for airmail outside Europe.

The maximum subscription you can have is 4 issues,which is 4 times the Price of one issue.

"IF YOU WANT TO BE AGGRESSIVE PICK UP AN ELECTRIC GUITAR"

The Models originally formed as The Beastly Cads 5 months ago. At their first gig in Harrow and they got a big response...they got chucked off.

They changed their name to The MODELS a few months back and now look like getting a single realeased real soon... the incredible "FREEZE".

The line-up hasn't changed, it's still MARCO;lead guitar ,CLIFF FOX;guitar and vocals; MICK ALLEN; bass and TERRY DAY ; drums.

HISTORY

MARCO did that one stint with Siouxsie and the Banshees at the 100 PUNK FEST, he did have a meaningless job selling clothes, but other than that he's just hanging around.

MICK and CLIFFare still at college doing A's while TERRY'S been a worker since 'e left school.

They haven't lived very spectacular lives in Harrow. Harrow's like anywhere else. Next.

INFLUENCES ?

MICK - US!

MARCO - Yeah! it was out of trying to resurrect Harrow.

MICK - We play out of our own feelings.

WATERGATE

CLIFF - When we first started we were very lighthearted - but since we-'ve been around and met people in the music bussiness we've found out what crooks they are,- and that's what's made us a bit more serious.

MARCO - We were so naive, we thought everyone was honest!

CLIFF -People are even payed to do good reviews.

MARCO -We used to read reviews and say 'Oh yeah, they seem a good band.'

CLIFF -People are being payed ...you can pay £25 and get a good review. And it doesn't stop at music it's in everything.

THEIR MUSIC

TERRY -Atfirst when we formed, we didn't know what to play...

MARCO -WE just picked a few songs we like.

CLIFF - We had no direction.

MARCO -And they all turned out to be LOU REED and DAVID BOWIE songs.

MARCO and CLIFF are the main song - writers. Their music is just what it is, it's nothing pretentious, they've learnt to play, they practice, they get the feel of a song, get some lyrics and work it in

to shape like any band.

MICK - It's so blatant what we're play - ing that it doesn't need explaining. It's nothing intellectual it is perfectly straightforward.

"NAZI PARTY"

Viv Goldman of Sounds refuses to even see the band play because of the title of this song. Though she wrote,

> "Every time the MODELS sing 'Nazi Party', they should consign them-selves to the ovens for irresponsibility."

CLIFF - THE SONGS A CYNICAL LOOK AT ALL THE SILLY PUNKS WHO WEAR NAZI ARMBANDS.

> If she thinks that we stand for the Nazi ideal of the forties she's thicker than we thought.

But Viv's right when she says kidsdont normally catch any lyrics other than the chorus. Viv defends what she wrote by saying

> "I never suggested the Models are Nazis, I only said that people in general don't listen to every word in lyrics. So the bands cynicism might get lost, while the audience cheerfully march out of the gig singing that they want to form their own Nazi Party... and that aint no joke! "

3

"WE'VE GOT SERIOUS VIEWS BUT WE BELIEVE YOU SHOULD ENJOY YOURSELF"

"I JUST CAN'T HELP THINKING, NOW THAT IT'S A LOAD OF BOLLOCKS. JUST THINKING, 'THAT REVIEW MIGHT HAVE BEEN FIXED- IT MIGHT NOT- BUT IT COULD HAVE BEEN."

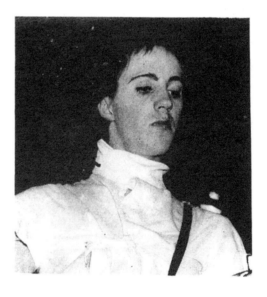

Lastly, is there anything you think people ought to know about you?
Marco - Na, they've just got to come along and see us...and ask us questions afterwards if they want.

'Thousands of people didn't take a stand They died like flies under Fascist hands "FREEZE".
CLIFF - The parallel between then and now: people not exercising their rights and being stepped on and used.

STEVE MICK

ALL MODELS PKS BY HARRY T. MURLOWSKI.

YES, YOU MISSED IT...
THE DAMNED IN GREAT MALVERN.

WINTER GARDENS SAT. 26TH MARCH 1977.

Christ ! it's them . Ruddy Helli -
as if the Cortinas weren't enough. blime
-ly these suicide fanatics are as sharp
and overwhelming as ever . they bulldoze
-d straight through everything-the shuft
-ies didn't no what hit 'em.
  "Feel Alright" had Dave racing across
the stage to the different mics, his eye
-s flashing. Nah, the kids down here are
great and they've all got the album.
  Dave and Brian bring their arms up hig
-h and down again at the end of the same
chords it's incredible to feel and see
the action. The song ends with the Cap-
-tain swinging his arm gently out across
to the audience looking like a part of
some cabaret on the London Palladium.
  OOohy. fucking 'ell The Damned are as
neat as the day they first scared the
living daylights out of their audience.
As always , their sets powerful and in-
-teresting -you don't wanna look away
in case you miss something.That's what's
great about the Damned, no one can just
stand there and count mistakes,you don't
notice that kind of shit 'cos you're gul
-ping in amazement.
  Rats symbols are set on fire . 'Ole
Rat's symbols lark is like some bleedin'
extravaganza by Carl Palmer you could im
-agine Rat going round and round on his
drums with all coloured lights flashing
and bits of fire here and there like
something out of Battersea Funfair. But
it wasn't anything that stupid, the flam
-ing symbols was effective and elbowed
Rat into the centre of attention, until
Dave grasped the symbols on the other
side of his drumkit and lifted 'em in
the air as if he was going to smash some
-one in face with 'em.
  But before all that tosh "born TO KILL
has RAT standing up in order to whack th
-e drums into the sound he demands-as if
he's beating some cunt to death. Ray's
throwing himself all over the stage like
on supersonic,while Bri wrings out his
great 'star' guitar break bits, and the
songs burnt to death.
  The kids here are being brought up to
date-Rat chucks out his sweat shirt as a
souvenir. T There's no time to breath
  "This one's called FAN CLUB"
It's slammed out with dave scampering
this way and that like a paranoic vam-
-pire, trapped-creeping this way again
-looking evilly from side to side and
scurrying from left of the stage to the

right and climbing back on for conclu-
-sion.
  "This one's our new single
                'MEAT, MEAT, MEAT!'"
Everybody's cheering, flinging them-
-selves inthe air, their eardrums are
being busted- yet fuck who cares?All
the pent-up feelings- the frustration
is tumbling out and anything can hap-
-pen in this tense atmosphere, but it's
great, we're all tormented into dancing
right up to the abrubt ending.No, NO-
you can't cheer- there's no time.
  "Chic I'll beat her!" is the scream
for "Stretcher Bearer" and the sheer
avalanche of power is unbearable - it
nearly knocks ya block off! HONEST!
Yer feel CRAZY
  "This one's called SHUT YA FACE!"
yells BRIAN, staring out to see who's
gonna answer ...but no one does. Abrupt-
-ly Dave stops singing and Bri picks
up the chant-half mumbling, half talk-
-ing.
  "Sick of being SICK" cuts out ,then
Rat's drumming comes to the fore...
"Is She Really Going Out With Him!"
At the end Ray falls flat on his back -
half gimic,half knackered.
  You should see Dave's black hair dren
-ched with sweat dangling in short strin
gy

5

Pic Jill Fishmanovsky.

Pic by Harry

Pic by Harry

Pic by HARRY

THE DAMNED IN NEW YORK AT CBGB's

I've been in NYC almost 4 months, and during that time I've been quite disappointed with the music scene here. I'm tempted to go into a big rave about all the shitty bands I've seen and the rip-offs I've endured, but my aim here is to tell all you S.G. readers how the Damned happened in here at Easter for 4 nights, and went over so well that they're returning by popular demand to CBGB's from April 21-24.

Being a British punk band, the first time in NYC they had certain expectations to live up to. They already had a few fans who follow the English scene avidly and the 1st night audience was full of musicians. CBGB's is about 3 times as big as the Roxy and 3 times the price means that people actually sit at tables or the bar, resulting in a subdued atmosphere and a lot of poseurs.

You can imagine how excited I was when I knew they were coming, and they didn't disappoint me. Last time I saw them was 5 mnths before at the Hope & Anchor.

Playing in front of a very partisan audience, they came on and most people just sat there at their tables - I was standing at the side of the stage and couldn't resist pogo-dancing to "Feel Alright". Each song came out much faster than on the album - they did 2 strong sets, leaving the CBGB crowd not wanting to believe what they'd seen.

On Easter Sunday the Dead Boys had tightened up their act since the 1st night which put pressure on the Damned - who responded by combining chaos and fine musicianship in a really tight 25 minute set. Brian slurring into the mike "This is our new single" and they burst into "Neat, Neat, Neat" - later, Rat jumped from behind his drums and introduced himself by saying "If ya turn on the electricity we'll play some more fuckin' music".

Cream cakes were thrown by the band and the audience returned a few bottles and glasses - just a few, so nobody was hit or hurt. The captain played his bass like no other bassist anywhere - staggering, stumbling, tripping and shouting "For me fan club" into the mike and never missing a note. He and Dave looked as though they'd knock each other off stage, but never did.

I won't go on with clichés about Daves fine vocals or Rat's energetic drumming - when ya gotta get a bit of some loud live music - go see the Damned. They finished the set with "So messed up" and didn't have the encore habit - I broke 2 beer bottles banging them against the wall making requests. The band simply went wild, saying "we're fuckin' here in NYC from London" - leaving me hoping a lot more U.K. bands will follow 'cause they're much more exciting than the local stuff.

FROM STEVE READ IN NEW YORK

Yeah! CBGB's 5½ with a magnifying glass

ANOTHER TOWN SMOULDERING?

strands as he sreams the lyrics- yuk'.
His make-up is hideous, he looks lur-
-rid and pale as if he's been dead for
months. But meantime , the Captain's
sneaked up again , and at the finish
he lobs a strap and some kid snatches
it amidst a thicket of arms.

Good 'ole "New Rose" never fails to
get 'em stomping and the impetus is
pushed on without a moments notice by
"Stab Your Back". "So Messed Up" has
Dave diving off the front of the stage
agin,-hey!. Rat's SYmbols- yer this is
where 'es burning 'em.

The symbols are chucked to the front
and the Captain slings his guitar across
his back and twists round and round the
mic screaming and screaming. Yes, as u-
-sual it's chaos. The song starts up a-
-gain, but quickly finishes.

Ray rips his jacket and guitar off
andthrows the lot clean across the stage.
Then they clear off the stage as if they
are all running for their lives.

But no they're not frightened to death
they return for "Fish". Rat stands by
his drums, lifts his hands and claps -
getting a bigger echo from us after ev-
-ery clap.Dave pogo's and knocks a mic
over as he scats across the stage sing-
-ing. With the P.A. squealing with feedback and the song suddenly changig to an
abrubt chorus of "Stab Your Back", the
band bugger off for good.

LEAVING Great Malvern Smouldering
and the kids with the memory of a gig
THEY'LL NEVER FORGET!

STEVE MICK

6

ALL DAMNED PICS. BY
JILL FURMANOVSKY.

CORTINAS

Without warning The Cortinas hit the stage and started tearing through their set.a Automatically, everybody surges out of the bar towards the blare.

"Fascist Dictator" is rammed out with ferocity at a gruelling pace to kids who-'ve read all the scandel caused by "PUNK ROCK" and have come out of curiosity.

Nothing like it had been heard before at the Winter Gardens. It wasn't no sleazy little joint neither- looked more like the bleedin' Alexandria Palace with just as bad accoustics. Place looked more at home for "The Black and White Minstrel Show" than The Damned and Cortinas.

The gig already felt unusual and special- it felt fresh and raw like the early days. The atmosphere had that desparate edginess our music feeds on and reflects.

The Cortinas are only a young band but you can sense their importance to the scene , because their musics got our ideas and our direction behind it. Their music is furious -a battering ram of sheer energy - enough energy to wake fuckin' zombies .

"I Wanna Be Sawn" and Nick Sheppard's still swerving all over the place on rhythm guitar, while, strangely, Mike Fewins on lead remains taut and motion-less. His eyes staring fixedly on his chords, rarely looking up 'cept when he can stop playing for a tick and have a break. He's totally immersed in play-ing - and playing it right. Yet that doesn't interfere with the bands total exuberance.

The band sounded very blary in the big echey hall which the group didn't like one bit but , funtunately, the bad sound blended well with the group on this occa-sion -because by the power you'd expect 'em to have amillion watts and some dyn-mite behind 'em.

"Yer we come from Bristol " "PLAY IT IN THE SUBWAY" Slips violently out. Dexter shuffles, jumps and jerks to the left of the stage while Nick's al -ways moving like some hungry caged ani-mal. At the centre of the stage up front is hefty Jeremy Valentine , the band's spokesman and vocalist., and behind him is little Dan Swann the drummer. We're all happy tottering to the tune in a lively fever - but it's not enough... "THANKYOU YOU APPATHETIC BASTARDS - ARE YOU STONED OR WHAT ?" taunts Jeremy full of disdain.

TOES BY JILL.

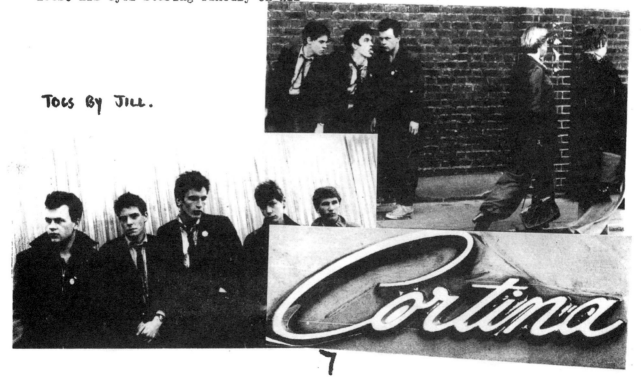

JOHNNY CORTINAS

Suddenly, a mic stand topples into us,
chopped down by Nick as he sinks to the
floor and sprawls about still playing.

"This One's about going home having
your girlfriend — fucking her— it's
called"I WANNA HAVE IT WITH YOU".It's
intro stop and starts but it grows into a bleedin' whirlwind.

In the thick of it it's more of a
hellhole than the ROXY on a packed
night. It stinks of sweat and kids are
just stripping off their jackets and
jumping around.

Then up front barges some signfuckers
out for a good laugh yobbing up their
fingers to the rhyt hm . Jeremy smiles
as he clings to the mic for a breather-
then he leans off and barks.

"WHY DON'T YOU GO BACK TO THE DISCO
        YOU OXFORD FAGS".

Next, "DEFIANT POSE" is a killer, and
Jeremy spits out the lyrics like Iggy
Pop.The guitars clangy strumming is just
right for the song. But little Dan Swann
swatting fiercely on drums begins to tire
under the demanding pace and gets a little
weak at times, but it hardly shows.Dan
tries hard to keep up with Dexter to give
the songs the tough backing rhythm they
need and he never lets up for the life of
him.

There's a really heavy scene looming...
"WHY DON'T YOU FUCK OFF TO THE DISCO'S —
YOU THINK YOU'RE SO FUCKING CLEVER YOU
CUNTS! "

growls Valentine.

The next one, "GLORIA"has aslower more
plodding beat to it than the original —
but it's powerful alright!

"LET ME INTRODUCE TO YOU ON BASS —
        JOHNNY FUCKOFF !"

It's great, they're ALL johnny's.
After each johnny's introduced, he does
'es bit, like 'ole Dexter wrestles sky-
wards,hopping up, twisting and playing
his bass at the same time. Johnny the
drummer head-butts his symbols and drums.
Johnny guitarist Nick, on the other hand,
is much the same as ever...whirling about
like a nutter! Mike Fewins our Johnny
lead guitarist just stands there and plays
afamous old Hendrix riff looking like a
dummy from Madame Tousards with an
anxious face.

Then Johnny vocalist Jeremy Valentine
sends the whole band shifting in tur —
moil as he finnally introduces himself.

Jeremy shouts and quacks out the lyrics
to the next song "TOKIO JOE" and you can
barely make out the words, but it's with
the same gruff feeling, you can tell.

They all great songs — some of which
are gonna rate as classics in '77. **8**

"Here's to all you boring people who
    watch TELEVISION all night —
    it's called TELEVISION FAMILIES."
This is their last song and it's just
great.By this time kids are yelping and
jumping around. While Mike's still wearing his dirty mac on, and jeremy's got
his protective fire helmet on. The bass
twangs and the vibration lingers and
moves like a stodgy wave which Nick jump
over as if it was something real that
could trip him over or cut his legs off.

The song storms to an end and they
clear off. It was bleedin' well worth
the journey and THE CORTINAS were only
the support band! **STEVE MICK**

MIKE FEWINS.
PIC BY HARRY.

THE TRUTH→

THE CLASH

THE CLASH (CBS album).

Janie Jones/Remote Control/I'm So Bored With the U.S.A/White Riot/Hate & War/What's My Name?/Deny/London's Burning/Career Opportunities/Cheat/Protex Blue/Police & Thieves/48 Hours/Garageland.

Right,I'm 20.I've lived in London for 18 of those 20 years.We've moved about four or five times but it's always been into other council flats.I left school at 17 a got a job in a bank.First I was a clerk then I was a computer operator.I wern't very good at that so they made me a clerk again.In July'76 I saved my life and I left the bank.If it ain't had been for SG and all the music I'd still be in that same ol'fucking job.Oh yeah,perhaps I'd have gone up a grade or taken some banking exams maybe.Wow, really exciting stuff.I was lucky'cause I got out of it.I still live in a council flat but I survive...just.

There's a million kids still doing what I was doing.They're going to their steady jobs in the morning.They look forward to their lunch break when they go down the pub and have a roll and a pint with the lads. In the afternoon they look forward to going home.When they get home they'll have their tea then either watch TV,take a bird to the pictures,go out with the lads or play with themselves in their bedroom.They go to bed at about 12 and then it starts all over again the next morning.At the weekend they spend most of their time in discos,pubs or at a football match where they'll kick some cunts head in.They'll try to make the most of the two days.They're always fucked up. On Monday morning they look forward to the next weekend-they wish their lifes away.

Life is a pile of shit.I mean,real life stinks.I'm not talking about if you live in Devon or the Isle Of Wight. I mean London,Birmingham,Manchester,Glasgow. In the city life is terrible.I feel sorry for all the young kids who've got to grow up in it'cause it's gonna get worse.

THE CLASH ALBUM IS LIKE A MIRROR.IT REFLECTS ALL THE SHIT.IT SHOWS US THE TRUTH.TO ME,IT IS THE MOST IMPORTANT ALBUM EVER RELEASED. IT'S AS IF I'M LOOKING AT MY LIFE IN A FILM. A STORY OF LIFE IN LONDON.PLAYING IN AND OUT OF THE FLATS.A SCHOOL THAT DIDN'T EVEN KNOW WHAT AN O-LEVEL WAS.A JOB THAT SAT ME BE-HIND A DESK AND NICKED MY BRAIN.ALL THAT SHIT IS NO LONGER IN THE DARK.

THE CLASH TELLS THE TRUTH!

Mark P.

JOE →

"London's Burning.London's Burning.

All across the town,all across the night,
Everybody's driving with four headlights,
Black or white,turn it on,face the new religion,
Everybody's sitting round watching television,
London's burning with boredom,
London's burning,dial 999!

Up and down the Westway,in and out the lights,
What a great traffic system,it's so bright!
I can't think of a better way to spend the night,
Than speeding around underneath the yellow lights,
London's burning with boredom,
London's borning,dial 999!

But now I'm in the subway,looking for the flat,
This one leads to this block,this one leads to that,
The wind howls through the blocks looking for a home,
But I run through the empty stone'cos I'm all alone,
London's burning with boredom,
London's burning,dial 999!

London's Burning!"
(Strummer/Jones).

London's Burning!!

9

"BACK TO THE STREETS"

PIC. BY CAROLINE COON.

YAP /YAP / YAP   Generation X need Drummer Phone Stuart: 723·4053
The LURKERS are fun...O.K?..CHELSEA's got a new guitarist and bassist- should be on
the road soon...Some geezer phoned up to say you've got to turn up for 'ROCK AGAINST
RACIALISM' on MAY 4th?...check, bands include GENERATION Xand ASWAD... Bleedin' 'ell
this trash is getting more like an advertising page!
                    ADVERTISEMENT
A DRUMMER IS URGENTLY NEEDED BY THE' ERECT NIPPLES' contact SHANE 23,Atwood Road,SW6
or SHANN SCRATCH   ....Space cost £2oo SHANE .
Be at the NOTINGHAM PUNK you dopoes it's the event of the decade; featuring MARK'S
notorious ALTERNATIVE T.V. also includes G. X . CORTINAS, MODELS and CHELSEA...
ON MAY 6th kids. A RED STICKER TO THE CLASH it's the only REAL album I've heard.
(stupid persil deal with NME).∴. Adverts drummer Lorrie Driver got jumped on at
   Sheppards Bush, his thumb got hurt but he'll be alright...Wanted, BASS player and
   drummer ring DREW 699-2961... oh yer, good ole WILLY wants a drummer for her band
   REMOTE yer, so start rehearsing and get those fuckin' biscuit tins out!...BUY your
   CHERRY VANILLA TEE shirts £2 including postage to JOTOGLOW, 27, á DRYDEN CHAMBERS,
   OXFORD STREET...What? Capital Radio still upset 'cos someone sprayed "White Riot"
   over their nice big Capital building. Yer, and why wont they play the best and
   most important rock album of th e decade?...well, Capital fuckin' Radio, there's
   more to come...'e, what's all this 'bout Jessie 'ector thinkin' 'es God? Yes, well
S.P JOHN TOWE SACKED FROM GEN X?   **10** THANKX FOR THE VAN PETE, ZEN & THE REST
                                        OF THE CB's.

JOHNNY MOPED - JAM ALBUM

JOHNNY MOPED/SKREWDRIVER-Roxy Club(16/4/77).
                    The back of my legs still ache,
I tell ya.1 don't care there weren't more
than hundred people down there,the Roxy was
a great night on Saturday.I went ignorant of
both bands'cept in name and Steve had giving
the Skrewdriver single a fair review earlier.
When Skrewdriver come on into'Anti Social'
they were obviously gonna work hard for the
handful there.1t suprised me to learn that
this was their second proper gig(Man.Poly,
supporting Li'l Bob Story-two encores).Their
songs were sharp as staypress crease,the high
points being'9 to 5'(Yeah,I thought that
enal),'Jailbait'(their own),'No Pushover'and
the great'Gotta Be Young'.The band,Phil Wal-
msley-guitar,Kevin McKay-bass,John Grinton-
drums and Ian Stuart-vocals,he's a stocky
frontman whose veins stand right out on his
forehead-he puts that much into it(mind you
he sat down once on stage,for a very good
reason-"I was knackered",he said).I'd hate
anyone to try to read anything from the fact
they're from Blackpool or go looking for a
freak show of pretenders.They shift and 1
felt triffic.

"I'm Stan,and I'd like ya to
meet the only genius I know"was Johnny Moped
's intro and on rushed an orange boiler suit
with head attatched.Now,there is more stories
of this bloke than you know who but the people around him seemed fed up with this eccen-
tric tag.He's got a band behind him that he,
and you,can really sweat too.Dave-drums,or
that should be DRUMS,Fred Burk-bass and Slimey Toad-guitar.Altogether they're as tight as
a fist.They are all proud of being connected
with the Damned thru a mutual band called
Rot,but don't wear it like a badge,and included a perfect'New Rose'(with the entire(?)
Roxy going AH! on cue).To watch the man himself is a hard thing to put in words.Sure,
he's funny,he has to be-he's got more heck-
lers than Fozzie Bear-but 1 know,had the atmosphere not been like a lounge,this band0(
(and I say"band"in the same way that the old
Alice Cooper band was known,y'know-singer/
group,spotlight on leadman,earoles on group)
would have turned every head in the house.

"Walkin'down the road with my incendiary de-
vice/Lookin'for a lady,blow hereup with gel-
agnite/Stick it in her lugole/Watch it blow
her head apart/Stick it in her lugole/Stick
it in her other parts/Stick it in her lugole/
Stick it in her'ead"('Incendiary Device')
                    Alright,Jackson Browne it ain't
but you'll be singin'it after the first
chorus,easy money.Go and see him,it's hard to
write.He sings inlots of keys,dances with
the punters,spends time lookin'up his guitarist's crutch,does'Little Queeenie','Wild
Breed'and does great justice to EC's(that's
Eddie Cochran,div!)'Somethin'Else'and gives

11

lectures with brief question/answer sessions
and exites.The Toad was till they met and
assured me Johnny Moped was a nutcase.A
genius?I dunno,I'd love to have a proper
rabbit with'em.
                    Whether the Heartbreakers,
the Clash and Co.were there for the bands
or a swift half,1 dunno either(Stan did).
I do know it was a SATURDAY NIGHT,and this
time brown shoes did make it...(DB).

THE JAM-IN THE CITY(Polydor album).

Art School/I've Changed My Address/Slow
Down/I've Got By In Time/Away From the
Numbers/Batman/2)In the City/Sounds From
the Street/Non Stop Dancing/Time For Truth/
Takes My Love/Bricks and Mortar.
                    In context with the Jam's
style of music,this album's great!Honest,
it couldn't be more perfect,Jam fans must
get it.The band are really picking up now
and this album should establish'em nation-
ally.Weller's 'Bricks and Mortar'is my
favourite,a track which comes accross
powerfully.Yeah,of course,'In the City'is
as good as always too.Weller's other songs
all maintain that Who/Maximum R&B feel.All
ace tracks,but now that the Jam's getting
around I hope they broaden and strangthen
their style so that by the next album they
sound completly différant.(SM).

THE SAINTS-I'M STRANDED(EMI import album).
                    This could be called'I'm
Strained'.Most disappointing album of'77.
It drones on and on and doesn't even make
ya fancy turning it over let alone playing
again.Ted Nugent with a rocket up his arse.

COME A LONG WAY SINCE
SOHO MARKET.

`CHINESE ROCKs´ (中國石)
b/w Born to Lose

L.A.M.F.

out Now! you waiters on ~ TRACK RECORD

CAT. NO: 2094 135

PHONE OR WRITE
439-8646 ~ 5/6/7, CARNABY ST. TRACK RECORDS

STIFFS STRANGLERS IV

BUNCH OF STIFFS(Stiff album).

I Love My Label-Nick Lowe/Go the Whole Wide
World-Wreckless Eric/White Line Fever-Motor-
head/Less Than Zero-Elvis Costello/Little By
Little-Magic Michael/2)Jump For Joy-Stones
Masonry/Maybe-Jill Read/Jo Jo Gunne-Dave Ed-
munds/The Young Lords-Tyla Gang/Food-Takea-
ways(Tyla/Lowe/Edmunds/Larry Wallis).

Bonus track-Back To Schooldays:Graham Parker.

      Now that Stiff have got their
bleedin'distribution deal with Island they
think they can put out any old crap.Well,this
is the first of it.Out of the 11 tracks only
4 are worth playing again,Motorhead,Elvis
Costello,Tyla Gang and Graham Parker.The rest
are definetly Stiffs.
      Motorhead's track is a heavy
job which sounds a little like Deep Purple
but after that setback it rocks along in the
only way Lemmy knows.It was gonna be released
as a single but they never got around to it.
Elvis Costello's single's included on the
album and you can find a review of it elsewhere in this mag.I'll just add my praise.
The Tyla Gang track is incredible.Sean sings
like Dylan or Springsteen and the backing
jumps about like Little Feat or one of those
Nils Lofgren line-ups.Tyla deserves an album
release.His music is growing all the time.
The Parker track is a outake from some old
tapes and is excellant in it's simplicity.
It's better than the album version.
      The rest of the bunch is the
crap:Nick Lowe is boring,Stones Masonry is
an instrumental R&B workout featuring Martin
Stone,the Takeaways is a jokey Dylan take-
off and Wreckless Eric,Magic Michael,Dave
Edmunds and Jill Read are all over produced.
      This album is a waste of time.
I'm suprised Island agreed to put it out.I
hope Stiff sit down and think about their
next releases otherwise the original cuteness
of this label is gonna wear off.An Adverts'
single is out soon so that should be alright.
I hope they make it.
      Liven up Stiff. (Mark P).

THE STRANGLERS IV RATTUS NORVEGICUS
               (United Artists album)

Sometimes/Goodbye Toulouse/London Lady/
Princess Of the Streets/Hanging Around/
2)Peaches/(Get a)Grip(On Yourself)/Ugly/
Down In the Sewer(a)Falling(b)Down In the
Sewer(c)Trying To Get Out Again(d)Rats
Rally.

Free single-Peasant In the Big Shitty/
              Choosey Susie.

      Apart from the title this LP
is easy to understand.The natural progression of a band like the Stranglers is to
have a first album that sounds like this.
'Rattus Norvegicus'shows all their styles
and proves that their inclusion in the
lists of"new-wave"bands is bullshit.The
Stranglers are doing stuff that could have
been done in '68,'70 or'72.Progressive rock
will always be around.
      They write great songs-'Some-
times','Hanging Around','Grip',etc and
they make the best of them.This whole album
is excellant but I don't know why SG's
reviewing it.Yeah,I secretly like the
Stranglers'album.It's no longer a secret,
this band will be very succesful.America
will fall all over them.
      The Stranglers are qaint.They
sing about acne,rats,"getting laid","the
mersey tunnel",etc.They're incredibly
British,their type of humour comes from
their British upbringing and from a couple
of years touring,playing the pub circuit
and genarally taking the rough with the
smooth.
      Their sound is original and
they never fail to suprise with sound ef-
fects and interesting fills.The individual
members all have styles of their own.Hugh
Cornwell on guitar and vocals,Jean Jaques
Burnel on bass and vocals,Dave Greenfield
on keyboards(vocals on'Peasant In the Big
Shitty')and Jet Black on percussion.Jean's
bass is the killer,it forms the base for
most of the songs.The voices are good,espec-
ially when the lyrics allow for Hugh's odd
quirks(as in'Peaches'when he makes lots of
weird noises).I thought that'Down In the
Sewer could have been a lot better.The
stagesversion is much more adventuress but
it doesn't spoil the overall quality of the
album.
      One moan-why didn't the put
the free single tracks(limited edition of
10,000)on the album and leave off'Grip'and
'London Lady'which came out as a single last
month.Some kids ain't gonna hear the free
single which is a bit of a fucker.I don't
know who thought of that stupid"free single"
idea anyway.It's still a great album.
                  (Mark P).

The Clash

JOIN US ON THE WHITE RIOT — 77 TOUR

MAY		
Sun.	1st	Guildford, Civic
Mon.	2nd	Chester, Rascals
Tues.	3rd	Birmingham, Barbarellas
Wed.	4th	Swindon, The Affair Ballroom
Thurs.	5th	Liverpool, Erics.
Fri.	6th	Aberdeen, University
Sat.	7th	Edinburgh, Playhouse Theatre
Sun.	8th	Manchester, Electric Circus
Mon.	9th	London, Rainbow
Tues.	1nth	Kidderminster, Town Hall
Thurs.	12th	Nottingham, Palais
Sun.	15th	Plymouth, Fiesta

MAY		
Mon.	16th	Swansea, University
Tues.	17th	Leeds, Polytechnic
Thurs.	19th	Middlesborough, Rock Gardens
Fri.	20th	Newcastle, University
Sat.	21st	St. Albans, City Hall
Mon.	23rd	Stafford, Top Of The World
Tues.	24th	Cardiff, Top Rank
Wed.	25th	Brighton, Polytechnic
Thurs.	26th	Bristol, Colston Hall
Fri.	27th	West Runton, Pavillion
Sat.	28th	Canterbury, Odeon
Mon.	30th	Chelmsford, Chancellor Hall
		Dunstable, California Ballroom

... now out + THE LP + The CLASH

PIC BY SHIRLEY HILL

SKREWDRIVER-YOU'RE SO DUMB(Chiswick).
        Dan reckons this is the type
of track that used to make good B-sides and
now makes good A-sides.Great title but I
don't like this'cos it's a dollop,but it
grows on ya.These lads come from Bristol...
no Blackpool.I fuckin'hate records that grow
on ya.Still,if you like fast,inaudible lyrics
it's for you,punk!(SM).

EDDIE & THE HOT RODS-I MIGHT BE LYING(Island)
        I like this number.A must for
all Hot Rods fans.Not immediatly likable but
after a while-really enjoyable.Their sound's
got a lot stronger and although their lyrics
have never grabbed me,these are interesting
(and on the cover).Yeah,they're still Status
Quo-ish but it's their own fast,loud brand
of R&B.The flip side is worth a mention?-
'Ignore Them'.(SM).

RADIATORS(FROM SPACE)-TELEVISION SCREEN
                                    (Chiswick)
        Moronic Mess.(SM).

RADIO STARS-DIRTY PICTURES(Chiswick).
        Dunno what was designed to fit
with this-it's so contrived.Like interior
decoration,y'know-guitar bit here,piano line
there.Then stop-back to chorus.Yeah,it's alright if you like interior decoration.

"I'd like to take you in the attic,
 with my Kodak instamatic".

Yeah?...Go back to bed.(SM).

THUNDERTRAIN-Hot For Teacher(Jelly)
        Y'know them records that kill
a dance floor stone dead?This is one.There's
nothing in it that Status Quo ain't done
better by yards.The B-side is the death
rattle of Pat Travers.Well,that's another
group SG's gotta steer clear of.(DB).

Waddya want from pubrock,BLOOD(SM).

ELVIS COSTELLO-LESS THAN ZERO(Stiff).
        I've played this for about
two weeks so this is easy to write.If you're
into hard angry sounds and nothing else,see
you later.If not,roll back the carpet,roll
on the weekend and bop.
        It's Springsteen lyrics/voice
and a funky chacha.Hey Ray.(DB).

MAX WALL-ENGLAND'S GLORY(Stiff).
        Written by the same Ian Dury
of the Kilburns?Go to the back sleeve for a
name check.You're not on it?You must be a
jerk.Steve says he's off to give out song-
sheets at Millwall.Lyrics include Little
Titch,Billy Fury,Mr Pastry and a sex act
called Muffin the Mule.Still,any song that
mentions the dole,and the Board Of Trade
must be anti government.One to stagger from
the grave yard to.(DB/SM).

BLONDIE(Private Stock album).
X Offender/Little Girl Lies/In the Fleash/
Look Good In Blue/In the Sun/A Shark In
Jets Clothing/2)Man Overboard/Rip Her To
Shreds/Riflerange/Fung Fu Girls/Attack Of
the Giant Ants.

        Classy trash and pop at it's
best.It's one that's best to start on Side
2 and right from the bass intro on 'Man
Overboard' away ya go-Surfin' on the New
Wave.It's red hot bubblegum,the best being
the first three on side 2 and'In the Flesh'
and I love the line-"I'll give you some
head(and)shoulders to lie on"-in 'Look Good
In Blue!.I wont bore you with what Debbie
Harry is wearing on the sleeve,NME's already done that but she is beautiful to the
point of taking liberties.Again,music for
the legs not for the head.(DB).

13 BLONDIE

Plain Stupid Pinup No1.

TO MARK P.
& EVERYONE AT SNIFFIN GLUE
1-2-3-4

DONT PUNK OUT!!!

APRIL FOOL DAY

14 4/1/77

ROCK ON OK!

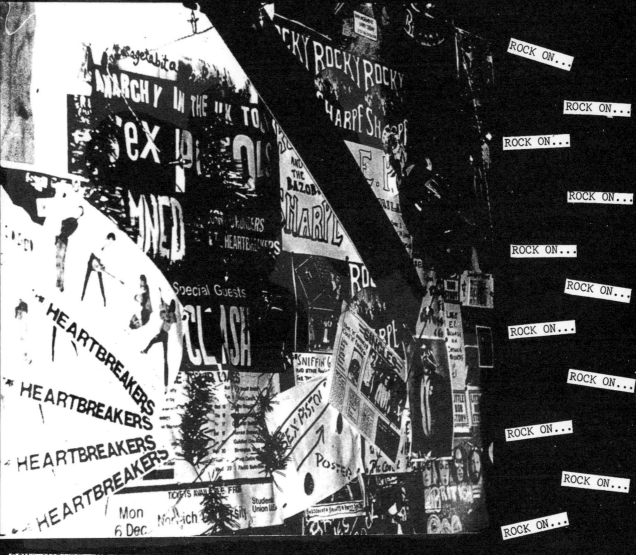

ROCK ON...
ROCK ON...
ROCK ON...
ROCK ON...
ROCK ON...
ROCK ON...
ROCK ON...
ROCK ON...
ROCK ON...
ROCK ON...
ROCK ON...
ROCK ON...

SOHO MARKET, NEWPORT COURT, off LEICESTER SQUARE TUBE....

3 KENTISH TOWN ROAD, CAMDEN TOWN TUBE....

93 GOLBOURNE ROAD, off PORTOBELLO ROAD. (Saturday only)....

AVAILABLE NOW... CLASH L.P.+45 EDDIE AND THE HOT RODS-I MIGHT BE LYING   TELIVISION

COMING SOON... CHISWICK... RADIATORS FROM SPACE   SCREWDRIVER RINGS MOTORHEAD   101'ERS, KEYS TO YOUR HEART

STEP FORWARDS-45'S... CORTINAS CHELSEA   MODELS   JOHNNY MOPED
                                                                      COUNT BISHOPS L.P.

SKYDOG... FLAMING GROOVIES   STIFFS... ADVERTS
          OUTAKE 45   M.C.5-BORDERLINE

EDDIE AND THE HOT RODS LIVE E.P.   HEARTBREAKERS CHINESE ROCKS

SNIFFIN' GLUE...

30p

AND OTHER ROCK'N'ROLL HABITS FOR DEPTFORD YOBS! ⑩ JUNE-1977.

STEVE MICK'S GOT THE SACK AND WE GET BACK TO THE STREETS. THE GLUE: <u>STILL</u> DEPTFORD YOBS!

PIC BY JILL FURMANOVSKY.

CHELSEA + JOHNNY MOPED
+ JOHN CALE, WHITE RIOT TOUR.

S.G. 10

HARRY.   MARK.   DANNY.

YER, STILL DEPTFORD YOBS!

Front cover and above photo by Jill
                                    Furmanovsky.

THANKS FOR AN IDEA, CHALKIE.
    FROM JILL

What made it all possible:

MARK P.

HARRY T.MURLOWSKI.

DANNY BAKER.

JILL FURMANOWSKY.

ERICA ECHENBERG.

Also: Caroline Coon,Stan,Phil,the music.
+ EDDIE D. +MARK+JAN CHAPMAN.
Oh yeah,STEVE MICK got the sack last week.
There will be crying in the streets.Wah!!

NEW ADDRESS:
SNIFFIN' GLUE,
28 DRYDEN CHAMBERS,
119 OXFORD STREET,
LONDON. W.1.

BULLETS - IN.

Lets sort all this shit out:

1.'Sniffin' Glue's getting like a newspaper'(Stranglers-Sounds).If people want some cockney sparra chic scruffy ornament,thats true.We print what we can afford,what we like,and what we think.Not because,like this weeks T-shirt,it looks and sounds right. We dont go after any fashionable'look'.When you see an Eagles review,turn it in.

2.'How can Mark P. have a record company and still say..'(Record Mirror reader).Mark's so called company is Step Forward,a new wave label,who he advises what to sign;there's no big few bob involved..an' thats another thing,I noticed we're having to apologise for having a circulation.Listen mate,if we ever do see a taste for workin' seven days a week,you aint gonna see this bloke puttin' it in the church poor box cos he feels guilty.I spose you would!Anyrate,gettin' back to Step Forward,I reckon its healthier Mark doin' the signin' than some fat wanker business man who just sees the scene as a way of lengthening his pool.

3.National Front. The Evenin' News says the Front are manipulatin' the new wave. I don't need to say what bollocks that is. Some cruds say that NF in power would shake people out of their apathy. Well,cruds,how would you express this new found anger? It aint only the blacks who'll be shut up. So a big FUCKOFF to NF,Lablibcon,Commies, Socialist fuckin' workers,the head in sand brigade,the lot.And the poxy Evenin' News can quote that!

4.'How comes groups like Clash/Pistols sign with big companies?' Theres no point screamin' to the converted on privatly owned/distributed labels that could sell about two hundred,is there? We wanna be heard,fuck being a cult.

5.Have you noticed how amused the other press is to find out punks like other types of music? Look sunshine,we don't need mum,dad or Sniffin'Glue to let us know what to dance to,BUT the new wave is more than music to you and me,its our megaphone for Youth.Positive Youth. Spelt P-U-N-K and put over as rock'n'roll,right. Sniffin' Glue should be guitar shaped.

DANNY BAKER.

PIC BY ERICA ECHENBERG.

THIS IS A PHOTO OF MARK P. WITH STEVE MICK AND THE REASON STEVE WAS SACKED FROM 'SNIFFIN' GLUE' - HER NAMES ALICE.

2

TELEVISION ARE HERE

at the Hammersmith Odeon

Sat. & Sun. 28th & 29th MAY

Their Album MARQUEE MOON K52046

Elektra

MAIL ORDER - MAIL ORDER

Alright. This is about our much abused mail order bits. Cunts go 'ah,yer wankers wiv ya fucking business,just like Melody Maker.' It aint. A lot of kids,(in a lot of countrys) write to us,so this is to save us shelling out on all them stamps.Anyrate we bin screwing it up in the air. We're about two months behind as it happens,an' we aint sent it out,(just like them loon pants or posters deals),so what we're sayin' is hang about cos week beginning 23rd May,its all gonna start 'appening,so watch it.

So: Prices per mag (inc.P&P)
        40p for the UK and Eire
        50p for Europe and seamail to the rest of world
        65p for outside Europe(airmail)
    Maximum subscription ya can have is 4 issues,which is
    4 times one issues price....(clever eh?)

And get'old o'this. A new address,we're in some naked rooms in a doss house off Oxford Street. An' Marks screamed to tell yer to put ORDERS on subscriptions cos he sometimes mistakes 'em for 'is fan mail. SO,the new place(now open to female members of the public,come early-stay late) is;
        28, Dryden Chambers
           119,Oxford Street
                W.1.
                            28,Dryden Chambers
                              119,Oxford Street,
                                   W.1.

    By co-incidence this is also the address of the Mark P. International Fan Club.
    (London Branch) Soon available,T-shirts,posters,badges and little noddy Marks for
    the back of ya car.......

MAIL ORDER - MAIL ORDER

CHELSEA

Interview with Gene October of Chelsea.

SG:Where does Henry come from?

Gene:Well,I got a friend who works in Capital Radio called Nicky Horne,right.I walked up to Capital one day to try and get'em to play 'White Riot'.We got chatting and I told him I needed a bass player and there was this guy who answers the phones,you know,the phone in."Oh",he says"I'm a bass player".He auditioned,we liked him and that was that.

SG:D'you reckon you'll ever play the Rainbow?

Gene:We'll get up to that level.I mean,you keep stating-"I made you"-,I think you made the Clash and the Pistols.You know,a lot of papers made the Pistols what they are.The hype that they are,I mean,you can only make us by giving us front cover.Which is a fact, it adds a bit of style to the band.This band needs style because it's taken a lot of second best.There ain't much interest taken in it...

SG:Why do you think that's happened?

Gene:...because there's too much happening with Clash and the Pistols.Now the Pistols have gone by everybody's concentrating on the Clash and when Clash wern't doing something it was the Damned,right?

SG:Really,they're the first wave of bands and you're,sort of like,heading the new new-wave.

Gene:I mean,the Clash have been around for a year,at least and,sure they deserve it.

3

They've been pumping in there.They instigated.Mick Jones said to me,"I don't want to be a follower,I want to be an instigator". Which he has achieved.Everybody needs some body to lead'em.Until they're able to make up their own minds as to what goes.You'll always find this in life.Since rock began there's always been leaders.Then you get to a stage when you're able to make up your own mind and get it on.

SG:The stuff you're doing...d'you hope to influence kids in your audience?

Gene:I hope to instigate something if I can.I wanna take it away from the rough side that it's got and I wanna add a bit of smoothness to it,a bit of polish.A bit of style.There's too many of these"punk-bands" being looked on as thickos.

SG:Are the new guys(James and Henry)bringing in any new ideas?

Gene:The newest song-"Get Out and Walk"-was partly James.

SG:What about the old songs like'The Right To Work','The Loner'etc.Does that still relate with what you're into with the new members?

Gene:Sure,we havn't even started...I havn't even got my message over.One gets accused of being a poseur,one gets accused of writing stuff'cause that's the thing to write about.I've had all that..."I don't take drugs and I don't drink beer"...I mean, for too long the rock music business...It got to the stage where you had to come from the Royal College Of so-and-so.It was getting really bad,you know?You got these people up on the stage,people who were speaking in a posh voice.It was a bit crazy.Rock comes from a dirty old playground,in the slums or the World's End,Chelsea.

SG:Where was you born?

Gene:In the East End,I was chucked in an orphanage.
                    NEXT QUESTION.

Gene:I went to see the Jam at the Red Cow.I think that guy Paul Weller,fucking good. Kids shouldn't be put off by the fucking suits,the honest statement of that guy was like..."yeah,we'd like to play the Earl's Court stadium one day".Not many would admit to that.

SG:Do you look as far as that?

Gene:Sure but there's a danger that we'll get away from what we set out to do.

SG:What d'you reckon"we set out to do"?

Gene:We set out to not be like this fucking lot that have just gone.There's a danger that we'll end up just like'em.In our big

RollsRoyce's and our big penthouses,know what I mean?Without ever doing anything,you know,really we havn't achieved anything yet. As far as a government or anything like that. I mean,hippies did achieve quite a bit.They got out on the streets,they were prepared to fight on the streets.Red Lion Square,things like that.Have we ever done anything like that.The scene hasn't come together,it's got to come together.They've got to realise what they've got to do and do it.Don't talk about it but do it!There's a lot of talk but no action.

SG:The press are frightened of the music...

Gene:Well,fuck me I was!I was frightened when I first saw the Clash at the ICA I was shit scared.To see a punk show is very frightening,it's the music.It's very heavy,the vibe in the music and the vibe in the audience is very frightening for a first-time onlooker.

SG:The press at the moment are trying to crush the scene...

Gene:It's like old cunts,frustrated old cunts who try to re-live what they went through in the sixties.They say"That ain't as good as..." you know?You should be writing for NME or something like that.This scene will produce it's own journalists,it's own clothes shops, you know what I mean?It will create it's own thing.I mean,at the Hope & Anchor we had some guy standing there in a suit,he'd just come out the office and he was shouting,"Rubbish, Rubbish!".I mean,what does the guy know! Everybody's thinking,"Is it just a fad?",I say they are a load of doubting Thomases 'cause this is gonna be the biggest thing...forget the sixties.It's just like the Teds,some of them look fucking great but a lot of them are kids.You know,why don't they create something of their own.They've got this image but they should do it their way,not the way that their father.Their father's probably got his drapes still in it's mothballs.Yeah, son those were the days...that's what they're saying.

SG:This scene is the only scene where the kids are actually calling the cards.

Gene:We'd like to think.To a certain extent but with a lot of compromise.

SG:There's gotta be some compromise to play places like the Rainbow...

Gene:Yeah,but what the fuck have the Sex Pistols gone through what they've gone through for?Has it been a waste of fucking time? It isn't a waste of time but it is when people turn around and compromise with what they fucking tried to bring down.When people are prepared to lick people's arses and they wer'nt.The Pistols wer'nt prepared to lick anyone's fucking arse.

4

SG:Who do you think has compromised then?

Gene:You know I can't mention names,I couldn't slout could I?

SG:Well,if not names...what have they done to compromise,I mean,what's your idea of "to compromise"?Cause you're obviously gonna come up against that and you're gonna be faced with a decision.

Gene:Be faced with decisions but I don't want to come against this until I feel that I've achieved something,done something for my time.Yeah,I don't want the kids to look back and say,"1977,oh yeah it was great but what did they achieve.They came on with all this talk at first but what did they achieve".

THE RIGHT TO WORK.

Gene:The right to work,fuck the unions I say...

SG:Is that what that song's about then?

Gene:Yeah,fuck the unions."Your father worked on this dock,you'll work on this dock". "If you don't sign with the fucking union, you don't get the job!".Big brother.

SG:What about a song like'the Loner'.It's personnal to you isn't it?

Gene:It's personnal to me but also I reckon there's a lot of loners.A lot of kids who die when they're 14,15...just die,no feelings. I personally died a long time ago.This big build up of what life is supposed to be.In the 17th Century when the kids went to work when he was 12 wasa better way of doing it.

G:Didn't you think much of your schooling?

Gene:I thought it was a complete waste of time.I thought it was a joke.It was a fucking send up.Waste of money,a joke...learning about the"Great Britisn Empire".1 don't wanna know about it,why they rubbing that into me? There ain't one left.I don't wanna know about it.What can I say to these fucking Americans that come over here.Silly cunts!

SG:Do you resent the Americans coming over here and becoming part of the scene?

Gene:I resent their usage of the fucking scene,right,that's what I resent.They always have been bandwagoners...don't tell me Lou Reed was ever a punk.He was just a fucking queen into singing about queens.He was cashing in on the camp scene.Bowie was cashing in on the Iggy scene.Iggy was the only true one.Iggy was the punk,not Reed,not fucking Bowie.Patti Smith's just a frustrated groupie she'd love to be Keith Richard.She'd love to be Keith Richard's wife but he told her to get stuffed!

SG:What about all these smaller bands,I mean, I havn't got that much bread have they?Like Vanilla,Wayne County,Heartbreakers...

Gene:So are a lot of million other people in the world.Millions and millions of people ain't got any money.You've only gotta walk down the East End...they're all starving.

CHELSEA: L to R - CAREY FORTUNE, JAMES STEVENSON, GENE + HENRY DAZE.

SG:What sort of stuff did you listen to... any music you listened to when you was growing up?

Gene:The Who,the early Stones...I never did rate the Americans.I mean,they just ain't got no knowhow...they've been too well looked after when they were kids.They had too many pancake sandwiches,too much jam in their blood...too much treacle...too much popcorn!

JAMES STEVESON - GUITAR

SG:One thing good about this scene is that the Clash are a London band,Chelsea are a London band.It's never been like that since the Who,the Kinks,the Stones and Mott the Hoople.

CHELSEA ARE A LONDON BAND!

SG:You got any ideas for any new songs?

Gene:Yeah,I've got quite a few at the moment. Due to the fact that I have to manage this band all the time.I have to put 100% into it,arrange the gigs...we need a manager.But I'm not interested in a guy with a limo'or anything like that.I'm interested in a guy who knows what we're about,who understands what we're about.With all that I've not got much time to think about new songs.

A Chelsea single is being released soon on the Step-Forward Reacords label.The A-side is'Right To Work'and on the flip-'The Loner'. They'll make it sooner or bater.

Mild mannered reporter.

CHELSEA PHOTOS BY H.T. MURLOWSKI.

5

THE CLASH, THE BUZZCOCKS, THE SUBWAY SECT AND OTHERS AT THE RAINBOW!

The CLASH at the Rainbow went like this:

"He's in love with rock'n'roll,wooaghhh!
He's in love with getting stoned,woooagh!
He's in love with Janie Jones,wooaggga!
He don't like his boring job,no-ooo!

He knows what he's gotta do and he knows he's gonna have fun with you,lucky lady!
And he knows when the evening comes,when his job is done he'll be over in the car for you!

In his in-tray,lots of work and the boss at his firm always thinks he shirks!
But he's just like everyone,he's got a Ford Cortina that just wont run without fuel,
                                                        fill her up Jacko!

He got an invoice,it don't quite fit,there's no payola in his alphabetical file,
                                                'cept for the Government man!
This time he's gonna really tell the boss,he's gonna really let him know exactly
                                                how he feels,pretty bad!

Let them know,let them knooooww!"

                    (Joe Strummer/Mick Jones).

This was the gig when the kids won.
"As the Clash's Joe Strummer sang a song called'White Riot'fans smashed up 200 seats"
Yeah,the Clash caused a riot. So what,I'm glad that people are scared of rock'n'roll again.
From my view,down the front on Jone's side,the gig was a killer.Mick was slightly restrained'cause of his bad finger but Joe Strummer's maniac performance made up for it.From the opener-'London's Burning'- he was shaking all over the stage.Unlike Iggy in March,Joe talk to the kids,he was with'em and leading them.When he refused to stop the show,when asked by some official,it meant everything.I just hope the Clash stay human, they'll never turn into a product.No way!
The rest of the gig was just as memorable.The first group I saw was the Subway Sect.There's no good or bad states with this mob.They are just an experience,although the audience were pretty subdued during the band's set.The applause was sparse but the music was excellent.'Eastern European'was the best song:

"I take no exceptance of those hoardings I
                                    see,
As I run along a street I prefer not to
                                    take it,
I prefer quotes directed at me.

Cigarettes,they look at me,
And tell me I'm an Americane,
But my recent dreams advise me,
They'd be extra life,
If I were Eastern European,
Then I can concede".
                    (Vic Godard).

VIC GODARD - SUBWAY SECT.

Yes,the Subway Sect are a wonderful band.
The Buzzcocks were also great. The new line-up is getting better and better.I reckon'16'is the strongest song and'Orgasm Addict'needs to come out as a single.Garth-on bass-looked very cool in shades,even though he is a big lump.
The Jam were...I didn't see'em, I was in the bar.I also got there to late to see the Prefects.Next time the Clash have just got to destroy Hammersmith Odeon!
                                    Mark P.

VIC PIC BY CAROLINE COON.

6

STARS FADE AND DIE BUT CULT HEROES LIVE ON...
JOHN CALE WILL LIVE ON!

JOHN CALE

PICS BY JILL + HARRY.

YOUR RABBIT

The cover of the new HEART-BREAKERS single is a complete joke.Two pics stuck together trying to pass as one.No way.The records on at the moment though and we're all boppin'around to it, "I'm living on a Chinese rock..!"plus 'Born To Lose'.LAMF...Mark P. impressions to order,just put on yer record and away he goes...meet the TALKING HEADS in Rough Trade the other day.David's a very quiet lad,Chris is'comical',Tina's lovely and the new guy,Jerry Harrison (ex MODERN LOVERS)is interesting.They'll be an interview in SG11..some good new releases soon-the DAMNED single-'Sick Of Being Sick'/'Stretcher Case,Baby'and EDDIE AND THE HOT RODS'Live at the Rainbow'EP.From Chiswick there's gonna be singles by JOHNNY MOPED,MOTORHEAD and RINGS.Step-Forward records are gonna release a MODELS single soon-'The Freeze'/'Man Of the Year'.A SEX PISTOLS album which will show the bastards that it's all been worth it is in the can.Oh,yeah by the way,we're really glad that the PISTOLS have gone with Virgin.They may have Mike Oldfield,Gong,Can and all the other'hippies'but they've always put out what they want,and you can always bowl in and chat up the boss-Richard Branson-for some freebees'cos he's ok(whatever that means)...BLONDIE come and saw us the other day,an' if we hadn't gone to print the next day we'd have done a bit on 'em,anyrate they did say they were interested in whats happenin' here and great to talk to,an' said they'd like people to dance rather than anylise what they do,so now ya know...we have reason to believe SNIFFIN'GLUE is being bootlegged in the States.Watch it or we'll get Peter Grant on to yer...just wait 'til you see the Step-Forward label,you better get ya shades ready.It's a multicoloured blinder...Baker's Keith Emerson impression ain't bad either...recent sets on JOHN PEEL's radio show have been the CLASH,DAMNED,GEN X,ADVERTS,JAM.So, any night you're not doing anything at ten...where's the fiver,JOHN...and fuck NICKY HORNE...more TALKING HEADS:their album will be ready in September.Jerry Harrison reckons there's only a little bit of brass and a few suprises,David Bryne on oboe?A RAMONES/TALKING HEADS thing is gonna be in SG11(again?)...also a mention 999 who are really good.GENE OCTOBER tell's me that the lead singer used to be in the KILBURN & HIGH ROADS.. meanwhile the SG staff are all dossing on the office floor tonight-back to the fuckin'streets?You bet we are...

8

WE MAY BE WHITE BUT WE'RE ALRIGHT

It had to happen,a reggae bit! Yes,for the first time in SG's history we've got one.There's gonna be one every month.It's gonna be called'Reggae Album Of the Month''cos that's what it's called. Rush out and buy every album we mention in this column.

PETE TOSH WITH WORD,SOUND & POWER:
                    Equal Rights(Virgin)

Get Up,Stand Up/Downpressor Man/I Am That I Am/Stepping Razor/Equal Rights/African/ Jah Guide/Apartheid.

In case you don't know it, Winston Hubert McIntosh-who can apparently open the heavens if he gets mad-was one of the original Wailers along with Marley and Bunny Livingstone.He's still knocking out the best reggae around.It's heavier than his last album-'Legalise It'-and it is definately my favourite black album so far this year.
The opener-which Tosh wrote with Marley and is on the Wailer's 'Burnin'album-skips along great,Al Anderson filling in the spaces with some tasty guitar.My fav lyrics of all time:
"Most people think great God will come from the skies/Take away everything and make everybody high/But if you know what life is worth you would look for yours right here on earth/And now we seen the light we gonna stand up for our rights".
                    (Bob Marley/Pete Tosh)
This song sets the feeling for most of the album.Tosh sings from down there...not some high horse.Most of the songs are political but some are incredibly personnal like'I Am That I Am'. The song basically says-'don't try to change me'.'Stepping Razor's a rocker Anderson tearing out a seering intro. Again,Tosh is great:
"If you are a bully treat me good/I'm like a stepping razor,watch my sides-I'm dangerous"
        (Tosh).
                    Throughout the album,bass lines are provided by Robbie Shakespeare-the best and the drumming by Sly Dunbar. If you can't get into the lyrics,their shifting rythmns will murder yer.
        'African'came out as a single not long ago.A reggae classic,it's one for the juke boxes and if they're ever looking for a national anthem when all the blacks unite,this is it. "No mind your nationality,you have got the identity of an African".(Tosh).
                    Sometimes it makes me wish I was black.Buy it.
                    Mark P.

DANNY BAKER GRAPPLES WITH THE SINGLES, ALL 16 OF 'EM!

THE CLASH:Remote Control/London's
    Burning(Live at Dunstable)CBS
I spose for us mob the B side is the
A side,if ya see what I mean. Anyrate
it's out.

THE POLICE:Fall Out/Nothing Acheived
(illegal) Good to see a new label,but
this is like a sort of Highway Star,an'
I never did like Highway Star.
Did you?

THE MARBLES:RedLights/Fire and Smoke
(Ork-Marbles) Whatsallthisabout? No
idea what this has to do with us.
Fuckin'cheap lousy pop tune,thats probably got clever lyrics or hidden send
up. American. The B side had people running in saying'leave me out',not on the
record,in here I mean.

ALEX CHILTON:(1)Free Again/Singer not the
song(2)Take me home and make me like it/
All the Time/Summertime Blues.(Ork)33⅓
    This bloke was in Big Star,who I
liked once,but after this I wonder if
they've aged well. On this pony record
player I can't tell if the vocals are as
weak as they sound, mind you Clash come
over just as good so I don't see why this
geyser shouldn't. Well up from the Marble
's but that means fuck all. Poprock.

ROKY ERICKSON:Bermuda/Interpreter(Virgin)
With this and the Pistols,someone at Vir
gin knows his singles.One of the 13th floor Elevators (Poxy history),sounds like
Gene Pitney backed by Blue Oyster Cult.
Fast an' easy to mime to, get this cos
its good.

THE STRANGLERS:Peaches/Go Buddy Go.
(UA) They 'ad a go at us last week,but
it was in Sounds,so it don't count. Both
A sides but I still reckon Peaches by a
short head,and prefer it all to the LP
which,not like this,ya can't play all the
way through. Go Buddy Go aint been out
before, yeah we're playin' it again now
good,good single.'Oh shit,we missed the
charabanc'.Or sharabang. Fuck me,my spel-
lings gone right downhill.

TV SMITH - ADVERTS (Pic- H.T. MURLOWSKI)

THE ADVERTS:One Chord Wonders/Quickstep.
(STIFF) I really like the Adverts,(Gary
Gilmores Eyes is a classic) as ever the
drums and bass way up front,for a group
who,(all join in on this cliche)—you either
love or hate. Great track,'specially the
lyrics,but will do lousy as a single, good
B side ennall.

THE USERS:Sick of You/In love with Today.
(RAW) Sort of record that gets right up
peoples noses,cos its so obviously straight
forward,wallop. Damnedish, fast,with the
singer tryin' to sound disgusted. I think
I like this,even if it does go on a bit.
Bore on the label though,cos its not only
got a producer,BUT,an executive producer.
Next stop's a fuckin' spiritual advisor.

THE RAMONES:She na is a punk rocker/Comm-
ando/I don't care.(Sire)
If the Beach Boys were alive today they
would have done records like this.Nobody
needs tellin' about Ramones records,do they
They take all the bovva to put out a 12"
disc and finish about inch and half into
the plate! Makes a lot of the records here
sound naff. We got no.003637.

the stranglers

MORE GRAPPLING WITH D.B.

CHELSEA:Right to Work/Loner
(Step Forward);Oh it's Mark P's
label,its bound to get a good review
in SG,what a carve up.
Well look,whether they're signed to
Telefunken or what,Chelsea are a major
new wave force-FACT. An' you can't arg-
ue bout a fact see. I don't owe Mark or
no-one no favours,but if you miss this
cos of anything,well.....well just don't
miss it thats all. Anarchy,White Riot,
and now Right to Work.   Got it.

Cortinas:Fascist Dictator/Television
Families(Step Forward);New Wave fast
and furious,I reckon TV Families is
the better,in the Saints vein but
with more brains,edge and anyrate
Marks got his boot on me neck.
('let 'em know I don't sign shit')
This single is proof.

SEX PISTOLS:God Save the Queen/~~No
Feelings~~(Virgin); The ol' singles col-
omn aint fuckin' about this month is it?
No hook in this like 'anarchy' but the
end bit with'no future'makes sure this
is just as good,but then,we all knew that
already.It might not actually be on
Virgin tho'.

**THE B-SIDE AIN'T 'NO FEELINGS',
IT'S 'DID YOU NO WRONG'.**

THAT HIDEOUS STRENGTH:Night at Space Opera/
Call me Energy/Locomotive.(Aware)
I wouldn't ask anyone to buy this,but if
the bloke turns round to ring something up,
know what I mean? Dopey,deranged tracks
that are a good crack while they last, a
few Spike Jones bits among the Lou Reeds,
but nothing to hunt for.

COUNT BISHOPS:Baby your wrong/Stay Free.
(Chiswick);First record with their new aussie singer,on a sort of uninspired Thin
Lizzie workout. Forget it.
StopPress:::The first SG record to be thrown
from our third story window.We'll let ya
know what type of crud picks it up.

Motorhead:White Line Fever/Leavin'Here.
(Skydog) Was to be released by Stiff,an'
we like it,so there. Nothing shakering,but
the B side,got us all pretendin' to play.
Didn't end up in Holland Street.

Judy nylon (Pic by N.T. Mralowska).

SNATCH:Stanley/I.R.T.(Bomp) ; We fucking
LOVE this. And it's acoustic. No drums,no
bass,nothing. The type of acoustic track
that'd make Dory Previn shave off her beard.
Recorded in London,but by Judy Nylon and
Pat Palladin who're from New York,but don't
hold it against 'em. Worth Gettin'.

Weymouth guitarist wants bassist/
drummer/vocals etc;Tony on 71397,
early July.

Drummer and lead guitar wanted by
Simon-300 0890

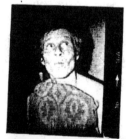

Pics By Eddie Duggan
Except Queen Pic (Not The Group!)by Royal Crawler.

10

JOHNNY MOPED
VOCALS
+ THINGS.
SLIMEY TOAD
GUITAR.
FRED BURK
BASS.
DAVE BURK
DRUMS.

"National Rockstar said we were the Monty Python of Punk,y'know,I just coll-apsed when I read that,people expect me to tell jokes or somethin',...I mean course I'll react when the shout out,just as long as they know we are playing good stuff, which most of 'em don't."

By their own words, that is the main thing that gets the Mopeds back up. No Heavy Politics.No Shafts of Wisdom. Just so long as they can 'play the next gig', and carry on backing Johnny.

ST:"I mean I've played with hundreds of singers,even as Toad of Toad Hall in a Yorkshire theatre, but when I heard him sing I knew I had to play in his band,really"

The rest of the band are all of the same opinion,and leave JM to most of the talking.(As it happens he was schtum for the first twenty minutes,and found walking around BTM's offices a better crack than rabbitin' to us)

It's common knowledge that the group that the group are sort of a brother to The Damned, DB:"We'd sit in my bedroom in Addiscombe,the Captain too,and just jam this 'orrible avante-garde jazz stuff and see what sounded good on the tape afterward, it was when the Damned were formed we decided to get this up."

JM:"It took me ages to adjust to this new scene,like,sleepless nights or waking up like a bear with a sore 'ead. I mean I'd see people like Rotten and know that I'd have to mould my voice 'round to that style,cos I aint always sung like this.....'cept maybe Hard Lovin' Man. I try to put so much into it,but all we seem to get is a label for being a novelty act. Once to keep the audience happy I'd give 'em this..I dunno.. ecology preservation talk,an' the next concert all I got was 'tell us about whales Johnny', so I said 'd'you mean the Taffy place or what?'."

Tell us about y'songs Johnny.

"I just love that fast,hard formula,and although I try to be different I could never move away from that.The lyrics I like to use to give more balls to the hook like in No One,but I don't think people know how much go into 'em"

But it's not like,say with Clash, that the lyrics an' rock can stand separate an' still get appreciated, y'need both to see how good the song can be,ennit?

JM:"No I don't think so at all,I think you're disillusioned. Y'see a song like 'Incendiary Device' is fairly personal against women, most of my songs are about boilers." Got that NME.

'Walkin' down the road with my Incendiary Device/Lookin' for a lady blow her up with gelegnite/Stick it in her lughole,watch it blow her head apart/Stick it in her lughole,stick it in her other parts./(Incendiary Device)

How far can you get today bein' so anti woman?

JM: "No we're not anti woman at all.....jus' the battleaxes not the attractive ones." Oh.

V.D. Boiler is contagious/V.D. Boiler is outrageous/(VD Boiler)

"Y'see I've been fucked up before,plenty of times,me mother once hated this woman I was knockin' about with who was 43,and had done a spell in a mental home,things like that.

11

PANIC BUTTON!

"But I'm not a hater or nothing,I need women around me to write songs about."
    What annoys <u>you</u> then.
"The value and reliance of money,probably cos I only get about nineteen quid a week,"
(thats seven more than I do ole son)-"an' I'd like to see somebody in power pull their
finger out in power,cos words don't change nothing, but mainly money I reckon, mind
you I have a job handlin' me dole money at the moment."
    ST:"I hate the big boys who don't care about kids, Eric Burdon an' Chas Chandler
made me feel like this, the really stitched me up, they're horrible.."
    JM:"They're animals.." Collapse of punk party.
  So what about New Wave?(64 dollars)

Johnny with Suney.

ST:" Well,obviously its got to be aimed at
   makin' kids more aware,that Mark P. bit,
   the truth,was what its about I really
   wanna write a song after readin' that, y'
   see Johnny can't see it tho' thats what it
   done to him,the system."
FB:(Who apart from havin' bin a telephone
   kiosk thug,has been a Jehovahs Witness,
   straight up)"As far as I can see it's all
   down to money,a commercial thing,all over"
   So how does SG explain itself?
FB:"No,the managers,the bizniss,it's all down
   to money tho' ennit? Although I agree
   that without New Wave we wouldn't have
   got a chance to make a record, I don't
   go along with the politics of it all"
   But surely the fact you've made a
   record is the politics!
FB:"But the bizniss put us on record"
   Goin' round 'n' round.
JM:"I'm just so glad that kids don't have t'
   be pissed off with 'acid' or 'progressive'
   rock any more..it's alive again,an' music
   is the best way to express,the only way
   as far as I'm concerned,feelings. An' 77
   kids are aggresive,an' they are angry,its
   such a release."

Despite the bands apparent disinterest in social lyrics,Johnny quoted these words to
'Panic Button'
          'All you tomcats haven't got any bread/Smashing up the suburbs cos you
          aint bein' fed/Bettin' on the horses cos y'need to pay the rent/Leapin'
          over barriers,fag machines get bent/Tension and Unrest Panic Button has
          bin pressed/Stabbed my teacher when I was young/Stole mothers money for
          my fruit gums/Never learnt much always on a run/Whats wrong now? Well
          I'm always gettin' drunk/I feel left out,always called a punk/Not gonna
          work/Gonna have some fun/Maybe cause a riot/I'm gonna hit and run/
          Tension and Unrest Panic Button has been pressed.'
JM:"We've got this deal with Chiswick (1st single No One/Incendiary Device) but at the
   moment its pretty vague."
ST:"The contracts forever being drawn up,y'know? They're talkin' of a second LP,an'
   the first aint together yet! Still we're on the Roxy album when that comes out."
DB:"Yeah its funny,groups keep comin' up who're on it too, and sayin' 'what percent-
   age you lot on?'"
Who do you like today?
JM:"The Damned and the Pistols are like cliches now,but they were there at the begin-
   ning" (cont'd)

MORE MOPED

JM: "Yeah they're so great. X-Ray Specs are bloody great. The Monitors. But in the past I aint really been inflenced by no one, not that I know in anycase. Today tho' I'm influenced by so many punk singers. Funilly enough I was in a cafe in Cambden with some of the Damned and two of the Clash come in., but like me they didn't have a lot to say for 'emself."
    Now theres one to bounce around.

ST; "If people come up to us, we'd never talk politics. We're just into gettin' off"? So what do you wanna do for yourself an' yer audience?

JM: "Just as long as we can keep playin's enough for me, but I want people to know th hard side of the band, an..I just...I just wanna ripple through 'em like a pack of steel balls"

So thats it then. A great band to see, (get the live tape if ya can), a really good night out. The 'boilers' bit seemed a bit strange to say the least, (beware low kicking Julie Burchills), and if you see the band at the bar don't ask 'em how they see the flames over London, and especially I wouldn't recommend asking 'em to tell you a joke, cos like they say, 'We're not that sort of a band."

                                                            Danny Baker.

FRED BUCK + JOHNNY.   MOPED PICS
                       13 BY MICHEAL CLIFFORD.

A STEP-FORWARD Record

Released 3rd. June

Singles

THE CORTINAS

FASCIST DICTATOR   TELEVISION FAMILIES

CHELSEA   RIGHT TO WORK   THE LONER

Don't Forget!

THE CORTINAS

ALSO AVAILABLE BY POST FROM:

A STEP FORWARD RECORDS
27 Dryden Chambers,
119 Oxford Street,
London W.1.

PRICE 70p (INCLUD P+P)
MAKE CHEQUES AND
POSTAL ORDERS OUT TO FAULTY PRODUCTS.

CHELSEA

ERICA'S HANG-UP: THE BUZZCOCKS.

AND WE'RE GLAD SHE'S BACK!

IN THE ROXY DRESSING ROOM.

From the PREFECTS;a big fuck off to
the kid what nicked our bass+to the
girl what split our bassists head
open with a pint mug.

L→R: PETE SHELLEY · JOHN MAHER · STEVE DIGGLE · GARTH
LEAD VOCALS, GUITAR.   DRUMS.   GUITAR, VOCALS.   BASS.

Sex Pistols' God Save The Queen.
It won't be on the new album and it may not be
out at all for very long.
So get it while you can.
Sex Pistols' God Save The Queen.
Available only as a single from Saturday May 28th
at shops with the sign.

Virgin Records VS181

SNIFFIN' GLUE

AND OTHER SELF-DEFENCE HABITS...
JULY '77

STUFF YOUR CHEAP COMENTS.........CAUSE WE KNOW WHAT WE FEEL...

SO TELL US.....
WHAT D'YA THINK

ISSUE NUMBER 11

THESE 'LL GET UP YER NOSE

Patti Smith Group
'RADIO ETHIOPIA'
SPARTY 1001

'Rock and Roll Heart'
LOU REED
ARTY 142

The Hollywood Stars
'All the kids on the street'
ARISTA 103

SG11

...when the two ones clash...

SG11.
     The whole point of this issue is cos the contemporary attitude (look it up)
is that the entire new wave is just shouting for the sake of it. So we said to
the people around,alright,number elevens yours,we wont touch what ya do,and
heres your chance to state the case.All the ones that got to us on time,(hey Tony)
are here,and what you make of it if you let us know will go into 12.
     Its not to say we like or go along with any of this,(I'll take one Clash
for any ten Radio Ethiopia's,),but this is exactly what we got back.

                    A LETTER
     At the Vortex last night(4/7) threw bouncers beat up and threw out a friend
of mine for no other reason than he was having a good time and jumping about.
     THE BOUNCERS:
'Lined up in front of the stage during the Heartbreakers(not Buzzcocks)-unnecessary
this would be unheard of at the Marquee-and caused a great crush at the front.
THEY were continually intimidating the kids,verbal abuse,blowing smoke into faces,
etc.,
AFTER managing to get my friend back in the club after the first attack,on the
second I began a long row with one bouncer,during which I told him if he wanted to .
do the strong arm heavy bit he should be in the NF heavy brigade.He told me he
already was and only saw his job tonight as to beat up'unruly' kids.
     I need hardly say that both the manager and Track Records people were most
disinterested.
     I would like to urge all groups to look carefully at any clubs 'security'
before submitting new wave fans to this. Love XXX.

     This letter was given to Mark after the first Vortex new wave gig,and Mark
says that its a wierd tactic that no bouncers were lined up during the Buzzcocks do.
I'd just say that its a mistake to consider all NF members a drooling twenty stone
thugs. Mostly they're our mums and dads.

                    SUCH INARTICULATE JOURNALISM
          Has anyone seen that 'punk' article in,wait for this,Harpers and Queen.
Its a real snob 'oh lets play working class' shallow pig shit 'we've examined it
for a week and understand it all deahs' bunch of crap. It says things like'fanzines
can say fuck but little else', and we apparently are terrified of sounding 'inter
leckshul'(sic). But my dears the first thing they taught us at private school was
if one is going to try to communicate with these people (who by the way still eat
with their fingers) one must forget all ones degrees and make one sound as if one
was dragged up,and feels positivly sickened by magazines that say 'let them eat
fish and dripping' between ads for Cartiers. So fucking Harpers and fucking Queen
fucking ask any fucking East end fucking guttersnipe to in future fucking speak
properly like fucking you and be prepared to get your stole soiled. (BY the way
Clash are terribly naive..so now ya know)
     The sickest thing is the Zandra Rhodes 'punk chic' look which now our privil-
aged cousins are able to buy. LET THEM KNOW.

               SNIFFIN GLUE:DANNY BAKER
                    HARRY T MURLOWSKI
SPECIAL SG11 contributors ; MARK P/Sandy Robertson/Steve(Rough Trade/Savage Pencil/
Mick Jones/Robin Crocker/J.Gorton/Jon Savage/Erica Echenberg/Chelsea

          SPECIAL MESSAGE FOR EDDIE D./WE LOST YOUR BIT AT THE CRUCIAL TIME/DONT DO
YA. NUT/IT'LL GET IN THE NEXT/
                              27 Dryden Chambers,119 Oxford Street
                                             London W1

THERE IS NO 'NEW WAVE'
It's only in the minds of
the music press/record companies.
Yeah,we are all to blame.
THERE IS STILL ENERGY & COMMITMENT
TAKE IT/USE IT/GIVE IT BACK.
Look around/outside · think/DO

FIGHT - you will have to.
BEFORE IT'S TOO LATE - & we
become Hitler Germany.or Stalin Russ
Time's running out for us/everyone.
DON'T GIVE UP WITHIN A YEAR. (YET?)
No eezi-wrap solutions.Sorry
messageendsmessageends

FUTURE'S LOOKING PRETTY BLEAK

HIGH-RISK FACTOR AT OPTIMUM

J.S.
30/6

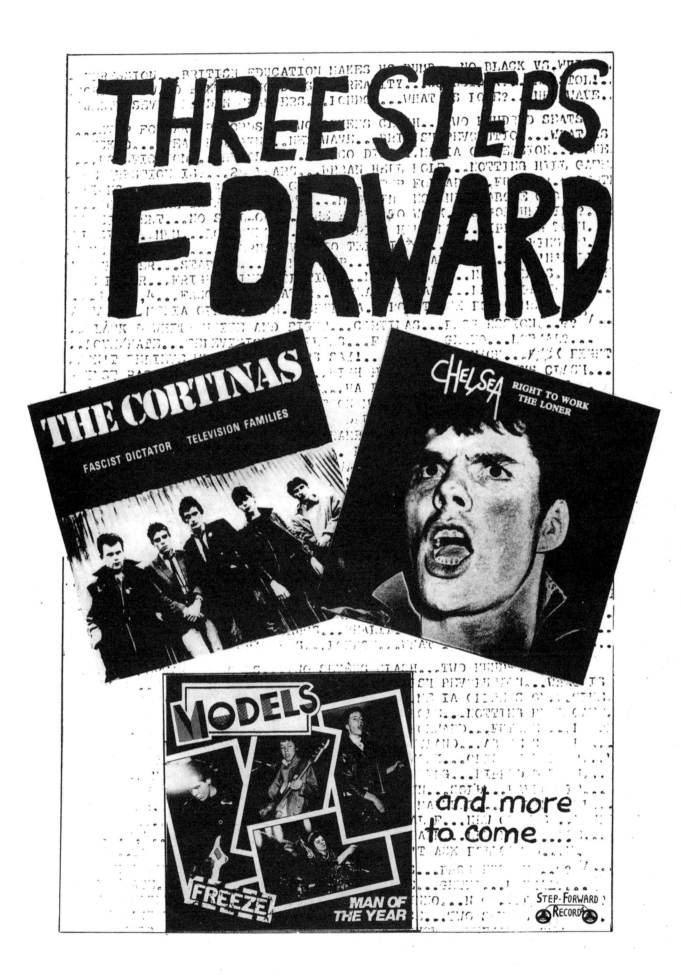

QUESTION: THE SCENE?

THE WORLD IS YOURS AS WELL AS OURS,BUT IN THE LAST ANALYSIS,IT IS YOURS.YOU YOUNG PEOPLE;
FULL OF VIGOUR AND VITALITY,ARE IN THE BLOOM OF LIFE,LIKE THE SUN AT EIGHT OR NINE IN THE
MORNING.OUR HOPE IS PLACED ON YOU.

MAO TSE TUNG

O.K.You might be wondering what the fuck
Chairman Mao is doing in Sniffin'Glue.Well,
I was asked to write what I felt about the
scene.And Chairman Mao is saying what the
young should be doing.O.K.stick safety pins
in yer nose,i don't care if you stick them
up your arse.What I do care about is,EVERY-
ONE OF YOU MOTHERFUCKERS SHOULD BE A POTEN-
TIAL H-BOMB,NOT A FUCKING CLOTHES HANGER.
You're the victims of yourself.Alot of you
believe what you read about yourselves in
papers like the Sun,Daily Mirror and the so-
called left wing rags like the Guardian.Are
you that apathetic that you don't understand
the lyrics of'Anarchy','Remote Control'.

You shout about being the Blank Generation,
shout about getting beaten up by Teds.But
you don't shout about being exploited,by
record companies,fashion houses,newspapers
or anything that will determine your future
existance.You don't want to end up like the
Hippies do you?

Fight for the right to maintain
your individuality,fight for the right to be
able to walk down a street unmolested by the
authority that <u>was</u> designed to protect us
that has turned into the moron machine you
all know could devour us all.The war has
been started by <u>them</u>,they have prevented the
people from hearing the Pistols,they are now
trying to prevent it from appearing in the
charts altho it has outsold all other
records in the county,but what are you doing,
fuck all.

IF YOU WANNA FIGHT <u>UNITE</u> FIGHT
BACK AT THE LIES,don't take it like every
other minority group,show them and yourselves
that you do mean what you say,suprise yerself
Punk,hit back stop posing.

Steve at Rough Trade.

TWO
DIFFERENT
VIEWS

ROCK N' ROLL GLOO

THE SCENE?

ER WELL I HMM..

ER - SHIT...

IT'S ER FUCKIN' WEIRD!

NO I MEAN ER... HEE HEE!

AH FUCK IT!

GLOO?

Dear Readers,
Seriously tho - the whole Kaboodle
of New Wave is pretty fab my
vinyl habit is growing as I hope
you all are. Long live the revolution.

© 1977 SAVAGE PENCIL
WITH RESPECT TO
R. CRUMB MY HERO

Savage Pencil

A COMMUNIQUE FROM CLASH CITY

BIRMINGHAM: Strummer announcemant, "We have just been told that Remote Control is to be our next single."

PLYMOUTH: (Worse than the Armada), Jones and Crocker chased by local police for loitering disguised as punks. When eventually apprehended and challenged they reply, "The Spaniards are coming."

BRISTOL: Opposite Colston Hall the Lord Mayor leaves function, entering his Rolls Royce, he is greeted by Strummer and Crocker, "Only punks wear chains"........"Mayor of punk." A nearby police officer trots over, "Show a little respect boys" he pleads.

AMSTERDAM: Three funk bands, one country and western singer and The Clash appear at media party. The reaction of the Bols Advocaat set is mainly one of hysterical laughter.

SWINDON: Heir to furniture fortune is assisted into outdoor pool to see if he sinks, he is thereafter referred to as "Trout."

ST. ALBANS POLICE STATION: Post gig shock! Strummer and Nicky confess under interrogation to wilful theft of eleven Holiday Inn pillows.

CHELMSFORD: Jones storms out of dressing room as local councillor is ushered in. Strummer and Paul promptly hurl abuse and bottle tops at the politician who sanctioned the show.

DUNSTABLE: Drunk, Paul and Crocker horrify party-goers by "canning" an innocent Prefect. A case of mistaken I.D.

MARBLE ARCH: St. John's Ambulance in attendance as Clash video is shown at Virgin record shop.

DON'T LET THE SUNDAY PAPERS TELL YOU HOW TO BEHAVE OR IT'LL ALL BE OVER BY CHRISTMAS.   SPRAY YOUR OWN GRAFFITI.

MICK JONES
ROBIN CROCKER

'These people are the wreckers of civilisation'

MUSIC FROM THE DEATH FACTORY

When these suave good lookers set up their own group after years of working the club circuits, a whole new experience hit the music scene. For here at last were personalities and talents capable of entertaining any audience with noticeable ease and success. Thats just one of the qualities that makes them stars.

Genesis P-Orridge Bass guitar, vocals
Cosey Fanni Tutti Lead guitar
Chris Carter Keyboards
Peter Christopherson Tapes and machines

THROBBING GRISTLE L.P.

The Second Annual Report
of
Throbbing Gristle.   IR0002

Recordings made in the year ending 20th August 77.

Manufactured and Distributed by
Industrial Records, 10 Martello Street, London E.8   £5

AVAILABLE FROM all GOOD record shops from:-
September 1st 1977. OR if they say that they
haven't got it, order it direct by mail from
industrial Records at thee above address or
get your shop to phone up **01-254-9178** and er
order some for you and your friends. Places
wishing to book THROBBING GRISTLE to play it
live also contact Industrial Records,London.

suspected foul play, but it transpired that she had tried to kill herself with an axe and tried to stab herself with a knife. Both of these injuries were trivial and had not caused her death. She had finally resorted to gassing herself and death was ultimately due to carbon monoxide poisoning which was revealed by a high level of carboxyhaemoglobin in her blood.

ERICA'S HANG-UP No. 4

DEDICATED TO TUPPENCE (WHAT A SCHNITZ)

3 MINUTE SERVICE

PHOTOS

"Photo..."

FACE OF THE ASSASIN

ART/RAT

HAPPY ANNIVERSARY DAMNED • WATCH IT BANANAS!

SPEED LONDON PRESS...

AND WE DON'T CARE

See I consider meself a great bloke,
(anyone who considers themselves to be
'an ordinary type of geyser' I wouldn't
wanna know; Joe Rank is a wanker),and for
a while I got confused,I was into that
sort of blind hate/passion bit and burn
down the manor that punk newcomers can find
on page one of their How its Done;New Wave
Manual.

So alright,not so much a movement, more
a bleedin' good club is how it stands.
I'm nineteen and white and in London don't
nobody tell me thats not as good as it gets,
but only if its coupled with thinking, and
I'm working nights on that. So when I hear
'shitty life,council estates,on the dole'
anguish, I wanna say,no mate, thats a fash
ion,that type of opression is mainly en-
forced by personal laziness, and if you aint
got it in ya to get positive and use people
rather than harmless abusing em then you
deserve to stay static. Dont wait for the
next Clash album to find out what your att-
itudes are,and I aint such a prat to go on
about my 'Bermondsey hell hole'when I only
see mine maybe twice a week, but it seems to
me thats all some kids wanna know.
      Its like,alright,the estates are dismal
but anyone who's got any spark is alive enough to get active and out, jack that job and
take those chances. Why are kids working away
their youth because they might be secure
when they're forty? What would you rather have?
Be middle aged and look at your semi detatched
and say 'well here I am', or be able to say
when I was young nobody told me, I did what I
wanted,when I wanted. Ya gotta use the right
years. Apprenticeships aint no fun. You don't
call nobody 'sir'.
      Look around at the unfortunates. The
cruds that are fodder for the council Estates '87. Y'know that sort of Lord John/
Ravels/Normal sort of bloke('ere Dave d'ya
see Iove thy Neighbour last night,really
funny it was) that type of shirt outside of
blazer with the typist on his arm going to
see the film hes been waiting for weeks to
come local,harmless. I couldn't give tuppence
for his mob,they were stillborn,their only
ambition is to be forty,and of course anyone
not like them is either immature, or the
dreaded queer. "huh huh,when them Sex Pistols
can fill the Earls Court and make an album
like Hotel California let me know,I mean
they can't even play" Yeah sure,crud,and
they're Russians,and they think Hitler was
OK,and Bill Grundy is really the press
officer. Mind you he's right about they can't
play.

His father's seen to that.

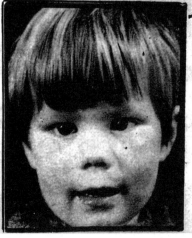

This young
chappie
plays in
a rock band!
He lives in
Bristol,
and likes
hitting
things

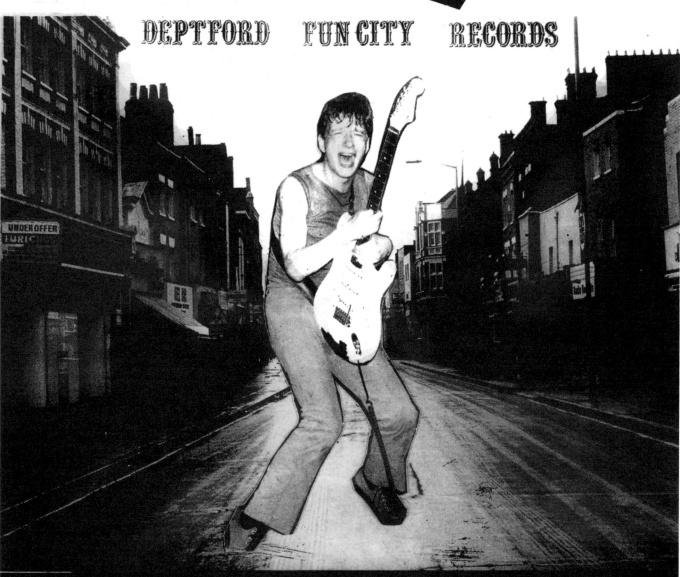

SQUEEZE

DEPTFORD FUN CITY RECORDS

FIRST RELEASE

PACKET of THREE

So dont waste your time on cardigan
youth,they dont mean,or want to be,any-
thing, close your eyes and that lot will go
away.

However sometimes, some idiot gets you
so wild you've got to have a dig. This was
Beat(Songwriting and Recording) review of the
Clash album.

'Sorry boys this is a music magazine,
teach yourself infantile brain damage
is ten floors down..out the window'
Can you imagine the type of bank clerk
who wrote that,all alone and shit scared in his musical South Africa. Beat on the
Brat? More like a Prat on the Beat. If Clash
had nothing to do with Beat why did silly
knackers feel need to 'write'about it? Cos
his musical'knowledge' dont mean shit, ya can
know every note and how to play 'em on the
most obscure import outtake snob rock album
you can name but all you are is a filing cab-
inet afraid to go against 'people who know'.
I bet this bloke is one of them who checks to
see what session men and producer(s) an lp
has before he likes it,and if a 'respected'
group gets oh TOTP he says 'oh they sent it
all up'.

D'you know something mister?
Fuck you.

See,thats why I love new wave. Its that
certain mob of nutcases who give the ol'
fingeroo to the twats,its being involved
with the blue touch paper of the eighties,
knowing your hundred percent right,saying
this is it and no cunt stops me. Except if
your in a band of course,then the opression
is real and not imaginary. If the new wave
has any balls,the bands could forget all that
A hates B and B wont appear with C,and C hates
A's bassist...and remember some of the propo-
ganda. When ATV played the Marquee some 'punks'
saw fit to throw their(plastic albeit) pint
mugs at Mark P and call out 'wanker' etc in
the breaks. Next morning ya hear about the
blokes beating the Pistols and wonder what
those glass throwers get off on.

Its all money and ego right? Fair enough
let ye cast the first stone and all that, but
most of the time these mouths that speak
'the truth' are just a bunch of unmarried marr-
aige councellors if ya see what I mean. Are
you with us brothers? No we're with the Woolwich.

Another thing thats gone a bit flat is the
drive from the audiences which gave up new bands, people are just coming to concerts
for the night again. We've got STARS,stars,and audiences again,and crowds remain
subserviant and just nudge their mates when they see a FACE at the bar. I mean Rotten
Strummer,etc are just you and you and you,and its not their fault or nothing,but they
are finding themselves being held,if not in awe,a sort of respectful hate, by people
who're gonna be the first to say 'oh hes big headed and aloof now! Its like when
Robert Plant was down the Roxy once,the crowd dared not venture within His presence

GET FUNKED

for fear of rebuke,but like if he was John Smiff or something and you walked over and he told you to piss off, I mean a cunt is a cunt whether he earns two billion or tuppence ha'penny,but don't take yourself for less than mortal cos if you don't meet and talk with the people who you consider 'leaders',you'll always be prepared to take the backseat and your ideas are always gonna be orders from above. We're all fucked more or less,the difference is whether you lay back and accept it cos you dont want

We as a band are going in one direction.We believe in the right of the individual to choose for himself what he wants to do,and to help others acheive the same.Chelsea as a group,are a group because everyone writes and contributes to the end product and believes in what they are doing. Totally. We are not fashionable,we dont follow trends, and by signing with an independent label,we'll continue to pursue our own direction.

We dont disagree with the Ted image,but can't understand their recent violence,we fail to see why kids aren't united, and opposing the discredited and corrupt system we live under. For the first time,govt bisiness men,etc,are worried by the emergence of a youth movement that is openly critical of them and not afraid of the risks involved.These people are on our blacklists.OK. We are sickened by the irresponsibility of the media,not only with their general'coverage' but with the blown up headlines....'

GENE OCTOBER
CAREY FORTUNE HENRY DAZE
JAMES STEVENSON

.......CHELSEA.......

no trouble. All the meek are gonna inherit is a nuclear family. It seems to me that,like,at school it was the sap who read the book while'the men' fought the system from the back of the bog door or by not turning up, that concept still carries on but nobodies attempted to seperate fighting and avoiding. Alright so you were probably just as well off reading the graffiti as to have sailed with Vasco de Garma in the history room but that waste of time and lack of effort was what resulted in the slack minds of south london,and then acceptance of jobs that would make the new wave throw up. Why they give Shakespeare to'read and evaluate' I dont know,perhaps the Essential Lenny Bruce would've given the spark and by now the NF wouldn't have such a hold.

Same as I say there's the twenty year old forty year olds who should be forced to donate their youth energy to people who appreciate it,people who aint got no bottle 'cos what am I gonna be doin' in ten years', posers,losers,nutters and then the new wave.

Thats us,and behind that bog door are you thinkin' readin' or just havin' a wank?

Tell your little brother.

Danny Baker

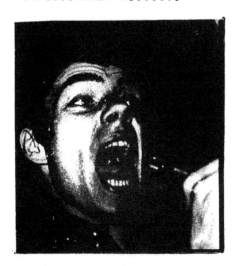

Punk or Hippie ?.....
Answers on a postcard
please.

ALL PICS ON THIS PAGE ARE BY GORTON IN NYC.

ALL THE WAY FROM New York IN TRUE PUNK STYLE .... THAT'S WHY THIS PAGE STINKS!

THIS IS THE FUN PAGE 'COS IT'S THE DAMNED

'O! NOTHING EARTHLY..'-Poe

THE SCENE/How I see it:Since the late 60's there has been a
generally stagnant and incestuous rock n roll industrial
complex,albeit with a few outposts of creativity,(we all
know who they were,no need for lists of names). Inbreeding
has resulted in musico/genetic debility and instability.
BUT:In the last couple of years,in New York/London partic-
-ularly,there has been a sudden cell regeneration,via fresh
input. HOWEVER:This does not represent an entirely unified
movement,which in some ways is good because,a)variety is the
spice of life,and b)different strokes for different folks is
a fair maxim. IN NEW YORK:Musicianship is mostly of a higher
standard,group members older and more affluent,and therefore
less interested in 'social protest' than in art/music. They
create these in much more varied formats/patterns than in
LONDON:Where,due to **socio/economic** conditions,the music is
younger,badly played(mostly),and overtly political. A lot
of English kids are scornful of the Americans' artiness,which
they see as student dilettantism,unconnected with real life.
However,this is where they miss the point.Groups like the
Clash are operating on a straightforward political level,which
is a lower strata of thought,an elaboration of the 'who ate my
porridge' argument. They represent something which those in
power have seen before,and can be easily assimilated,controlled,
dealt with and even incorporated into existing structures.(There's
always a place for a token revolutionary). People like Patti Smith
Group,Television,etc,are infinitely more threatening to the
current social orders,because they turn their backs on them to
present symbolist visions of ecstasy,the desire to become God.
This is a subtler magic,and one that is incomprehensible to
those in control of purely physical realities.

If Clash win their struggle,all they'll have is a bigger
slice of cake.

If Television/Smith Group win theirs,they'll be beyond all
that,heading for the stars.

I know which idea excites ME more.

recommended reading:Anything by Colin Wilson,especially 'The
Outsider' and 'Introduction to the New Existentialism'.

SANDY ROBERTSON/WHITE STUFF.

---

quotable quotes

patti smith in '73 on why she doesn't read contemporary female writers:
"Most women writers today are like the new black poets,they can't get out
of what they are."

jonathan richman in '75:"We're all full of beauty just waiting
to explode. It's always springtime."

"Get out"

RED STUFF

RELEASED ON

THE ELECTRIC CHAIRS

STUCK ON YOU   THE LAST TIME   PARANOIA PARADISE   E.P.

RICHMAN + LOVERS ARE BACK!

ROCK'N'ROLL WITH THE MODERN LOVERS
(Beserkley album)

Tracks: The Sweeping Wind(Kwa Ti Feng)/Ice
Cream Man/Rockin'Rockin'Leprechauns/Summer
Morning/Afternoon/Fly Into the Mystery/South
American Folk Song/Roller Coaster By the Sea/
Dodge Veg-O-Matic/Egyptian Reggae/Coomyah/The
Wheels On the Bus/Angels Watching Over Me.

Jonathan Richman-lead vocals,guitar.
Leroy Radcliffe-guitar.
"Curly"Keranen+accoustic bass.
D.Sharpe-percussion.

Thank god for music like
this.Music that doesn't mean anything but fun!
Yes,Jonathan is the only guy who can get me
into this mood.His music's from the country,
from morning walks through the fields...my
god,this is silly.Why beat about the bush.This
is right at the other end of the credability
scale from the Clash.Not one slice of concrete
on this album.It's so soft and nice that I
actually feel happy listening to it,yer-happy
remember what it's all about.When you was a
kid you used to play in the park and when you
went down to the seaside you used to sit in
the sand and wish that yer holiday would never
end.When your mum asked you to go home you'd
bawl and scream-"I don't wanna go home,mummy".
Yeah,go back to the sea-
side with the Modern Lovers.Go back to 1966
when all you cared about was yer holidays(I
can remember,that's all I cared about).
It's a crime that this
guy is just a'cult-figure'.Every time he brings
out an album it's time to say,rock'n'roll is
still alive.You know,rock'n'roll American
Graffiti style before Dylan and all the other
deep thinkers got hold of it.Christ,this LP
sounds like rock'n'roll before even Chuck
Berry got hold of it.Yeah,it's very primitive
medievil even!

The album is dominated by a
folky accoustic guitar sound.The drumming is
very sparce and the recording sounds like
the early Sun records.Best tracks are the
trad.Chinese folk song-'Sweeping Wind','Ice
Cream Man','Afternoon','South American Folk
Song','Roller Coaster By the Sea'...hold on
they're all fuckin'great.It's impossible to
play just one track,once it's on the player
it stays on.
You know,I reckon what the
Lovers are doing is so advanced that even
they don't know what they're doing.It's not
as if Richman has been boppin'like this all
through his career.I mean,the first album
was very dooming(or dark,mysterious even).
He seems to have gone back in time,perhaps
he's gone round the bend.He might think he's
in the '50's,and the other Lovers are playing
along with the game.With all this advanced
technology in rock music these days,even
the electric guitar misaprehension(?)(You
know,"if it's dearer it must be better").
Bollocks to that,it's harder and more interesting to make the use of cheaper stuff.
I'd advise any follower of any
music to listen to Richman.Listen good and
hard'cause it'll probably do you a lot of
good.In this day an'age we need some fun,
yes fun...running in the fields,playing
foota'in the playground,all that crap.I
could go on forever about it but I don't
need to...just listen to this...please.
Don't be hip and say that it's corny and
childidh,don't miss out...'cause when you
start missing and ignoring everything that
ain't hard-punk you miss the point of the
new-wave completely.
To me,the new-wave means free-
domm,don't restrict yerself.Just fall in
love with the Modern Lovers!
Mark P.

YEAH,
THE USUAL
PICS OF
RICHMAN.
STILL,
WHO
REALLY
CARES?

≋ Rail Express Parcels

British Railways Board   Consignment Note

Goods for conveyance by Red Star Parcel Service.

Receive and convey by the passenger trains nominated below from ....
station the undermentioned goods subject to the Board's General Conditions of Carriage at :

IMPORTANT NOTICE TO SENDER

Label parcels to show consignee's name and destination station only. Show name of firm or individual but not both. Do not show consignee's postal address.

Advise your customer quickly, and make sure he knows the name the label.

Enter each package weight separately.

Red Star

Board's ...

Owner's risk.

Board's risk, as damageable goods not properly protected by packing

SIGN ALONGSIDE CONDITION THAT IS REQUIRED AND INSERT DATE.

The Board will use their best endeavours to carry the goods on the trains shown below but whether or not they do so the goods will be conveyed subject to the Board's General Conditions of Carriage whereby the Board limit their liability for loss, damage, delay, etc. at the rate of £100 per tonne and subject to a minimum limit of £10 per consignment.

§IF DECLARED WEIGHT IS LESS NOT KILOGRAMS TICK HERE

Sender's name and full address

For official use

Rly. Pro. No. X   Received by

Time

M

N/L

Consignee	Destination station	Train Time	Description Pkgs, contents and marks	No.of Pkgs.	§ Wt. of each pkg. kilograms	Pkgs.	Weight	Rate Code	Charges £	Tfc. Code	Code	Extra Charges Amount
						B B	C	D	E	F	(3) C	D	N/L
						B B	C	D	E	F	(3) C	D	N/L
						B B	C	D	E	F	(3) C	D	N/L
						B B	C	D	E	F	(3) C	D	N/L
						B B	C	D	E	F	(3) C	D	N/L
						B B	C	D	E	F	(3) C	D	N/L
						B B	C	D	E	F	(3) C	D	N/L
						B B	C	D	E	F	(3) C	D	N/L
						B B	C	D	E	F	(3) C	D	N/L
						B B	C	D	E	F	(3) C	D	N/L
						B B	C	D	E	F	(3) C	D	N/L
						B B	C	D	E	F	(3) C	D	N/L

(Handwritten across form: "Bizarre Michael are obnoxious all out to lunch!")

PARAGRAPH

People say why don't you do more,get active. I say I am active to myself,and I gotta know a whole lot more about things before I show how naive I can be. Which is probably why most bits I do in Glue are he,him,bloke,geysers. Articles by men on women always get me as like those 'demonstrations' thru London against Veitnam or South Africa or whatever which the police say as long as no one gets offended and you all march orderly and smile and sing,you can do it. Cos like most blokes I know will swing on this side of the Stranglers lyrics for the same reasons that journalists like some new wave, and if women fight they dont need men for lawyers.Men'll only pass laws that in effect just get all the blokes in a room and then the boss'll say'Alright guys we gotta keep that womans vote here so in future if you piss on a woman you aint got the right no more to tell her up front. Do it but try not to let her know,OK?'. Which is why at election times the TV man always reminds our mums that his party gave 'em some screwy law for you gals,and makes it sound like a favour rather than a right. I dont pretend to know the hardship of women,which isn't to say I dont care or wanna listen,same as I don't know what on earth being black can get you(now a black woman IS REALLY scary), all I know is that I won't lick arse by saying the right words because of either fashion or economics. Most girls I know find the hard assed Lib movement,(maybe that should be TV's hard ass..etc)just as boring as men giving the old 'sisters unite' bit. Anyway I should imagine that if women do ever get that equality,it won't matter if I'd written a ten volume set and lectured all me life from a soapbox, we's all gonna get it in the balls lads! Sort of in the same way the government of us is run by people who have NO IDEA NO IDEA NO IDEA of what life in the flats is like. The other week the prime minister did a walk about round Rotherhithe,where I live. Now if someone talks to me about living in a castle or pissing away thousands its the same as talking to me of walking on the moon.Which is to say its just words ,I mean the only way I know the USA exists is cos they told me in school and its forever on the box,I know it is there but have no concept of commuting back and forth for fun like some people do. So if the PM walks amongst the twenty-five stories and that,he's just reading the brochure. All he sees are doors and windows,windows,doors and happy faces waving the union jack,cos they dont want the neighbours,(in this case Jim Callaghan),to see they haven't got on in life. I mean they polish the doorstep,paint the doors,get their hair done,and when he's gone say, 'Pompous bastard whats he know about living round here' And that little band of people with the banners being pushed about by the police are the 'nutcases' ending up in the meatwagon. A disgrace to the disgrace. I mean how many times does the visiting VIP, go over to the crowd and say'I'd like to talk with you..' nah,he just averts his gaze to the red white and blue and exchanges nothings with the silly mayor. Everyone the rich have ever known have always been people with trusts or just plain money,so how could they know a weekly wage as anything more than as what 'some people have to live on'. Why should being born on that side give you seventy years of menial labour. Ignorance is bliss was obviously thought up by someone very clever,probably titled. No,ignorance is the goverments national sedative.
We gotta let them know,LET THEM KNOW.
IF i'm wrong or whatever,please somebody tell me.

Danny Baker

New school not needed

...s for a new three-form ...ablished

weekend.
Lady Marsha wore a dramatic crinoline dress made from 30 yards of ivory wild silk, with a lace train embroidered with seed pearls. She had a family necklace of sapphires and diamonds and carried a prayer book.
Her dress was spec-

New York Dolls

Album 6641 631

Before anyone discovered New Wave Rock,
The Dolls were inventing it.

SNIFFIN' GLUE
-ANNIVERSARY-

AND OTHER ROCK 'N' ROLL HABITS.....
FOR AROUND AUG/SEPT '77

·12·

ALTERNATIVE T.V'S 'LOVE LIES LIMP' - INSIDE. SG'S PROFIT BLOWING TEASER COZ WE'RE THE BEST.

PIC. ERICA ECHENBURG.

"HEY LITTLE RICH BOY TAKE A GOOD LOOK AT ME"

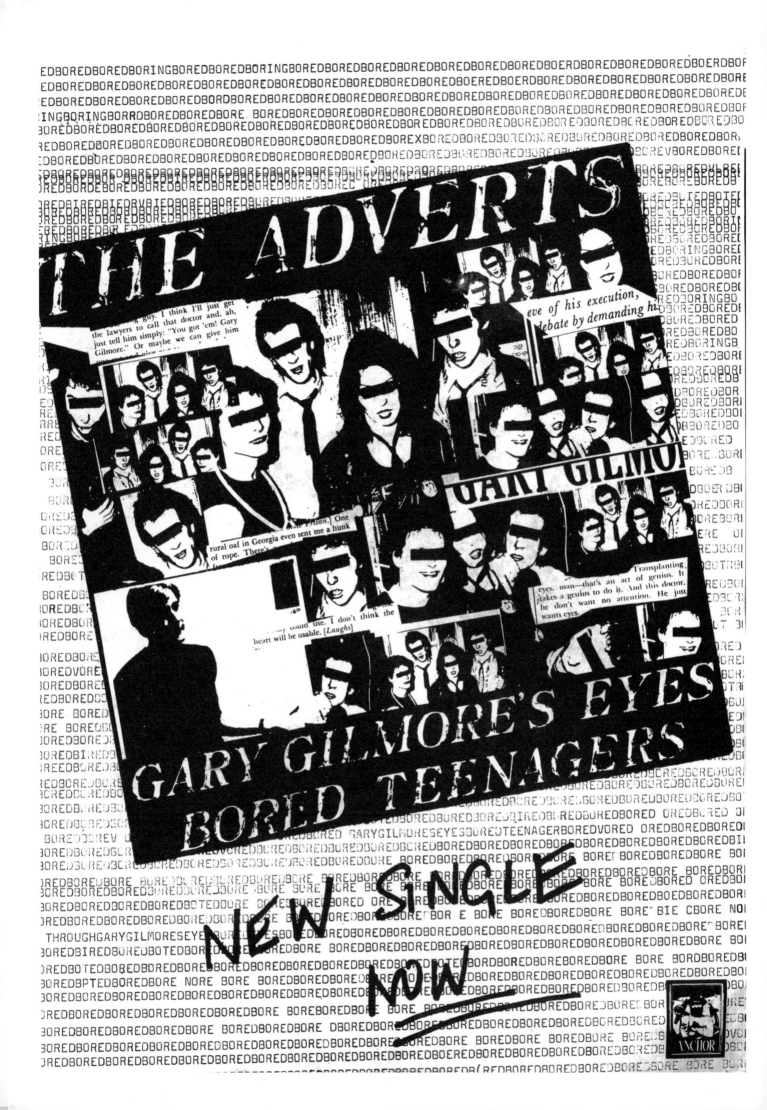

SG 12
ANNIVERSARY ISH.

PIC:HARRY.T.MURLOWSKI

Issue 12. (Or fifteen if ya count 3½,7¼ and Sniffin'Snow).
We got a fair bit of response to eleven,(I liked the line somebody wrote,in answer to
Sandy Robertson's bit,about if Clash _lose_ their struggle then Patti Smith won't be able to
continue hers but unfortunatly we lost the actual letter along with a rake of others when
our offices were turned over one night last week)a lot though were re runs of whats alread
bin said and its alright to know theres a lot going the same way.

There should be a single free in this issue,(aint sure at time of typing),which is
of Marks band. Pouring back the profits. God,we're so moral.

Sniffin Glue:Danny Baker/Mark P (he aint sure if he's comin' or goin')/Harry Murlowski. thanks;angie/erica/suesie(though I aint sure why),and Tony whose initial escapes
concertoftheyeargoestoalternativetvfortheirdukepubgigseeitaintjustthespotsincognito.

ROUGH TRADE

Geoff,Richard and Steve,directors of the Rough Trade
Multi Million pound Conglomerate wish to announce that they
are now trading in the best reggae records that can be found
as well as the hardest core hard core glue stained sounds
of the new wave.

Anyoneeinterested in acquiring these records as a wholesale item,
as a mail order customer or from the shop itself.....

Please write or call at ROUGH TRADE,202,Kensington Park Road,
London,W.11.   phone 01-727-4312

Remember:This is the organisation that doesn't give a shit
about Joe Public.

ROUGH TRADE

ROUGH TRAD+

It's time to wake up and emerge from the cocoon. When the new-wave first took shape it drew strength, in the search for a solid identity, from the'everything that went before was shit' attitude. It bolstered the force of the music and brought the seventies to life. Rock'n'roll ain't just started and the new-wave _is_ the rock'n'roll of today. It's not the only influence, with bands like Clash and the Slits looking to reggae for much of their inspiration, but the Pistols, the Ramones and many more are power-packed seventies rock'n'roll bands.

As a D.J. I attempt to turn new-wave gigs into rock'n'roll experiences. The Heartbreakers are always a great band to work with, because Eddie Cochran is as fundamental to their outlook as are the Pistols. For the sake of us all, let's hope that their proposed gig with Snakin' Stevens proves to be a success.

Of course for many people into the new bands, Presley, Carl Perkins, the Beatles, Stones, Seeds, Who ..... were making their most vital sounds before musical awareness set in. But what's that matter. Iggy, MC5 and the New York Dolls have all found favour with people not there the first time around. It's all down to an appreciation of what they were saying and how they were saying it, in their own times. Music is a perfect medium for shoving two fingers up at the establishment. Once it becomes respectable it loses all its potency. That's what occurred during the seventies. All the aggression had faded and rock stars seemed more interested in becoming tax exiles or partying it up with royalty than looking after their fans who, after all had put them on the top.

What they needed was a firm boot up the arse. And that's what they got. No more farting about, just raw, honest rockin', brought back on the intimate level of the band and their audience. Back to the roots, expressed in a contemporary manner. Yes the music of today has a sound of its' own, but the underlying spirit is the same. Frustration and boredom. Unlike recent trends though this time its spewed out from deprivation, from low wages and long dole queues.

Make no mistake, this ain't the first new-wave, and if it's the last, then what's the point carrying on. But things have to move on. If they stand still they become extinct. Take Presley, known to most of us in his flash Las Vegas or all-American boy eras. But in the fifties he was an outrage, who offended the public morality and was looked upon as a corrupting influence. It's ironic that straight society and its' media that today slags off Johnny Rotten and mourns the death of Elivs, once considered Presley a social outcast. Short memories they've got!

It is sometimes this bigotry towards the sounds of the fifties and sixties that brings about strange reactions at new-wave gigs to the inclusion of such material. You don't have to have been there to enjoy it. We're all children of rock'n'roll. It's so exciting being involved with music right there and now, but rock'n'roll hasn't started in the seventies, neither, I hope, has it ended.

BARRY MYERS

Real Rock 'n' Roll is rebel Music
'f Rock 'n' Roll. Aint rebel Music
then it Aint Real Rock 'n' Roll.

Animal Justice

JOHN CALE

Side 1 **Memphis**
Chicken Shit
Side 2 **Hedda Gabbler**

IL003

Distribution:
Mail Order from
ILLEGAL PRODUCTS
17 Dryden Chambers,
119, Oxford St.
London, W1

£1-25 + 15p. postage

A BIT ON CHISWICK

Right,this bit isn't going to be a detailed history of CHISWICK and it ain't even up to date but I just thought that they deserved a thing in the mag seeing as,in the early days,they were the only guys who wanted to know about SG.

The first CHISWICK record came out in 1975 and it was:

THE COUNT BISHOPS-SPEEDBALL(EP SW1).

At the time the band were a 4 piece,Mike Spenser-vocals,harp,Paul Balbi-drums,Steve Lewins-bass,Johnny Guitar-guitar, & Zen-guitar.The were the best R&B band in the country and still are.This EP features 4 standards-'Route 66','I Aint Got You', 'Beautiful Delilah'and'Teenage Letter'.It was a great start.I remember going into Rock On in Soho Market and seeing the dopey little CHISWICK label.What's this?I asked and he told me it was his label.The geezer I asked was Roger Armstrong.He started Chiswick with Ted Carroll.They were on their way.

MIKE SPENSER IN STUDIO

PIC: MIKE BEAL.

VINCE TAYLOR-BRAND NEW CADILLAC(S2).

Yes,Rock'n'roll at it's best.Just don't ask questions why Chiswick released it. It was made in 1959 and it's one of the best couple of minutes of rock music i've ever heard in my life.B-side is a slower job - 'Pledging My Love'.The best was yet to come.

THE 101'ERS-KEYS TO YOUR HEART(S3).

Strummer before he was STRUMMER. By the time this had been released the 101'ers had split.'Keys'is,I reckon,the best pub-rock song ever recorded.The flip,'5 Star Rock'n' Roll Petrol',confirms that even if Joe didn't form a band called the Heartdrops,who were to become the Clash,he would still be there. Do you get what I mean?

GORILLAS PICS - MIKE BEAL.

THE GORILLAS-SHE'S MY GAL(S4).

After months of waiting the Gorillas were finally released on the world (apart from doing a single with Penny Farthing as the Hammersmith Gorillas).'She's My Gal'is a rousing foot-stomper just like the old Slade singles.This band were gonna be big.They had the power and the songs to make a great album.Live they were great, they filled a gap which had long been open, for a fun rock band for teenagers.'Why Wait 'Til Tomorrow'is on the flip.

THE COUNT BISHOPS-TRAIN,TRAIN/TAKING IT EASY (S5).

The Bishops without Spenser,I couldn't believe it.They just about pass without him.Both songs are good but the vocals are weak,very weak...CHISWICK were cruising.

ROCKY SHARPE & THE RAZORS(EP SW6).

Don't worry about this EP.It don't need any help from noone.The Razors were finished when this was released.The cover's cute(really!)and the music is soft and boppin'.Great for late night walks in the park,'Drip Drop','What's Your Name', 'So Hard To Laugh'and'That's My Desire'.

A RAZOR.

CHISWICK BIT CONTD

LITTLE BOB STORY

LITTLE BOB STORY(SW7)
French mini bloke and band.Monte
de wotsit rock'n'roll with a neat sound.At
the time this was released Little Bob was
everywhere.Playing every gig in sight.At
first he was great but I reckon that he's
played too much.This is good to remember him
by.'I'm Crying','Come On Home',I Need Money'
and'Baby Don't Cry'.Great titles...

JESSE HECTOR OF THE GORILLAS

PIC: H.T. MARLOWSKI

THE GORILLAS-GATECRASHER(S8)
It was funny when this was re-
leased.I was expecting more but I didn't
think was as stunning as'She's My Gal'.It
was still going in the right direction but
Jesse Hector flipped and they broke up.I
mean,it was a pity'cause this band were one
of the best.
What it was all about was a
fucking great star-Jesse.This guy was amazing,
turning head-over-heels on stage while still
playing his guitar!He would have murdered'em
at the Rainbow.Yeah,if only he could have
got that far.The story ends with them doin'
'Gorilla Got Me'.It seems ages ago,it was so
recent.   END OF PART ONE.

RADIO STARS-DIRTY PICTURES(S9).
This is the only Chiswick I
just don't want to talk about.I consider
this to be their dark ages.Pass...

THE RADIATORS FROM SPACE-TELEVISION SCREEN
(S10).
In SG9 Steve Mick(remember this
housewife/owner)said this single was a
moronice mess.Well,it ain't that bad infact
it's more than interesting as is:

SKREWDRIVER-YOU'RE SO DUMB(S11).
I consider these two singles
CHISWICK's first ventures into"punk".The
Radiators are from Ireland and Skrewdriver
from Blackpool.Both singles are similar,
they're both hard and fast but they have
the same trouble,no suss.It's like if you
talk like this it's like you're trying to
be high and mighter or something but it's
a plain fact that altough both these bands
are comitted up to their highbrows they
are behind.I wished the Chiswick mob had
looked in London for new bands.Both these
bands sound as though they've been recorded
too early for their own good and that's a
shame.

THE COUNT BISHOPS-BABY YOU'RE WRONG(S12).
The new,new Bishops with
vocalist Dave Tice who comes from Australia
and looks like Paul Rogers(slightly).In
this context these tracks don't work(B-side
is'Stay Free)but on the album they're great.
I waited with baited breath and I had to
wait two months consoling myself with the
odd playing of the'Speedball'EP.

MORE CHISWICK

PK: MIKE BEAL.

ROGER ARMSTRONG LOOKING CONFUSED.

THE RINGS-I WANNA BE FREE(S14).
          Chirst,this is a burner.Goodm'yes
a classic R&B,fast,breakneck,ex-Fairies,now
split.Right game,the Gorillas,the 101'ers,
the Razors and now the Rings all split.Bad
luck ...I hope they have better luck with
MOTORHEAD!!!

MOTORHEAD-MOTORHEAD(S13)
          The best 12 inch ever released and
the most relevent ever released.Motorhead
needdd the space.This thing is pure power.
Somebody had to get them on plastic,I'm glad
it was Chiswick.Motorhead bring tears to
your eyes as they career through their theme
song.The name,by the way,is taken from'Motor
-head'Sherwood who was a sax player for the
Mothers Of Invention.

Look,all I can say about CHISWICK is listen to the fuckers and make yer own fucking mind

up or wait Giovanni Dadamo or any of them cunts tell you what to listen too...

right,this whole piece was an exercise in'how to bore the pants of you while reviewing

records that you've probably already heard or got". Writing is for cunts who are scared

to show the faces.They've learnt their craft in journalist school or English Language

and they can't wait to tell you what they think and half of you out there take it in,

don't believe a fucking word. It's not just the nationals that are bullshitting. Take

yer average fanzine (yes,there is a few about) writer. All he is is some frustrated

rock star who would love to grow up and became another teenage prodigy like Nick Kent

or Jane Suck. Well bollocks to that,if you want to fight,really fight,don't bullshit

yer way through print. That's why the GLUE should stop stop right now...stop right now...

IF YOU REALLY WANNA DESTROY,LEAVE YOUR JOB OR SCHOOL OR ANYTHING YOU ARE INVOLVED IN

AND GO AND SIT IN THE ROAD AND WAIT TILL A BIG LORRY COMES ALONG.THAT'S RIGHT DESTROY

YOURSELF YOU STUPID CUNT.STOP READING SG NOW AND BURN YOUR COPY,ALL BURNT COPIES ARE

TO BE LEFT IN ROUGH TRADE OR SENT TO US(YOU CAN AFFORD 7p).I want you to burn Sg 12

and burn it good. No I'm not mucking about I'm just beening HONEST,AND IT HURTS!!!!

A piece by MARK P.

"To be a Dictator you need absolute power"

A NIGHT AT THE VORTEX

August 29 at the Vortex turned out to be an unexpected killer, a magic night.What was so good about it? The Rich Kids, mate, that's what.

See Monday night's getting to be a high-light of the week. It's something to do with the Vortex being on but that ain't the sole reason...Monday is coming like a Vortex on wheels. But it's somewhere to go where ya get four bands for a quid but hard luck if you wanna drink and find you've only got forty pence left. But if you've flogged some albums in the afternoon then you'll be OK till two. Then you'll wonder what hit ya when youre standing in the street like you made it there via a scene change in the movies - yeah, when it's two o'clock and the bars close it's sweep 'em out time and no mistake.

As I said Monday's a highlight but not so much for the bands, unless it's the Slits or the Banshees. Up the pub at six, out three hours later legless and ready to take on the Vortex.

In the door, down the stairs ,into the bar then ...anything can happen and it often does. See we have fun,much to the disgust of the poserswho occasionally spare a cool,superior glance at the giggling huddle falling over and going WAAAYYYY!!! at every familiar face. "Look at them, not as cool as us, their hairs getting a bit long, too clean to be real punks" (and if you think that last one sounds far-fetched , honest it's true, some mohair meat-head said we were too clean to qualify.Boo Hoo)

These are the people who cheered with seld-indulgent glee when the news of Elvis Presley's death was announced. The posy sheep who flung glasses and gobbed at Danny Baker when he tried to explain that you shouldn't cheer when a geezer snuffs it and Elvis went through worse shit 20 years ago than you ever did.What-ever he did with his last I5 years Elvis was the bloke who started it all.Anyway soon the jeers turned to cheers and the girl with a face about as attractive as a bus accident who'd flung the glass at Dan's head wanted to kiss him.

These people make me sick. Posers revel-ling in the attention they're getting with their fancy dress. Yet they've got the New Conviction of a statue of Bert Weedon.

Anyway I'm going off the track. The four bands came and went in a haze - Chelsea went down well and Neo created a hard time for themselves when their singer started shout-ing about wanting to see some poets, but under his circumstances ∽ a barrage of abuse and glasses cos he was trying to be inject a bit of originality into the music- he can't be blamed for blowing his New Yawk cool.

All night we'd been hearing that Glen Matlock's new band the Rick Kids were gonna be playing after Chelsea.And they were gonna have an extra guitar on in the form of Mick Jones of The Clash.Wahoo! I'd been looking forward to seeing that lot for a long time.Although they formed some months ago they haven't been able to do too many gigs cos they need another guitarist, another Mick Jones ,going on the set they did on Monday. He fitted like a glove , and looked incredibly happy about it too, bouncing around the stage with a big grin flashing across his face at regular intervals.

The band were obviously really happy to be on a stage again and poured the lot into a succession of dynamic songs.

It's a very melodic sound but whacked out with the aggression of the early Small Faces and when topped with the stinging Jones guitar the effect is dynamite.I like the group's none-adherence to the Punk rulebook.I mean they got longish hair and the clothes weren't exactly Kings Road no it was good to see a group carving, their own image,not copying the Sun.

I s'pose the highlights of the set were the numbers I knew - the old Tommy James and the Shondells classic "I Think We're Alone Now" recently done again by the Rubinoos,which they delivered twice. It was great, after just half-an-hour rehearsal, brilliant, an d I hadn't felt as good for months when they were doing it.

The other familiar song was "Pretty Vacant". Mick Jones:"He wrote it so why shouldn't he do it". At this point Jimmy leapt up and took over the verses, 'cept he changed the words to tell the posy pogoers they're only here for the fancy dress party. I just CAN'T WAIT to see the Shams with a set of their own at this place. They'll demolish the crowd!

This ranked with the Slits as one of the best evenings yet down the Vortex, er I mean SETS...the only bit of the expedition wherev I can remember eveything what happened.

Kris Needs

Is that alright Dan?

THE ONLY ONES

LOVERS OF TODAY

Single Available Now

Vengeance Records

DISTRIBUTION
FAULTY PRODUCTS
27 Dryden Chambers,
119. Oxford St.
London, W1

MENACE

Screwed Up

Insane Society

OUT SEPT. 16

THE CLASH: RAINBOW.   PIC: JILL FURMANOVSKY

NEW WAVE

16 TRACKS
£2·45

Album 6300 902   Cassette 7199 005

RAMONES - JUDY IS A PUNK   DEAD BOYS - SONIC REDUCER

PATTI SMITH - PISS FACTORY   NEW YORK DOLLS - PERSONALITY CRISIS

RUNAWAYS - HOLLYWOOD   SKYHOOKS - HORROR MOVIE

LITTLE BOB STORY - ALL OR NOTHING

RICHARD HELL AND THE VOID-OIDS - LOVE COMES IN SPURTS

TALKING HEADS - LOVE GOES

THE BOOMTOWN RATS - LOOKIN' AFTER NO. 1   TO BUILDING ON FIRE

THE DAMNED - NEW ROSE   RAMONES - SUZY IS A HEADBANGER

DEAD BOYS - ALL THIS AND MORE   FLAMIN' GROOVIES - SHAKE SOME ACTION

RUNAWAYS - CHERRY BOMB   NEW YORK DOLLS - WHO ARE THE MYSTERY GIRLS?

THIS CANADIAN GEYSER COME TO LONDON + SAW GENERATION X

"Youth, Youth, Youth". I heard that chorus on a tape just once and spent the whole week mentally playing it over and over. Then I saw them live and added four more to my minds playlist. A week more and I was writing Gen X rule in underground stations. It must be love.

Y'see Generation X have assets that make you a fan overnight: incredibly well concieved melodic songs both live and, if you heard John Peels show, in the studio. And whether you like it or not, Generation X with the Ramones, are the seventies premier pop group. Both of these bands without the pre-

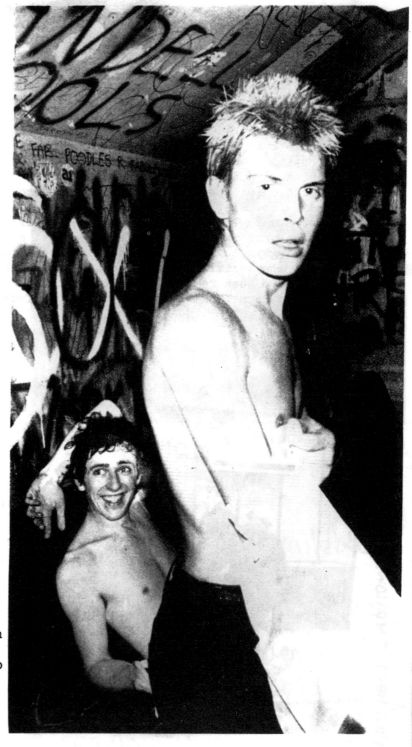

fabrication of the Chinnichap/Mike Leander epitomise what influences and ideas put to intelligent original use can achieve. An ideal mesh of new wave speed/energy in combination with attractive music and genuine lyrics, not just the insistent E flat shell shock chords most bands seem to be satisfied with.

Whereas the Ramones are thouroughly American, Gen X could be the 'New York' band that delivers on all the promises that overblown scene has broken in the wake of the Ramones prodigious debut.

Billy Idols voice constantly suprises me with its flexibility and range. Thrashing around stage during songs his face into contortions befitting of a generations crooner, (crooner I use, catch the opening of Listen), both guitarists play with a confidence that must reflect the pride in the material.

I don't usually bother with lyrics but what I've caught to songs like Listen, Above Love, Youth, and already a classic, Ready Steady Go, can't be dismissed with a routine adjective.

I know, I know, my enthusiasm is becoming redundant, but its not often these days a band makes you wish they could get it all down on vinyl.

And now some people look upon Gen X as black sheep because they're the 'pop group' of the lot, (apparently a label in disgrace), however when the detractors write a 'Youth' I'll listen to them. Pop may not fit the new wave image which is why Generation X are so important and impressive, they MAKE it fit and complement it in return.

Obviously when their singles show

.....up they'll just as likely appear on the cover of 19 as 'Sniffin Glue',Billy Idol may just be the guy to live up to his surname,and the band will outshine clearly the lesser lights and give stiff opposition to current 'names'. Whatever happens,if Generation X aren't chasing their contemporaries by the end of the year I'm going back to Mono.

Stu,their manager,tells me a lot of people are jealous of Generation X,and it doesn't surprise me a bit.

Listen to the ones who will change your world.

Jeremy G.

Yeah,it was all set wasn't it? My christ,the chance was there for the taking and we had a scene ready to take off. And they blew it,maaaaan.

Let me tell you what I'm talking about. On Tuesday the sixteenth at the Ambassador Dundee,fully advertised in local press/shops etc.,The Rezillos.

7·45.The people were a dozen strong fifteen minutes before the doors opened—or due to any way.We were still there at 9.05 and the doors opened then,by which time about four hundered people had gathered;since a quarter to nine some heavies had been prowling around informing us that,er,the Rezillos mightn't,er,turn up.

Once in we grabbed a table and a pint and waited. And waited. John-a mate/one of the Disco boys—came over and gave us some startling info. Seems Rezillos had been'delayed' cos Top of the Pops had asked to film them earlier. The promoter got up to quieten things down, and some morons lapped it up.

I met some nice people. Drank and got headache. People pogoing around the floor. It was a bad farce. To be so obviously used.

We need some swift moves to get us outa this mess. I'm keen,so should you be.

This non event came at a crucial time just as Dundee was getting a scene together and now needs time again to get back support/respect lost. I'm worried,but don't FORGET. Let them know. Let the Rezillos know! We aint to be mucked about with.

Rezillos have been re-appointed for the 22nd August.

I'll let ya know if we lose support or get fucked with again.

Alan Matheson 1977.

Best thing to do is get hold of a stage mike and let the assembly know. Whip it up.
DB

PIC: HARRY T. MURLOWSKI.

On the 26th July at Vortex there was the Vibrators supported by New Hearts, it was free admission and if you came early you got a couple of free drinks.

I understand CBS were footing the bill. During the Ants set there was the feel of a 'real' punk concert, but after that...

When it was finished (all the contracts signed), there were quite a few sad, frustrated punks left, including me. I mean, how can punks mingle so easily with all those buisness heavies?

As the new wave came through it attacked establishment in music and image, and to me, both have dissapeared into the business sponge. I still believe that bands like Jam, Damned and Clash have been had and so have we. That fucking sponge will get us all if something isn't done.

The image faired better at first, cos the music could be ignored by simply not listening to it, but the lifestyle was thrust at them on the street. Then that marvellous mouthpiece/propaganda machine for the ruling class, the press picked it up. The rich hate nothing more than people who refuse to listen to their lies. With all that 'punks=swastika=NF' getting the hoped shock reaction (booked your hos pital bed yet?) it forced the punks into an even tighter group. So then comes the action of getting the Youth groups fighting amongst themselves. Just another gang of yobs feuding on the street, all because the press say so. The energy is diverted and only when everybody is aware of this will we get back to the real aims of the new wave.

So Punk has lost much of its energy and the media has shown us what it can do. So its time we showed what we can do.

I think it would do the greatest benefit to stop buying records. (The Glue gets controversial and drastic eh?-DB/MP). Yeah, stop buying the records. Go and see the bands instead, cos I feel as soon as groups sign up they get the corporation dictating what goes and doesn't. To stop buying means that those greasy fat exects can't make a penny out of us. Plus with the vinyl market in full swing we can all become armchair punks and all the smaller bands will dissapear leaving another set of supergroups.

We need communication. If you've got something to say-say it, don't wait for a record to say it for you. Get out into the clubs, anywhere, and dance, sing, shout as long as you communicate.

Don't let them buy you out. Tony S.

Subway Sect Pic: Jill Furmanovsky

Mail Order.
Sniffin Glue is available
: bootleged in the States.
or: from 27 Dryden Chambers
119 Oxford St. London W.I.
35p UK. and Eire
50p Europe and seamail everywhere
else.
65p Airmail outside Europe.

"We're Sham 69,and we aint gonna tell ya to fuck off cos we want to have a great time, out that aint very fashionable is it? It's alright though,cos we're the support act and punks don't take no notice of support acts do they?"Acklam Hall

For the next few pages for fucks sake listen to the support act,and do yourself a favour.

*D'you know what a real 'punk' is?
A real punk today is the bloke with a
belt joining the legs of his trousers
together,or a girl in fishnet stockin's.
And they're the first people to shout
wanker at my band.Cos they're in their
little smug groups of fashion and they
look just like the Sunday People has told
them. They'll tell ya bands are selling
out to business too. Fuckin' snobs.
What was it last year?Bryan Ferry,Glen
Miller?"
Jimmy Pursey,Sham's frontman,is saying
this in a pub full of the mohair sweater
set.His voice is getting louder all the
time,and his eyes and voice carry emotion
I aint seen outside Joe Strummer. Every
so often,the frustration of a singer whose
band after eighteen months still supports
groups like the Rejects,comes top and he
will punch the wall hard during certain
sentences. There aint none of that,cool,
man with a mission,gosh I'm so relevent
shit that nine out of ten blokes find
need to wear.
"See,Dan,thats why we're still bottom
of the bill. Yer average crowd sees us
come on and even before we start they've
got us sussed as no hope bandwaggoners.
Then on'll stroll some band in all the
right togs introduce a song called,I
dunno,'Boring Labour Exchange',and everyone goes 'ah the right attitude,they
must be good,' but d'you reckon they
wrote that song cos they feel about it
or cos thats what they're expected to sing?
I mean surely an audience can see when
a groups acting. The first sign is to do
the old 'cor you lot are so boring.Why
dont you piss off' routine. I'd love just
once to see an audience walk out completly
on a band like that. I can't see what that
means. I never want to say piss off,thats
admitting defeat,I'm up there to try and
make people listen,I want them to hear,
how can you acheive anything playing for
yourself. If I sing 'Hey Little Rich Boy'
I don't want to sing it to me mates. I
want to sing it to the fucking ponces of
rich kids,I wanna rub their noses in the
shit I've had to put up with. If I want
to get at an apathetic crowd,I'll aim the
song at 'em. But just to go 'fuck off'
is to get all your supporters to go 'hurray',

PRIVATE

Sham69 pic.JillFurmanevsky.

"'slike Ripped n Torn fanzine which said something about how all the time I'm onstage
I'm trying to prove how working class I am and all them poncy NME letters about 'new elitsn
and stuff. Look,fuck it all, them type of people are gonna kill punk. They must really
think that I've read a few books on how to act. They want us all to go'way and calm down
cos they don't think I know what I'm talking about. What bollacks is that? If I say I hate
so and so,its cos I know I hate so and so. I know and thats all there is to it. But these
cunts think 'ah an obvious case of socio-bollocko fuckism caused by a disillusioned shit'
and they gonna get all artsy with words and tell bands this an'that an' for you know where
you are that gut level rock reaction,that is the only way I know,is gone.
        What was it that bloke wrote? Oh yeah that I shouldn't have had a dig at the middle
class cos they can't help where they're born either.

"Oh well sorry then,I understand now,how silly of me. I'll go away again.I didn't realize
that you can't speak out against something thats kept me at the piss hole end of the scale
while Lord Ponconby Allaenby little kids run up a drugs bill on more money than my dad,
YOUR DADS,ever earned in a year. Thats just how it is,is it. They come and see me cos I'm
this months trend. A bit of rough. Let me say something to all them people who try and
file my attitude under some 'ism' or another. My attitude might seem thick to you cos I
was brought up to be thick to keep rich cunts in money. If I don't show meself now,I
never will,cos nobodies ever wanted to know before and I aint that much of a prat to know
that in a couple of years I'll be on me arse again. What it is,see Dan,is that most of
these people are used to a sham,as in fake,with bands comin' on with well thought out
approaches,disguising what they mean to say in a load of wordy bollacks. Sham 69 speak
exactly what loads of geysers think and most important I THINK. And if Ripped and Torn or
all them fuckin students or people who write letters don't like it,well sorry darlin' thats
just the way it is.
        How bout this! We did the Other cinema at short notice,for the Time Out set. Anyrate
we were playin away and theres a few of the boys dancing in front and all the rest

JIMMY SHAM

stuck in the seats,y'know,a chewing
the pipe stalk an' all that,so I goes
to the mike and said,'I want you to know
who it is I'm playin' for. Its for these
people who come to have a laugh and dance
not you cunts just anylising my attitude'.

So,come the end of the set,they wanted
to ask questions while we stood there.

After a lot of shoutin' we says,
'alright,it'll be a laugh',but the first
question up is some aussie bird with
nothing about the words or songs but,

'I say,when you made a remark about
us being cunts,was it a direct anti
feminist reference?' I mean,(laughs)
fuck me.....thats why that type never
acheive fuck all 'cept depression.

I shoulda tolda that it was a term of
affection...'no lady I love cunts'

Then I reckon someone woulda said I'm
anti gay....

But thats what I mean,all this crap people mask things with. I just want to call
a spade a spade,(none in here is there!),
and people want to tell me different.

That bird reporter who asked me that
cos I'm a punk how much did I see the
Velvet Underground as an influence.

If you ask me punk goes back to,I
dunno,the geysers with the Vikings
goin' 'oh fuck I'm bein' whipped', its
just saying what you feel."

It probably don't come across in this
but Jim is probably the only bloke in
(or probably out) of punk that can make
me cry with laughter. He talks nearly as
fast as me and all the time wears an
expression that sometimes makes you wonder
if he's bothered about anything. As long
as you listen,though,its clear he means
it with more passion than it comes over
in print.

With that,all the time,he asks every
girl going past if she's alright. When a
row a business gents made for the bog,Jim
got there first and stood by the door like
a commisionaire and gave each one a napkin
and 'good morning sir',and told them the
water was on their desks and he hoped they
would be able to sort it all out. I tell ya,
every two minutes its a nudge on the arm and
*'ere watch this,we'll have a laugh here"

If you ask what kind of past the band's
had you'll need a packed lunch.

"We were playing this college,a while
back,when it was the old band,(only Albie
the bassist is still there),an' we're on
and all the students are chuckin' cans
an' stuff and theres a near riot. So I
does a stroll to the mike and says...

JILL FURMANOVSKY

"Look,you wankers,don't chuck anything 'less
you mean it-right!" An' a fuckin' great party
seven goes'wallop'to the side of me nut.

I was thinking 'what did I say that for for
fucks sake',an' I look over an' Albies got the
bass by the neck and swingin' it at this bunch
of geysers so I jump down an' I'm doin' the
old 'you're dead and you're dead,'bit pointin'
the finger at about thirty geysers,y'know.

All this time the rest of the band are playin' on up there!

I shouted here's your encore and give two
fingers and we've run off. And they chased us.
So we barracaded ourself into the dressin'
room which was at the top of some stairs,while
our manager went out to try and calm em down.

Anyrate as soon as he walked down some geyse
went 'whack' and laid him out,an' we've been
approached by the college secretary who tells
US to go and apologise. So I saw about four
of them fire buckets hangin'-two with sand
and two of water-we walks out and goes 'bosh'
all over the fuckin lot. The killer is that as
they're tryin' to get out of shot they're
tramplin all over our manager who's still on
the deck,an' he's groanin' 'fuck Sham 69...
fuck all of yer...'"

At this point the tape run out but the
stories flowed...the time they played a parent

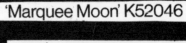

..teacher type institute,curtains opened,(curtains?), band playing intro and Jim with back
to crowd. When Jimmy turned to sing the opening verse I think most people noticed the fucking huge 'Lonely Nights' dildo strapped on to the front of his jeans. Curtains closed but
Jim ran in front of 'em till he was dragged off an' beat up.

"Yeah,we did all sorts of idiot stuff back then,playin standards to middle aged people,
thats all we were there for,the laugh.."

I said I weren't surprised people hardly book them now,and Jim stopped laughing.

"I know,but I wish it was something as basic as that. Take that Droitwitch thing. I hears
we're doin' it an' the band are feelin' great,y'know playing to a few people at last. So
there we are all ready an' that,till one day I sees a poster for it on a wall. And I'm reading down and down these bands I've necer heard of till I'm reading printed in Watford. So
I goes through it again. Do you know that was the first I knew that my band had been dropped
to make way for some new boys....some fuckin' business deal I spose.

Don't no one tell me punks about just gettin' up and playing. As it stands now its about
what business contract...what deal's gone on;all that. We tried to go on at the Vortex,just
cos we wanted to play,maybe some people even wanted to hear us,but what happens? Shit gets
kicked outa me for tryin' to nick guitars. But does anyone care? Do they fuck. Its gettin'
further and further away from street kids and if that sounds hippy or cliched thats too
fuckin' bad."

(Its about time I said that Sham 69 are playing the best live set around,and I spose
apart from anything else that's what matters,and since we did the interview that crowd
following the Shams is getting bigger by the performance. The hard thing nowdays if you
write about a band you genuinly think are among the big six,(whatever yours is),is that
always someone else is gonna think your writing it for some arse lick reason. When we did
Chelsea/Cortinas interviews all we got was letters saying how they're only in Glue cos
Step Forward signed 'em. I don't spose it had anything to do with them being good bands who
were otherwise ignored in the press had it? At this time Mark P is tryin' hard to get the
Shams to do a one off single for the label he signs good bands for. Shockin' aint it?)

I don't care if they surface on Step Forward,EMI or Deutsches Gramophone,I know the band
are strong enough to fuck any big biz trip,cos they feel like you and me and they know this
scene has more than its fair share of bad smells. But if Sham 69 go down without any recog-
nition,well,that'd be sickening.

We can sort a lot of this current shit out if we recognise the genuine from the
cruds who want our money and nothing else. I aint gonna say Sham 69 are THE ANSWER cos who
really believes that its all gonna fall into place one day,but they are part of what I
always thought this lark was about.

"I care about the people who come and see us,thats why I did the Roxy encore when only
four people clapped,I don't even think about the others.I care about what happens to my
band and geysers like us. I hope I don't come over like some whiter than white preacher or
some fuckin' man-who-wuz-wronged,cos that aint it. I aint got nothing to prove,but I got
plenty to say for meself,an' wether people think I'm a cunt or not is up to them.

It just mystifies me how kids can be satisfied with a scene that has got twisted so that
punks are judging you on your looks and how big your name's on the bill.

Punk's got so many followers who don't give a fuck what you say or think....so whats it
all about?"

Answers on Seditionaries notepaper only.

Danny Baker

CONT. HARRY.T.MURLOWSKY.

Bizzarre record's DISTRIBUTION

LARRY
DEREK
TIM

33. Praed st,
london w.2.

Phone   402—1939
          262—0616

RING FOR YOUR NEW
WHOLESALE CATALOGUE

FAST DESPATCH

SMALL ORDERS TAKEN
EXCELLENT TRADING TERMS

CHISWICK

ORK

STIFF

COMPREHENSIVE STOCK
CHEAPER PRICES

ILLEGAL

BOMP

DYNAMITE

STEP FOWARD

AND ALSO MISCELLANEOUS

FRENCH, DUTCH, U.S.

Phil sPector

St John's Ambulance Brigade at the Vortex: The strain's too much!!
Harry's Private joke's Pin-up No1.

K.N.

A DAY IN A LIFE

This page is about the records I bought on the 31st.August'77.Yes,I bought 'em...except no lies.

MOTORHEAD(Chiswick LP),IS POWERFUL.Headshakig madness,heavy,loud,we all love Motorhead,don't we.Most of it's fast and hard.It's good when it's turned up a long way.I like their energy and their guts,that's why I actually bought the thing.Tracks are:Motorhead/Vibrator/Lost Johnny/Iron Horse (b)Born To Lose/White Line Fever/Keep Us On the Road/The Watcher/Train Kept a Rollin'.I wouldn't get too near the bass speaker if I was you.This band take no prisoners!

THE FANTELS-Hooligan(Errol 45).I had this because of the title and it ain't bad.It's a very steady rocker with Mighty Diamonds type vocals.The dub on the flip is a gas.It's a great backing track.The drums sound like gun-fire.Yeah,"some like a'ooligan..."½

IAN DURY-Sex & Drugs & Rock & Roll(Stiff 45). Talk about funky.With the incredible"make my funk the p-funk"type bounce,this is a killa. Dury sings in his best Upminster accent.Buy it,keep it,love it..."Razzle In MMy Pocket" is the B-side and it's about teethin'.BUY17, or just one,at least.

ROOGALATOR-I Feel Good(I Got You)(Virgin45). The A-side is'Love and the Single Girl'but don't worry,it's crap.'I Feel Good'is great. The way they go into it after the freaky start is incredible.Get a listen to it even if you don't wanna lash out for the thing.

TRINITY-Tree Piece Suit (Lightening 45). One of,if not the best reggae single that's been released this year.It's got a great tune nice singing,sharp rocking and a brilliant toast.Get it or starve,fool.

TRINITY-Harvest Day(Hulk 45). Another from the'three piece suit'mob.Not as sharp as the other but still a cut above most of the pre-release stuff that's around at the moment.And get this,the flip is by BLACK BEARD AND THE PIRATES,even better than Factory Pleb and the Trouts,nearly.A really good single...find and catch!

DILLINGER-Flat Foot Hustlings(Third World 45) A long time out but it's got a great start- "My daddy was a dread old man and so he died with a shovel in 'is hand...",oh yeah,we're off.A true born hustler....another single to get or regret!The dub is fub!

DON'T GIVE ME NO MORE BULLSHIT,P!!!!

I ALSO GOT THE LURKERS, THE BOYS + 999 45's ! 50 WHAT?

PRINCE FAR I-   (White label album). I think it's called'Psalms In Dub'but I'm not sure.You can get it in Rough Trade and a couple of other shops in London.The first track is the Lord's Testament(reggae version) and it sets the scene for most of the album. Yeah,it's a plastic bible that goes round and round.It's an album you have to sit down with,you have to listen.Listen good and hard, it'll make up for all the time you missed from Sunday School(with capital letters).At £4.50 it's a struggle but try and get it,it's beautiful.Nice one,Far I!

THE COUNT BISHOPS(Chiswick album) Who put the bleeders' in this order?The Bishops make a good album that I've been listening to for weeks(I got a new one today).It's simple, honest and good.Good enough to help you come down from the heavens after Far I,just.No, it is a goodie and it's taken long enough to happen.Fave track is'Down the Road Apiece'.

JOHN CALE PICS MIKE BEAL.

JOHN CALE-Animal Justice(Illegal 12" 45). I didn't buy this cause the SG office is next door to Illegal and all that crowd.It was put in my hand with care.Even with is exciting story playing on my mind I think that this is a masterpiece."Heroes never die...",you bet they fuckin'don't! A-side:Chicken Shit-a up tempo rocker with great overdubbed voices,& Memphis-when Cale's viola comes in it's like fuckin'great.B-side:Hedda Gabler-don't ask me just listen.You've just got to buy this EP.

YOU DON'T HAVE TO READ THIS OF COURSE

Apart from being an American rock band who I never cared for,d'you know what Pavlovs Dog was? It was some dog the authorities or someone had trained to do things at the sound of a bell. Sort of brain washed.

I was in the Vortex when the DJ said Elvis Presley was dead. Loads of people cheered and said things like 'fuckin' great'. None of them,I'm sure,knew why. But thats what punks are sposed to do.....innit?

I could have seen it if there'd been a few'so whats',few shrugs 'n' that,cos if you really didn't think anything about someone it don't cut you up none when they peg out, but that night the Vortex had to be seen to be the mindless idiot the Sunday papers whip out on cue.

I got up on stage and grabbed a mike,cos I was so fuckin' wild about how dopey this whole set up is getting. But of course who's gonna listen when you can throw glasses at the target. There was one bloke tryin' to lead everybody in shouting 'off off off',plenty of shouts of 'cunt',and loads of glasses. See they had already made up their minds that I was talking about that fat geyser we've all grown up to know,and that was it. Punks read in the papers about how concerts are being banned left right and centre and how Mrs Whitehouse tries to stop you seeing something,or how records are banned cos certain people don't want them heard,and they go 'terrible,fascist,oppressive' and all the rest. Yet the same punks,when faced with something they think they don't like,are no fucking better than the coundillors who ban the Sex Pistols.

Punks are the same as the Government. We don't want to know. Shut it up.

If you don't believe me try getting on stage at a punk gig and talking against the agreed pose for the night.

If those people who at first booed me,then when the mood changed(after I was allowed to shout above the mindless insults) kept quiet,don't know what Elvis Presley did why are they following his music?

Back then it was Presley look alikes who got stick in the streets,who were the filth of the nation. Presley gave Youth a fuckin' voice for the first time,which died till we got it back again. Forget the man. I aint talking 'bout any one. I'm talking about youth rebellion which we were sposed to be about. Whatever the geyser we grew up to know did,(or didn't do),Elvis Presley gave bland/apathetic/oppresive society its first real kick up the arse. We're supposed to be doin' it now,but it seems that if we're given a club and some records we'll quieten down,and don't worry Mr Authority we'll deal with anyone who tries to step outa line,we'll throw some glasses at 'em.

Cos we really DON'T CARE.

Its all a big giggle aint it?

Well go on. Chuck glasses at me and let somebody else do that in Lewisham cos that aint your idea of 'fun'. Wear badges that say No Heroes. Yeah that was another thing. A girl grabbed the mike off me an' said,"We aint got no heroes" and as per brochure got a big cheer for it. Sure you've got no heroes. If the DJ would've said Joe Strummer had just been knifed to death you would have cheered too.....cos you've got no heroes..right?

The New Wave Reaction. It walks.It talks. It says No Heroes.

Shit,I bet you still think I'm talking bout Elvis Presley.

Danny Baker

"NO IDEA, LISTENING OR THE ROLLING STONES IN 1977"

Generation X new single
Your Generation Day by Day CHS 2165

generation   generation
  generation   generation
  generation   generation
   generation   generation
    generation   generation
     generationgeneration
      generatigeneration
       generagéneration
        genegeneration
         gegeneratdion
          generation
         gegeneratdion
        genegeneration
       generagéneration
      generatigeneration
     generationgeneration
    generation   generation
   generation   generation
  generation   generation
 generation   generation
generation   generation

Chrysalis
Mail order copies from Rough Trade Records
202 Kensington Park Road, London W. 11 (7274312)
70p + 10p P&P